"As is noted in this volume, despite the mid-twentieth-century prominence that Rouault enjoyed, his work is now lesser-known than contemporaries such as Henri Matisse and Marc Chagall, whose work and commissions often engaged with similar themes. The range and variety of engagements—both artistic and academic—with Rouault's work found in this book serve as a corrective to the partial neglect of his work and achievements, including his legacy in artists engaging with Christian themes, by demonstrating the richness, depth, and variety of his oeuvre and the many routes possible to connecting with it."

Jonathan Evens, associate vicar for partnership development at St Martin-in-the-Fields

"An important and richly layered new volume on one of the most important painters of the twentieth century—one whose commitment to Christ as the true image of God is unparalleled. Georges Rouault should be a household name for every believer who cares about the intersection of art and faith—and Wes Vander Lugt has assembled a deeply valuable resource to that end. The intellectual artistic hospitality of the many fine writers and thinkers in this book will serve to ensure that Rouault is remembered as a prophetic voice in the wilderness of modern art."

Bruce Herman, painter, writer, and educator

"We are living through one of the most challenging times in modern history. Many have either resorted to a 'gloom and doom' theology or are simply pretending that everything is fine. The artwork of Georges Rouault reminds us that being hopeful doesn't mean that we ignore the realities and challenges around us; rather, it means that we look in the face of our challenging circumstances with a realistic hope that comes from God alone. *A Prophet in the Darkness* is essential reading for how art can help us find realistic hope that is rooted in the Christian faith."

Winfield Bevins, director of Creo Arts, artist-in-residence at Asbury Seminary, and author of *Liturgical Mission*

"In this volume, Wesley Vander Lugt gathers prescient insights from theologians, art historians, and artists to celebrate artist George Rouault's life and legacy. It begins with a foreword by Sandra Bowden, whose extensive collection of prints from Rouault's *Miserere* series has, for more than two decades, stimulated renewed interest in the artist's vision, especially in the Christian community. The popular notion is that modern art was entirely opposed to Christian belief. Rouault's studio practice powerfully upends that view. These essays bear witness to Rouault's faithful making and believing through two world wars and seasons of dark personal struggle."

Cameron J. Anderson, Distinguished Fellow for Art and Literature at The Lumen Center in Madison, Wisconsin

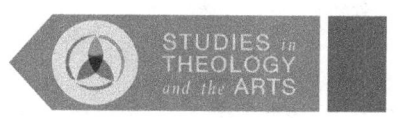

STUDIES in
THEOLOGY
and the ARTS

A PROPHET
IN THE
DARKNESS

EXPLORING THEOLOGY
IN THE ART OF
GEORGES ROUAULT

Wesley Vander Lugt, ed.

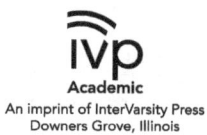

IVP
Academic
An imprint of InterVarsity Press
Downers Grove, Illinois

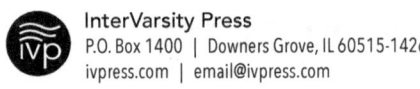

InterVarsity Press
P.O. Box 1400 | Downers Grove, IL 60515-1426
ivpress.com | email@ivpress.com

InterVarsity Press® is the publishing division of InterVarsity Christian Fellowship/USA®. For more information, visit intervarsity.org.

All Scripture quotations, unless otherwise indicated, are taken from The Holy Bible, New International Version®, NIV®. Copyright © 1973, 1978, 1984, 2011 by Biblica, Inc.™ Used by permission of Zondervan. All rights reserved worldwide. www.zondervan.com. The "NIV" and "New International Version" are trademarks registered in the United States Patent and Trademark Office by Biblica, Inc.™

While any stories in this book are true, some names and identifying information may have been changed to protect the privacy of individuals.

All Images by Georges Rouault © 2024 Artists Rights Society (ARS), New York / ADAGP, Paris.

The publisher cannot verify the accuracy or functionality of website URLs used in this book beyond the date of publication.

Cover design: David Fassett
Interior design: Daniel van Loon
Cover image: Courtesy of Bowden Collections. © 2024 Artists Rights Society (ARS), New York / ADAGP, Paris.

ISBN 978-1-5140-1105-8 (print) | ISBN 978-1-5140-1106-5 (digital)

Printed in the United States of America ∞

Library of Congress Cataloging-in-Publication Data
Names: Vander Lugt, Wesley, 1981- editor.
Title: A prophet in the darkness : exploring theology in the art of Georges
   Rouault / edited by Wesley Vander Lugt.
Description: Downers Grove, IL : IVP Academic, [2024] | Includes
   bibliographical references and index.
Identifiers: LCCN 2024022330 (print) | LCCN 2024022331 (ebook) | ISBN
   9781514011058 (paperback) | ISBN 9781514011065 (ebook)
Subjects: LCSH: Rouault, Georges, 1871-1958–Criticism and interpretation.
   | Theology in art. | BISAC: RELIGION / Christianity / Literature & the
   Arts | ART / Subjects & Themes / Religious
Classification: LCC N6853.R67 P76 2024 (print) | LCC N6853.R67 (ebook) |
   DDC 759.4–dc23/eng/20240620
LC record available at https://lccn.loc.gov/2024022330
LC ebook record available at https://lccn.loc.gov/2024022331

31   30   29   28   27   26   25   24 | 12   11   10   9   8   7   6   5   4   3   2   1

To all artists of faith

serving as prophets in the darkness.

May your kind increase.

Contents

Foreword

A Prophet in the Darkness

Sandra Bowden

It is critically important to revitalize what for centuries was taken for granted: that we can *see* the Bible and its stories. The Reformation nurtured a deep skepticism that places the visual arts for the most part outside the realm of the church. But a new confidence is emerging that we might once again be invited not only to hear but also to see the gospel and to embrace the visual arts in the life of the church.

Every generation of artists has wrestled with the challenge of visually presenting the Bible and its meaning in ways that create contemporary resonance. The role of the artist is to portray what cannot be seen with the eye alone, to uncover for us what we have not seen or have only imperfectly realized. Paul Klee says, "Art does not reproduce the visible; rather, it makes visible."[1] This is what the art of Georges Rouault (1871–1958) has done; his images have penetrated deeply into the human dilemma to find meaning and offer hope, helping us to see light in the darkness, making visible the invisible. This is why my husband and I believe Rouault's work is worth collecting and sharing with the Christian community and broader public.

The first piece in the Bowden Collections was *Obedient even unto death, death on the cross* (*Miserere*, plate 57; see fig. F.1), an intaglio from Rouault's *Miserere* series created in 1926.[2] In early 1980, I visited the home of an art dealer

---

[1] Paul Klee, *Creative Confession and Other Writing* (London: Tate, 2013), chap. 1, Kindle.
[2] An intaglio is a design engraved into the surface of a certain material, which in the case of the *Miserere* was copper, after which ink fills the engraved areas for printing. For more information on the Bowden Collections, visit www.bowdencollections.com. Hereafter, plates from the *Miserere* series will be indicated with a capital *M* and the number, such as M57 in this case. The titles of

in Connecticut who was hosting an exhibition of my work, and I noticed this Rouault hanging in the stairwell of her home. I asked where she got it, and I was curious because she was Jewish. Her father had been the manager of Brentano's print department in New York City and gave her this print because he believed it was an important work. She had been diagnosed with cancer and did not have long to live, and her children had told her that they would destroy the work when she was gone. So she asked whether I would purchase it from her, and it became our first Rouault and the first piece in our religious art collection. Thus, a most exciting journey began and continues to this day.

Many consider Rouault one of the most important religious painters of the last few centuries, his faith informing his art in remarkable ways. Holly Flora writes, "His works depict Christian subjects directly (both narrative and devotional), as well as metaphorically; a lonely clown rejected by society . . . becomes a present-day Man of Sorrows; a prostitute, stealing a moment of happiness with her child, stands for the Virgin Mary."[3] Rouault's work has been an inspiration and encouragement to many contemporary artists of faith as they have sought to wrestle with issues of faith and culture. He led the way in demonstrating how religious subjects can be tackled from a modern perspective. Moreover, most artists within the Christian community whom I know admire Rouault as a model of devotion and commitment—one who struggled artistically and spiritually with visual integrity.

At one point in the early twentieth century, Rouault's reputation rivaled that of Henri Matisse. He had two retrospectives at the Museum of Modern Art in New York, in 1945 and 1953. During the last half of the twentieth century, however, recognition of Rouault was often eclipsed by other figures, and he is no longer considered to be one of the major art figures of the twentieth century.[4] Only a handful of books have been published on his work since his death in 1958, and until just recently, few major museums have held exhibitions. Why might this be the case?

Rouault's works are rendered in English as translated from the French in Stephen Schloesser, ed., *Mystic Masque: Semblance and Reality in George Rouault, 1871–1958* (Boston: McMullen Museum of Art, 2008). Original French titles can be found in the image credits compiled at the end of the book.

[3]Holly Flora and Soo Yun Kang, *Georges Rouault's* Miserere et Guerre: *This Anguished World of Shadows*, exhibition catalogue (New York: Museum of Biblical Art, 2006), 9-10.

[4]Flora and Kang, *Georges Rouault's* Miserere et Guerre, 12.

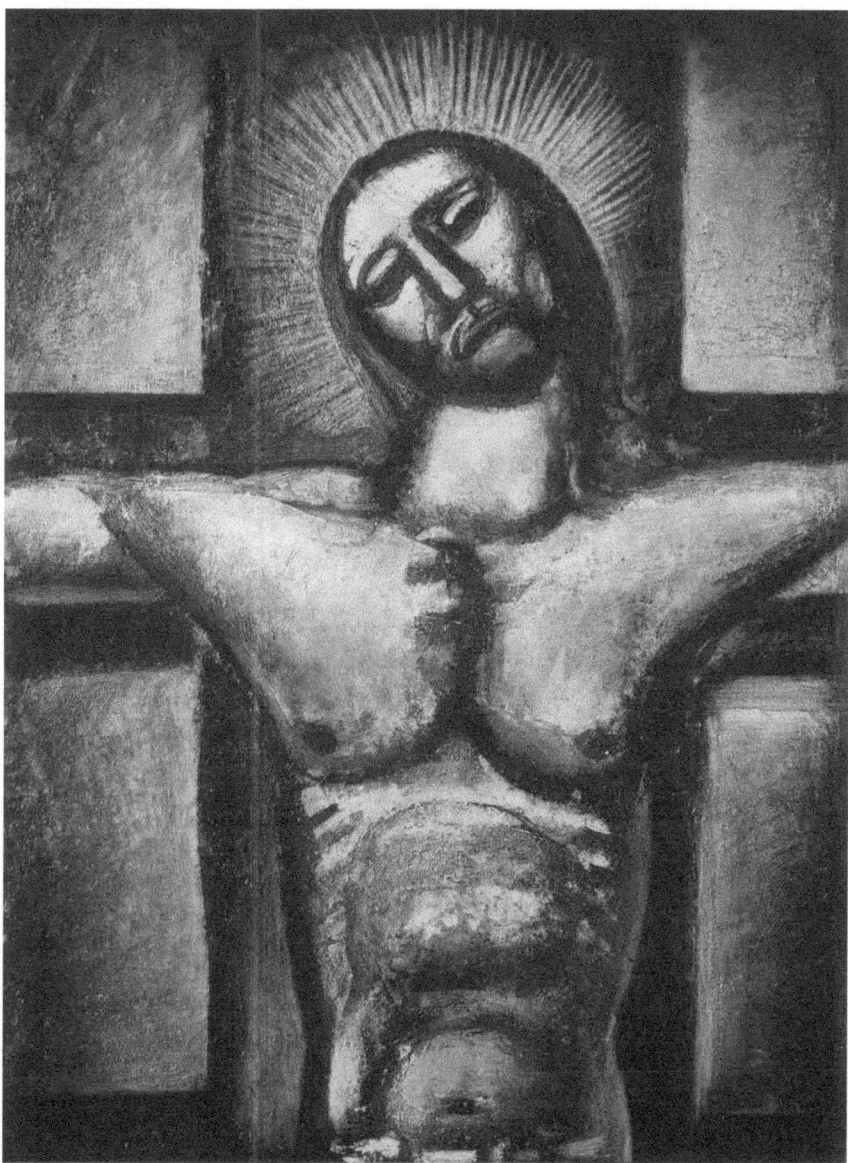

Figure F.1. Georges Rouault, *Obéissant jusqu'à la mort et à la mort de la croix (Obedient even unto death, death on the cross)*, *Miserere* plate 57, 1926. Etching on paper, 22 15/16 × 16 3/4

I believe this decline relates to the intense religious content and intent of Rouault's art, making it uncomfortable for contemporary critics and those in secular society to explore his work. It cannot be casually addressed and requires reviewers to engage theologically to interpret adequately. However, it is not only the secular world that has difficulty appreciating his art. For a good part of his life, the Catholic Church resisted the darkness of his art, since it was too far outside the sphere of the church's concept of sacred art. It was not until 1945 that Rouault received a church commission for two windows in the church of Notre-Dame de Toute Grâce du Plateau d'Assey in the French Alps—his only church commission. This is surprising given that Rouault's "faith is totally embodied in his art and his art exudes his faith."[5] Rouault was unabashedly a religious man, and he wrote, "My only ambition is to be able some day to paint a Christ so moving that those who see Him will be converted."[6]

Rouault was not just an artist but also a prophet calling his country and the world to see what was happening around them. Rouault lived through World War I and then witnessed what he viewed as a postwar decline in public and private morality. Rouault had compassion on those who were poor, prostitutes, clowns, and judges, all of whom were disregarded and discarded by society. He became a keen observer of life around him in the streets of Paris and everywhere he encountered humans in dire need of help. Rouault was aware of how society, the legal system, and the church neglected the oppressed and broken within their midst. He saw the downtrodden as types of the suffering Christ. As a kind of visual prophet, he focused his art on portrayals of suffering, particularly on the Passion of Christ, to challenge the church and society to see what he felt and observed. The works in the *Miserere* series, more than anywhere else in his work, portray the agony of human suffering and redemption through the suffering of Christ. Bill Dyrness writes, "There is an invitation implicit in these images: as Christ identified with the suffering of the world, you, me, all of us are called to go into the darkness."[7] We are asked to suffer with the poor, whether the financially poor, physically

---

[5]Ileana Marcoulesco, *Georges Rouault: The Inner Light* (Houston: Menil Collection, 1996), 3.
[6]Georges Rouault, *Miserere* (Boston: Trianon, 1963), 2.
[7]William Dyrness, "Seeing Through the Darkness: George Rouault's Vision of Christ," *Image* 67 (Winter 2020), https://imagejournal.org/article/seeing-through-the-darkness/.

poor, or spiritually poor. This is the work of the church. This is what is means to follow Jesus.

As we experience Rouault's work, he takes us into the darkness, but he does not leave us without light. That light is found in the Passion and in the face of Jesus. My hope is that Rouault's images will channel our meditations through the darkness so that, along with Rouault, we will see more fully the Christ who brings light into darkness.

Preface

Encountering Rouault

Wesley Vander Lugt

One of the best things about setting up a gallery exhibit is the amount of time you get to spend with the art. In fall 2022, as a part of my role at Gordon-Conwell Theological Seminary, I had the privilege of spending numerous hours with Georges Rouault's art through the process of unpacking, sorting, hanging, labeling, and then sitting back and enjoying dozens of works in "Seeing Christ in the Darkness: Georges Rouault as a Graphic Artist" from the Bowden Collections.[1] Having such sustained proximity to Rouault's art was a moving, formative, and expansive experience for me, especially since much of his work features marginalized subjects (clowns, prostitutes, refugees, laborers, and—most prominently—Jesus) presented in a simple, heavy style. If one is receptive, as I discovered, spending time with this artwork releases prayers of lament, longings for mercy, and empathy for the downtrodden.

Georges Rouault is unique among French modernist artists due to his deep Christian faith, emphasis on marginalized figures, heavy black contouring, and exploration of Christ's suffering. Despite his unique style and spiritual depth, theological engagement with Rouault has been limited to a few studies that are either out of print or difficult to obtain. This book seeks to bring Rouault out of the shadows and show how his empathetic imagination, honest lament, and christological concentration are a gift to all those who have experienced the pain of existence, those who desire to express this pain while

---

[1]See "Rouault: Seeing Christ in the Darkness," Bowden Collections, accessed March 18, 2024, www.bowdencollections.com/rouault-darkness.html.

maintaining hope, and those seeking a deeper understanding of the theological impulse of modernist art and Rouault's distinct contribution.

Each essay in this volume, except for Stephen Schloesser's, began as a presentation at a symposium hosted by Gordon-Conwell Theological Seminary
in Charlotte that corresponded with an exhibit of Rouault's work. While these
essays engage with Rouault's work from different angles, one unifying theme
is how Rouault's work displays our need for mercy within a world of anguish
and shadows. This emphasis is most evident in the *Miserere* series, a collection
of fifty-eight plates that began as drawings during the First World War, were
created as paintings and transferred onto copper plates in the 1920s, and finally
were printed after a long delay in 1948. Rouault viewed these prints as his most
significant and precious work, having imbued them with heartache, hope, and
the mercy offered through the sacrifice of Jesus. In his preface to the *Miserere*
series, Rouault confesses:

> Peace seems never to reign
> Over this anguished world
> Of shams and shadows[2]

Plate 27 of the *Miserere* (see fig. P.1) conveys this lament by picturing the blind
poet Orpheus with the title *There are tears in things . . . (Sunt lacrymae rerum . . .)*
from Virgil's *Aeneid*.[3] The original context of this phrase and Rouault's artistic
rendering both communicate that there are tears, sorrow, and misery at the
heart of reality, and for Rouault it was this state of things that led God in Christ
to suffer on the cross. The next line of poetry in Rouault's preface to the
Miserere is, "Jesus on the cross will tell you better than I."[4] Jesus on the cross is
both an expression of "this anguished world" and a gateway to refuge, hope,
and new life. While Rouault rarely portrayed the resurrection directly, the
reality of resurrection is nascent in the *Miserere*, especially in the plate directly
after *There are tears in things . . .*, which affirms, *"The one who believes in me, even
should he die, will live"* (M28; see web 2.1).[5]

---

[2]Georges Rouault, *Miserere* (Boston: Trianon, 1963), 8.

[3]The ellipses in some titles of Rouault's *Miserere* are intentional, sometimes linked as diptychs or
triptychs with following plates. Schloesser discusses this work in more detail in his essay.

[4]Rouault, *Miserere*, 8.

[5]Visit https://ivpress.com/rouault to access links to all the images not printed in the book. It is
recommended that you bookmark this page or keep the tab open so you can contemplate the images
as you read.

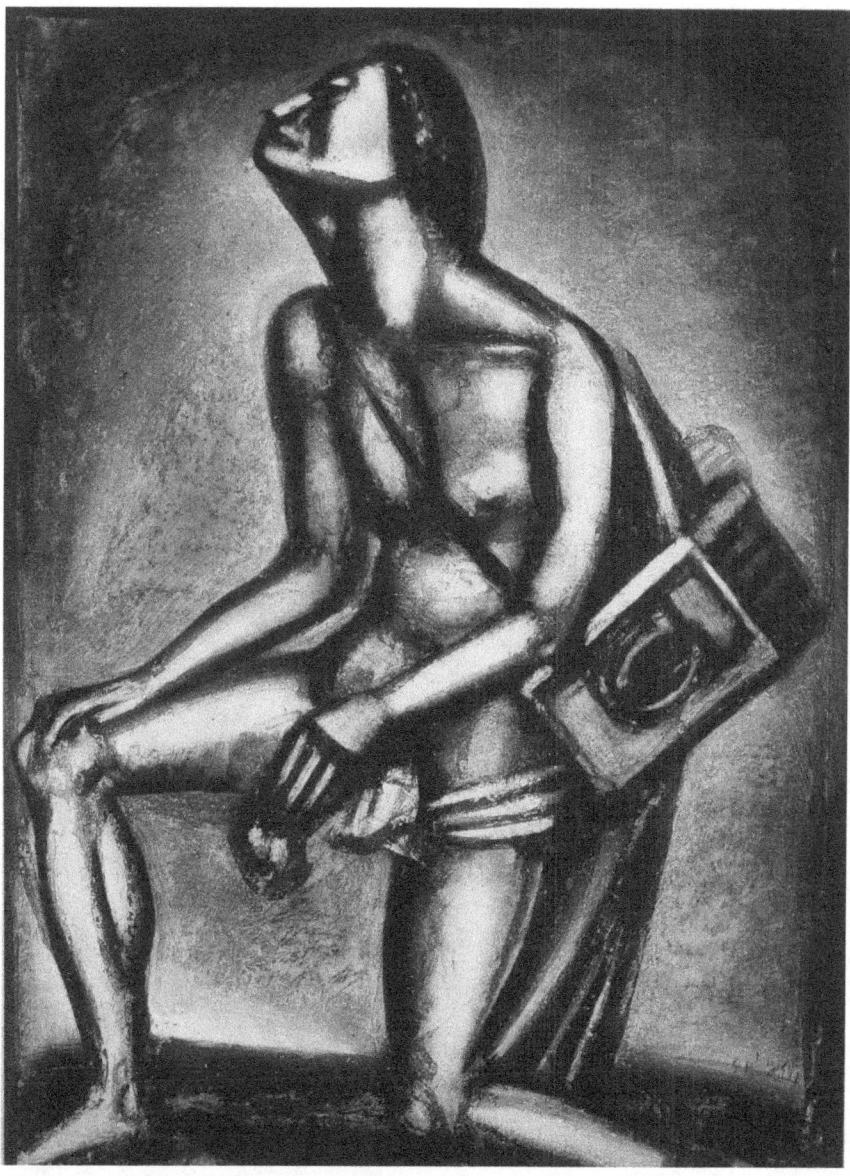

Figure P.1. Georges Rouault, *Sunt Lacrimae Rerum* (*There are tears in things . . .*), *Miserere* plate 27, 1922. Heliogravure with sugar-lift aquatint, drypoint, burnishing on paper, 22 7/8 × 16 9/16

Since Georges Rouault is often lesser known than his contemporaries Henri Matisse and Marc Chagall, it is fitting that the first essay in this volume is a biographical sketch by his great-grandson, Philippe Rouault. With insights passed down through generations, Philippe Rouault shows how Georges Rouault's artistic subjects and style were influenced by the terror of war, the death of friends and family, and personal suffering. Despite these difficulties, his Christian faith played a decisive role in the development of his unique aesthetic, which integrates lament and hope through a focus on the Passion of Christ.

Thomas Hibbs situates the gift of Rouault's art within the dynamics of our current ecological crisis and secular malaise. Drawing on the work on Jean-Luc Marion, he shows how within an anthropocentric paradigm, images typically operate as idols rather than icons, blocking our ability to encounter transcendence. In this environment, Rouault's work can make us more attentive to our disorders and can habituate us into a new pedagogy of desire. Rouault gives us a way to "see, feel, and say" things that run counter to the nihilism of our culture while avoiding sentimentality and grappling with the evil and affliction of the world.

Soo Y. Kang focuses on the experience and theology of poverty within Rouault's work as influenced by Rouault's mentor and writer Léon Bloy. She explains how Rouault's impoverished upbringing, combined with the power of Bloy's work, created empathy with the lowliest, which included not only the poor but also clowns, prostitutes, and other outcasts. Rouault once stated, "I am a silent friend of those who struggle in the deep furrow," whether that furrow is a literal furrow of mud, a social or vocational furrow of marginalization, or a spiritual furrow of despair. In this way, Kang demonstrates how Rouault's art embodies and anticipates Catholic social teaching on poverty, presenting what we might consider a visual preferential option for the poor.

Joel Klepac engages with the art of Rouault as both an artist and a therapist, integrating the wisdom of ascetic and Orthodox theology, internal family systems therapy, and the healing power of Rouault's images. He interprets the art of Rouault as a visual poetic that can evoke the viewer and hold them in dispassionate compassion (agape-apatheia), which makes possible the psychological integration of lost, abandoned, demonized, overworked, and exiled aspects of the self. As such, Klepac presents Rouault not only as a skilled artist but also as a psychological and spiritual healer who creates spaces for us as viewers to restore our own core, compassionate state.

Pamela Rossi-Keen draws on disparate disciplines of theology, art history, and community development to consider Rouault's art and impact through the lens of Walter Brueggemann's notion of prophetic imagination. By focusing on the abject of society and the dynamics of suffering, Rossi-Keen claims that Rouault's art carries prophetic weight, that he helps us see what and who we tend to ignore, perceiving the dignity as well as the tragedy of the bedraggled and hinting at the hope found in solidarity and mutual care. Rossi-Keen shows how this same kind of community-centered art is being prophetically deployed in her own community of postindustrial Pennsylvania and is contributing to the reinvigoration of community health and vibrancy.

James Romaine explores an aesthetics of empathy in the work of Rouault and sets this alongside the similar aesthetic of Romare Bearden. Romaine shows numerous parallels between Bearden and Rouault, including their sense of moral purpose, artistic methods, and subject matter. Despite his not being a practicing Christian like Rouault, Bearden's work bears similarity to Rouault's by his transformation of scenes from the American South into heroic narratives, his compulsion to integrate Christian motifs and themes into his work, and his contribution to the development of sacred art in the twentieth century. Romaine contends that both Bearden and Rouault depict scenes that contain empathetic dynamics that in turn encourage and develop the viewer's own sense of empathy.

William A. Dyrness addresses how many within the Christian tradition resist modern art and aesthetic shock, a dynamic present within Rouault's art. Dyrness shows how the reticent acceptance of Rouault's work within the Catholic Church and the lack of engagement within other religious traditions should be situated within broader antimodern trajectories. In addition, he investigates the irony of this resistance, especially given a growing awareness regarding the deeply religious roots and spiritual undercurrents of much modern art. Learning how to appreciate and engage with Rouault's art both aesthetically and theologically, therefore, can create new habits of attentiveness and receptivity toward modern art as a whole, which is a compelling alternative to more cynical and alarmist approaches.

Stephen Schloesser also engages with Rouault's art as quintessentially modern, with a focus on the *Miserere* series, which Rouault began in 1922, the year many scholars mark as the beginning of modernism. In doing so, Schloesser attends to the dynamics of appearance and reality in Rouault's work and his desire to show the world and its inhabitants as they really are in all their anguish and dignity. Schloesser presents Rouault as a visionary who helps us to encounter the beauty of a wounded world that requires the beauty of a wounded Savior. Rouault draws back the curtain and reveals the possibility of finding mercy amid tears.

In the final essay, I turn toward the question of reception and what makes the art of Georges Rouault resonate with the contemporary viewer. If anything, what the original symposium that gathered these scholars and artists together around the work of Rouault showed, and what I hope this volume will demonstrate, is that we can create the right conditions for resonance with Rouault's art through sustained presence, attentive perception, and adaptive response. What this requires, however, is the belief that the art of Rouault is valuable and that it has agency, that it continues to speak to us today, often in unexpected yet vital ways.

One of the elements that made the 2022 symposium unique and powerful was that several artists were invited to respond to Rouault's art with their own artistic expressions, both written and visual. Some artists created a new work as a resonant response to Rouault, while others identified an existing work with a strong connection to the themes and styles of Rouault. These artists then had the opportunity not only to show or present their work but also to give a short statement to provide a window into the creative process and artistic meaning. These are printed here as artistic interludes. In addition, I discovered at the symposium that Leslie Anne Bustard had written several poems in response to some specific works by Rouault. It is an honor to include two of those poems as an artistic conclusion in memory of her joyful presence and beautiful talents, which were cut short by her battle with cancer. Her poems, like Rouault's art, witness to the presence of Christ in both suffering and new life.

This volume presents the art of Rouault as a vast reservoir of theological wisdom and an enduring gift to help us lament the brokenness of the world while clinging to hope. Similar to how the Psalms give us holy permission to lament while affirming God's faithful presence, Rouault's art provides a guide for engaging with the glorious ruin of life in a way that keeps turning our attention toward the merciful agony of a crucified Messiah. In this anguished world of sorrows, shams, and shadows, tears may abound, but Rouault reminds us that God's mercy will carry us through.

Acknowledgments

My gratitude extends first and foremost to all the scholars and artists who agreed to present at the symposium in September 2022 at Gordon-Conwell Theological Seminary on the theme "Humanity Redeemed: Theology and the Art of Georges Rouault." The content, interaction, and overall experience of that weekend were incredibly rich, which is a testimony to those who presented as well as all who attended and participated. The way in which the artistic creations and statements illuminated the scholarly presentations and vice versa convinced me that this volume should be published and made available to a broader audience.

The symposium on Georges Rouault, which resulted in this book, was the first event of the newly formed Leighton Ford Initiative in Theology, the Arts, and Gospel Witness at Gordon-Conwell Theological Seminary. As such, I'm also deeply grateful for the leadership of Gordon-Conwell, most notably President Scott Sunquist, for believing in the power of the arts to form students, enrich the church, and propel participation in God's mission to make all things new. With his encouragement and the support of Dr. Brad Howell and Dr. Gerry Wheaton at the Charlotte campus where this initiative is based, I have been able to carve out the necessary time and energy to lead events and publish new work that will advance the burgeoning intersection between theology and the arts.

I also want to thank Robert and Sandra Bowden, who not only provided the collection of Georges Rouault's work for display at Gordon-Conwell but also were generous supporters of the symposium and the publication of this volume. We need more robust patronage of the arts within the church and theological education, and the Bowdens are a shining example of how that can be accomplished.

Finally, I'm grateful to former InterVarsity Press editor David McNutt for initially seeing the value of this book and for current editor Jon Boyd for seeing it through completion, along with Rebecca Carhart and the whole team at InterVarsity Press. It's an honor to have this volume on Georges Rouault included within the other remarkable contributions in the Studies in Theology and the Arts series.

Georges Rouault

A Personal Introduction

Philippe Rouault

Georges Rouault occupies a unique place among twentieth-century artists. He was at once an exceptional painter, draftsman, engraver, and writer. He found inspiration in the most mystical and humble subjects. His critical observation of society led him to tackle themes that remain current today: clowns and acrobats, judges and lawyers, prostitutes, migrants, and fugitives. Defying a century that was too callous for his taste, Rouault testified to an unfailing faith by illustrating the Passion of Christ. But this chapter is not primarily about the art of Rouault. Rather, my purpose is to provide a brief overview of his life along with some of the stories that have been handed down to me.

My great-grandfather Georges Rouault and my great-grandmother Marthe Le Sidaner lived together as husband and wife for half a century. They had four children and eleven grandchildren, and in my generation there are twenty-nine great-grandchildren. Georges-Henri Rouault was born in a cellar on May 27, 1871, during the tumultuous "Bloody Week" at the end of the Paris Commune, which occurred in the wake of France's defeat in the Franco-German War and the collapse of Napoleon III's Second Empire. A stray shell struck the house of his grandparents at 51 rue de la Villette in Paris, and the young expectant mother had to be moved into the cellar, where she gave birth to her second child. Georges Rouault kept a piece of this shell all his life. A month later, he was baptized in the Catholic Church of Saint Leu.

A frail little boy, Rouault spent a happy childhood in the working-class area of Belleville in Paris. He was a great admirer of his mother, Marie-Louise, initially a seamstress and later an administrator, who was up at dawn to take on additional work that helped pay for his education. His father, Alexandre, was born into a large family in the town of Monfort in Brittany. He worked as a carpenter and varnisher at the Pleyel piano workshop in Paris. As Rouault came from a relatively poor family, outings were rare, but occasionally a circus would come to town, and the clowns, riders, and acrobats made an impression on Rouault from an early age.

His maternal grandfather, Alexandre Champdavoine, was employed by the post office on the train between Paris and Marseille. He was an open-minded man who read Johann Wolfgang von Goethe and Baruch Spinoza and collected reproductions of Rembrandt, Édouard Manet, and Honoré Daumier. When Rouault was only four years old, his grandfather found him drawing on the kitchen tiles with chalk and was delighted to see that he had talent. He greatly encouraged Rouault. They also shared a love of reading, especially of Victor Hugo, whose funeral Rouault followed across Paris, riding on his grandfather's shoulders. Rouault was fifteen at the time his dearly loved grandfather died. From that time on he wore his portrait on a medallion and kept it all his life (see fig. 1.1). He was a happy child and an excellent pupil who loved sports and was appreciated by his teachers.

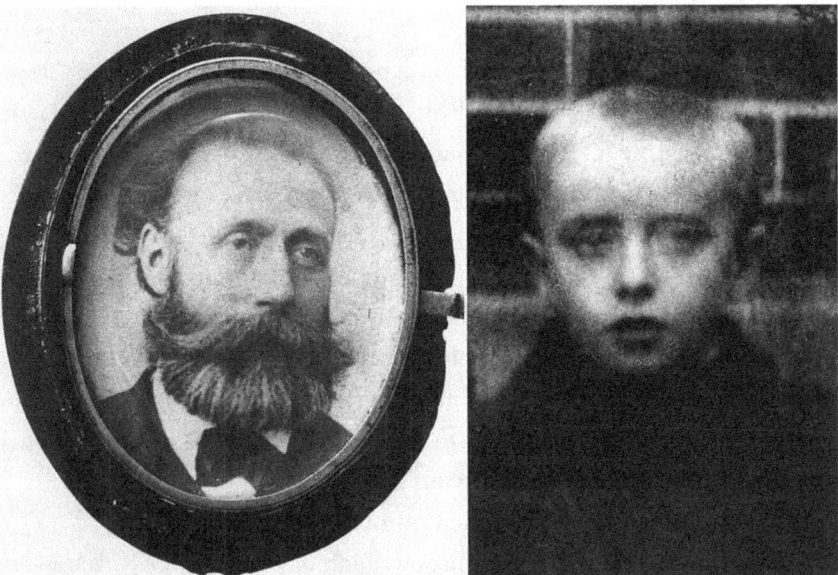

Figure 1.1. Rouault with his maternal grandfather

By the age of fourteen he was working as an apprentice to a glass painter, Tamoni, in order to earn a living. The work was hard, as he had to handle heavy lead plates. But he was full of energy. His love of sports served him well, as whenever he was sent on an errand he would keep the bus fare, preferring to run after the bus and use the money to buy paints. Following this, he went to work for prestigious glass painter and medieval windows restorer Georges Hirsch. He observed and was enraptured by the old stained-glass windows, which he meticulously detailed every day instead of having lunch. He called this his paradise hour. This period of learning seems to have been decisive and is often said to be the source of the heavy black lines that characterize Rouault's mature style. He rose at dawn to draw on an easel that his father had made for him, and in the evening he would walk to the other side of Paris to draw from antiques and from life at the School of Decorative Arts.

On December 3, 1890, when not yet twenty years old, Rouault entered the École de Beaux-Arts in Paris. For the first two years, his teacher, Elie Delauney, made him work on his drawing technique. He sat numerous exams but really wanted to paint. For that he had to wait until Delauney died and Gustave Moreau was nominated as her successor. Straight away, Rouault admired this exceptional teacher and quickly became his favorite pupil. The master sent his pupil to the opera and theater, opened his library to him, and insisted on the works of Blaise Pascal. Rouault, reflecting on his time in Gustave Moreau's studio, says, "I was mute; I would reply yes . . . no . . . that's all." But his fellow students gave quite a different opinion. One of them, Paul Baigneres, said, "We only heard him!" During this time, Henri Matisse and Rouault became very close, and their friendship lasted their whole lives. They wrote to each other for more than fifty years, and many of these letters are carefully preserved at the Rouault Foundation.[1]

Although Rouault won the Chevenard prize and the Fortin d'Ivry prize, Moreau was disappointed to see him ousted from the Prix de Rome and therefore encouraged him to continue working from his studio. After leaving the Beaux-Arts, Rouault continued to submit his work to Moreau as his patron, bringing him the fruit of his independent research, such as the painting

---

[1]Fondation Georges Rouault, https://rouault.org/en/.

le Paysage de nuit—translated *Night Landscape* but also known as *The brawl on the construction site*—from 1897 (see web 3.1). For many years, this painting was the property of Henry Simon, colonial minister during World War I, and is now part of the collection at the Musée d'Orsay.

In 1898, his beloved friend Moreau died of cancer. Before his death, he made Georges promise that he would never smoke, a promise he kept all his life. Rouault said, "My old master has left me. I wasn't a novice or student to him. But the happy confidant of his conscious thoughts." And so Rouault discovered solitude. He wrote, "If my art is harsh, it is probably due to this period of my existence."

Although he came from a Catholic family, Rouault waited to confirm his faith by taking Communion until the age of twenty-four, encouraged by Father Vallee, a Benedictine monk whom he met through René Piot, a classmate at the Beaux-Arts. Moreau, while not a practicing Christian, had a deep belief in the spiritual value of art and may have had some influence in Rouault's later decision. Rouault's faith can be seen clearly in his art, and form and color are central to his thinking.

Following the death of Moreau, Rouault suffered from depression: a moral, spiritual, and artistic crisis. In 1901, he found refuge at the Ligugé Abbey near Poitiers, where Catholic writer Joris-Karl Huysmans had invited a group of artists to join him (see fig. 1.2). But following the enactment of a law targeting certain associations, the Ligugé community had to be dissolved, and Rouault returned to Paris.

In 1903, Rouault was named curator of the Musée Gustave Moreau according to the wishes expressed in Moreau's will. Rouault had on-site accommodation and an office. This office, which was previously Moreau's, has now been refurbished as it was over one hundred years ago, and it is a moving experience to visit it at 14 rue de Rochefoucauld in Paris.

From this time on, American collectors such as John Quinn, attorney general in New York, and Walter Pach bought Rouault's paintings and ceramics. In France, Gustave Coquiot, Marcel Sambat and Georgette Agutte, Henri Simon, le Docteur Girardin, and Alfonse Druet bought paintings such as *La Peniche* (*The Houseboat*), *l'Escalier* (*The Staircase*), and *Le Clown au Bandoneon* (*The Clown on the Bandoneon*). Rouault then presented works at the Salon d'Automne and at the Salon des Indépendants. He soon became a

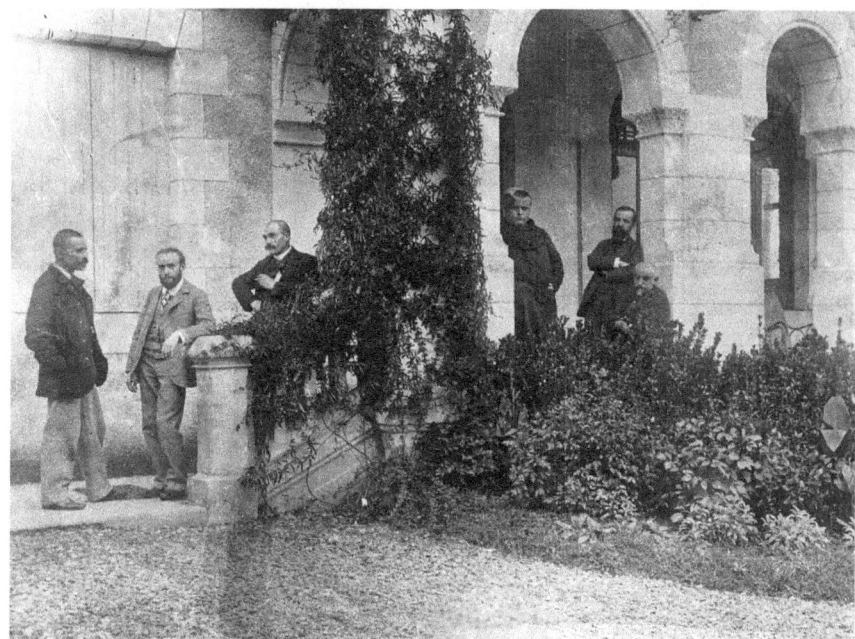

Figure 1.2. Rouault with others at Ligugé Abbey

member of the jury at the Salon d'Automne. His first individual exhibition of 183 works was held in the Galerie Druet in 1910.

Rouault seldom visited cafes and never really participated in the bohemian life of Paris, preferring to stay closer to Catholic circles. He took advantage of his role at the Gustave Moreau Museum to make new friends, first Léon Bloy, a Catholic writer, and then Thomist philosophers Jacques and Raïssa Maritain. The painter Edgar Degas came to meet him at the museum. He was also close to writers Jacques Rivière and Alain-Fournier (Rivière's brother-in-law) and artist André Lhote. In 1911, he met writer André Suarès, confiding in him and describing his inner creative torment. This was the beginning of a very long friendship, captured in their precious correspondence, which continued until 1948.

Rouault was particularly struck by the novel *La Femme pauvre* (*The Poor Woman*) by Léon Bloy. The book follows the miserable life of a woman named Clotilde who, animated by her strong faith, is able to endure all her sufferings, including those inflicted by Madame Poulot. In 1905 at the Salon d'Automne, Rouault shocked the public with dark and cartoonish paintings. Bloy reacted violently to the sight of the painting *Les Poulots* (see web 3.3), inspired by the characters from Bloy's book, which he found ugly. Nevertheless, the two men remained close friends until the writer's death in 1917.

After Rouault's parents came back to the family home from Algeria, where they had gone to help his sister Emilie following the death of her husband, his mother became his assistant, taking care of his mail and filing articles concerning him and his work. All of this documentation has been preserved and is available to consult at the Rouault Foundation.

In 1907, one of Rouault's friends declared, "No young girl from good society would want to marry you, my poor Rouault, with the painting you do." However, a year later, on January 27, 1908, at age thirty-six, Rouault married pianist Marthe Le Sidaner, the daughter of a sea captain and sister of painter Henri Le Sidaner. The young couple moved into the Gustave Moreau Museum, where their first child, Geneviève, was born in 1909. In 1910, before the birth of their next child, Isabelle, they left their lodgings at the museum and moved to the Rue Blanche in Paris. Then again in 1912, before the birth of their third child, Michel, they moved to Versailles. Marthe had given a concert there, which led to several new pupils, and for a long time they depended on her income from teaching piano.

It was also in Versailles that Rouault's father died, and he was profoundly affected. He said of his father, "As a man of common sense, he feared me being a painter. He would have wanted me to have a good job, whereas painters were very frowned upon at the time." He also wrote, "It was following the death of my father that I made a series called *Miserere*, in which I put the best of myself." In 1915, Agnès, Rouault's fourth and last child, was born.

Although he was a hard worker, Rouault remained very close to his children (see fig. 1.3). His daughter Geneviève recounts, "All four of us were disguised as clowns. He liked to paint our faces and knew how to comb and lacquer our hair. He read marvelously well. I remember 'The Gold-Bug' by Edgar Allen Poe which we listened to, lying on the floor in deep silence. Over the years we listened to him reading Victor Hugo, Balzac, Dickens (*David Copperfield*) and lastly Alain-Fournier. Sometimes, when we were in bed, not yet asleep, Papa would stand and read us poems that he had written for us" (see fig. 1.4).

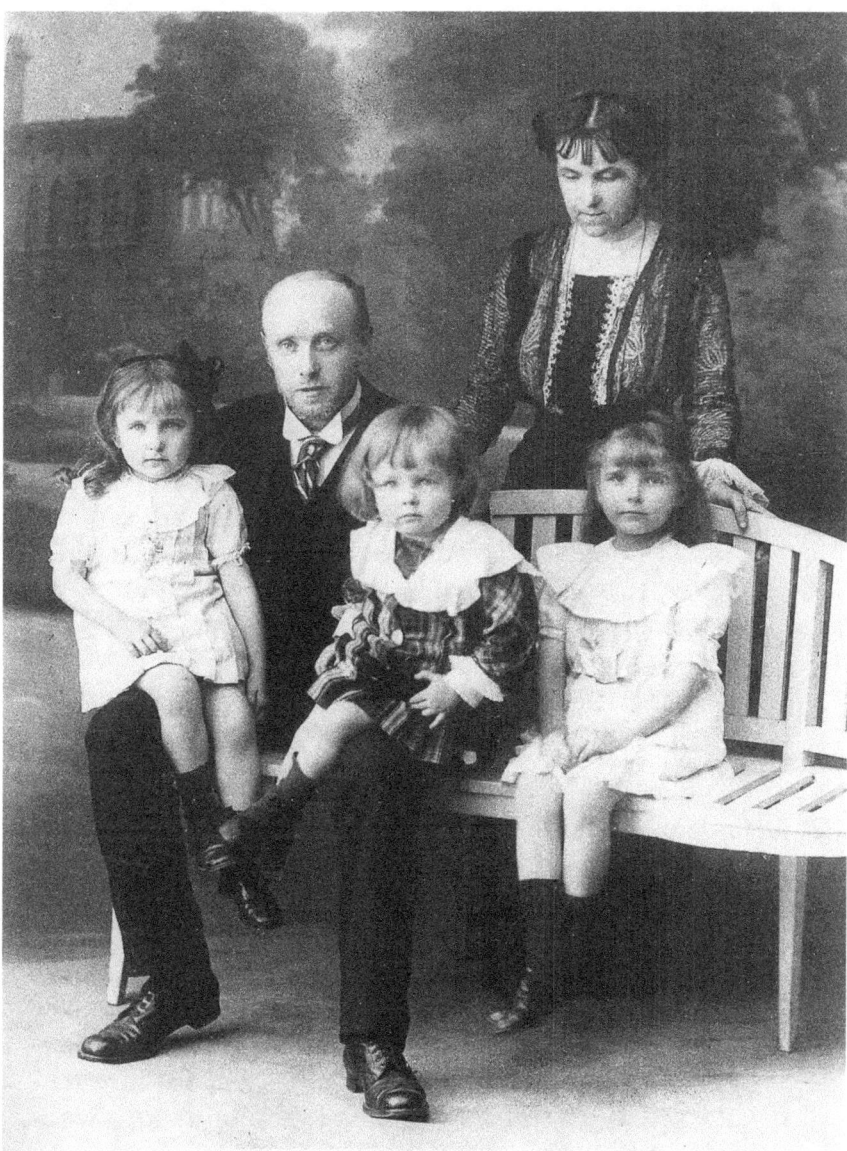

Figure 1.3. Rouault with his family

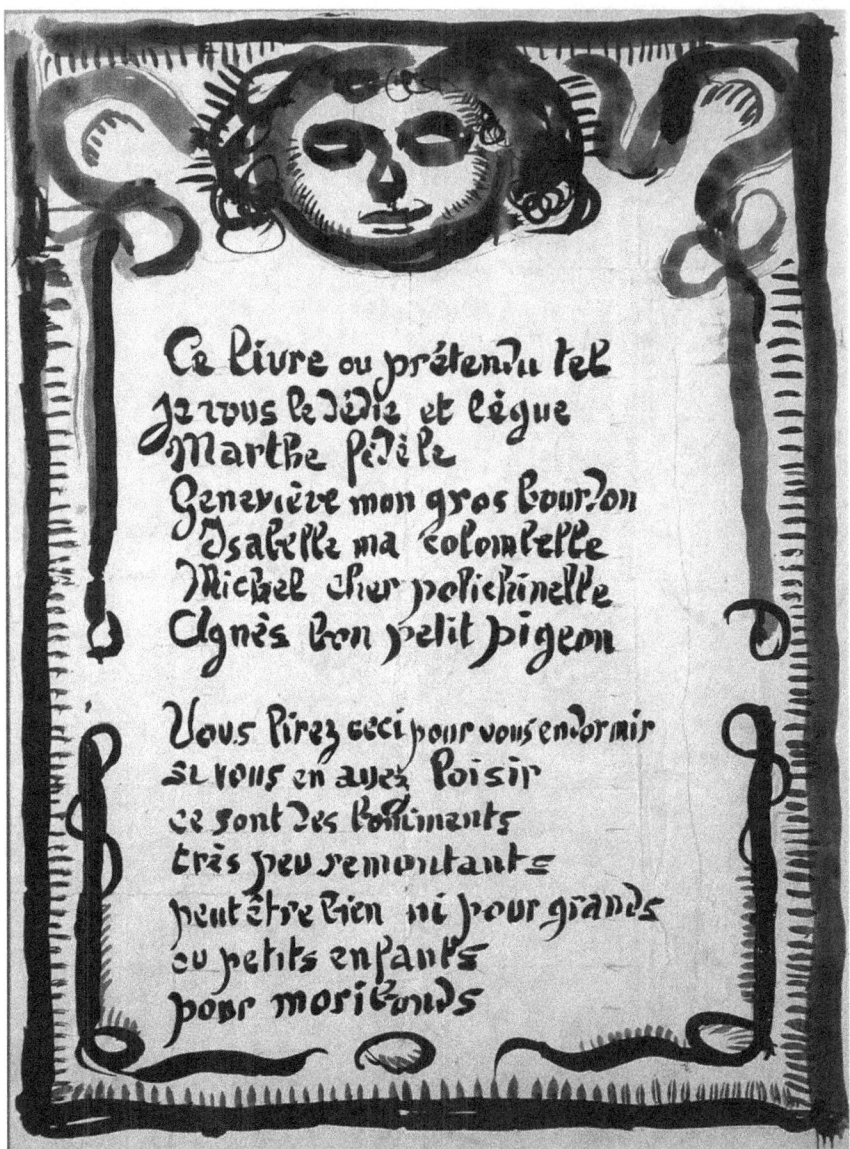

Figure 1.4. An original poem by Rouault

The year 1916 marked the beginning of Rouault's collaboration with Ambroise Vollard. In 1917, Vollard, who was one of the most prestigious art dealers in Paris, expressed a desire to buy Rouault's output. They had known each other for more than ten years, and Rouault agreed to give Vollard artistic exclusivity in return for a fixed salary, on the condition that he would have his whole life to finish the works he had already sketched out. The dealer made a studio available to Rouault on the top floor of his grand house. Rouault was gradually overwhelmed with work because he was required not only to paint but also to illustrate and produce books. The first book, *The Reincarnations of Pere Ubu*, was published in 1932, but Rouault had been working on it since 1917. The boards for the *Miserere* were drawn between 1922 and 1927, although the work was not published until 1948. In 1928, Rouault and Suarès completed a book project on which they had worked together for several years, but Vollard refused to publish the writings of Suarès. Though frustrated, Rouault agreed to replace the poetry of Suarès with his own writings, naming the finished book *The Circus of the Shooting Star*, published in 1938. *The Passion*, a book with writing and artwork, was published in 1939. During this period, Rouault painted less and focused on printmaking. He was more and more a prisoner in his studio, with his daughter Isabelle assisting him with administrative tasks.

His most well-known book, *Miserere*, represents in fifty-eight engravings the misery of the world and the mercy of God, evoking on one the one hand misery, pride, vice, and death and on the other hand patience, tenderness, and love. The images of Christ torn between these two contrary worlds are arranged in this book in a deeply thoughtful manner. This work, the realization of which required many years of labor, was born in the mind of Rouault in his youth but was not published until 1948 (see fig. 1.5).

In July 1939, Vollard died in a car accident, and Rouault was deeply moved. Barely a year after Vollard's death, Rouault wisely made an inventory of what he made and delivered to Vollard; it added up to around one hundred paintings. Vollard did not have any children, but he still had heirs, who sealed the studio so that Rouault could not get in to claim his work. World War II broke out, however, and Rouault had to wait to the end of the war for the trial against Vollard's heirs, who had appropriated everything in the studio and begun to sell it in America. Rouault argued with Vollard's heirs that the unfinished art that remained in the studio must be returned to him. It took a long time, but the court sided with Rouault, and the appeal court confirmed this ruling. This set a precedent for the rights of the artist, ensuring that, unless exhibited or put up for

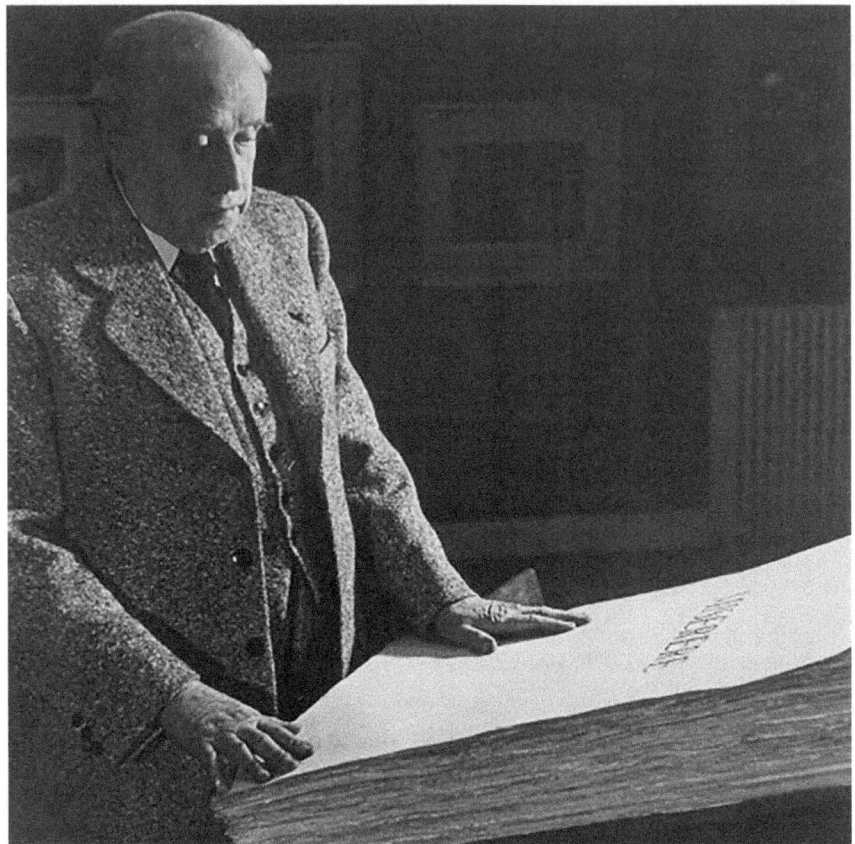

Figure 1.5. Rouault with *Miserere*

sale, artwork belonged freely to the artist. Rouault did not regain every-thing, as some works were already sold, but regarding the hundreds he did regain, he declared, "I am seventy years old; I can't finish everything myself, so out of respect for my art and to clearly show that I didn't do this for money, I will burn them." He burned over three hundred works in a factory chimney (see fig. 1.6).

Born under the bombardments, Rouault lived painfully through the two world wars. He illustrated the world's sufferings in the *Miserere* but also in paintings that are sadly still relevant today, such as *The Fugitives—Exodus* (see fig. 3.1), and *Man is wolf to man* (*Homo homini lupus*), which pictures a man hanged on gallows (see web 1.1). During World War II, Rouault left Paris for Beaumont-sur-Sarthe, then the south of France. After this

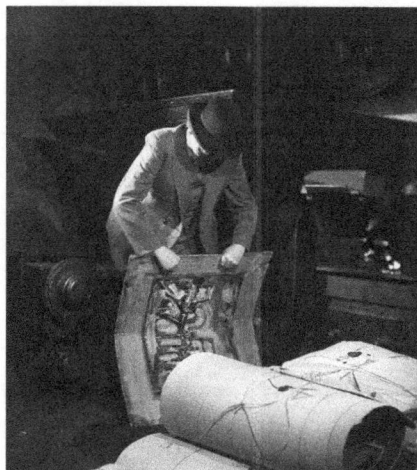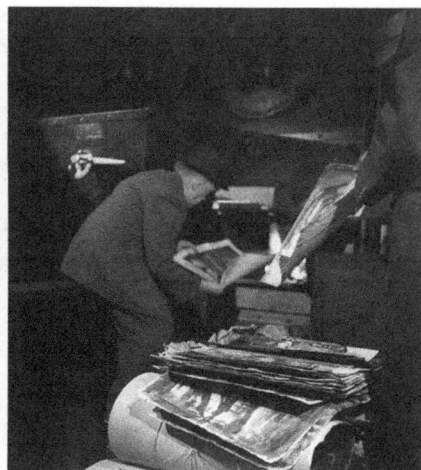

Figure 1.6. Rouault burning his work

difficult period, he lived and worked in the apartment near the Gare de Lyon in Paris. The last years of his life were lived in serenity, surrounded by his family.

After World War II, the Vatican became increasingly interested in Rouault and his work, and a room dedicated to Rouault was opened in the Vatican Museum. Rouault was elevated to the rank of commander in the order of Saint Gregory the Great. In 1957, when French President René Coty was received by Pope Pius XII, he presented the pope with Rouault's masterpiece, the *Miserere*, specially bound in white leather and stamped with the arms of the Sovereign Pontiff. In 1965, during a trip to the United States, Pope Paul VI donated Rouault's *Christ Crucified* to be hung in the headquarters of the United Nations (see web 1.2). In 2016, Pope Francis had a reproduction of *Head of Christ* (1937) from the Cleveland Museum made in the form of a medallion and distributed a copy to one hundred thousand young people gathered in Saint Peter's Square (see web 1.3).

After Vollard's death, when Rouault regained his liberty, he received numerous requests for stained-glass windows, but he chose to engage in only a few projects, assisted by Paul Bony, and preferred to work on his unfinished paintings. In 1949, the Catholic Church commissioned four windows that decorate the chapel of Notre Dame de Toute Grâce in Plateau d'Assy. Two more windows can be admired in the church of Fontaine-la-Soret in

Normandy. In addition, a stained-glass window is installed in a chapel built on the slopes of Mount Fuji in Japan.

Rouault painted until 1956, when he was eighty-five years old. *Sarah* is one of his last works and is part of the Rouault Foundation endowment (see web 1.4). She keeps watch over the studio and the archives that are carefully preserved in his apartment. Rouault died on February 13, 1958, and is one of the rare French artists to have had a state funeral. A commander of the Legion d'Honneur, he held many other French and foreign decorations. His works can be found in numerous museums across the world and have been shown in hundreds of exhibitions. In 1963, the family donated one thousand unfinished works from Rouault's studio to the state. An exhibition of these works took place at the Louvre in 1964. André Malraux also organized a presentation for General Charles de Gaulle at the presidential palace, where he personally thanked the family for the exceptional donation (see fig. 1.7). In 2021, a tribute to Georges Rouault was held at the Centre Pompidou on the 150th anniversary of his birth. The foundation in Paris manages the work and the archives and has a permanent staff. The Centre Pompidou permanently presents works from the donation in a Rouault room, and a Rouault Museum in Tokyo finances and presents themed exhibitions on the work of Rouault.

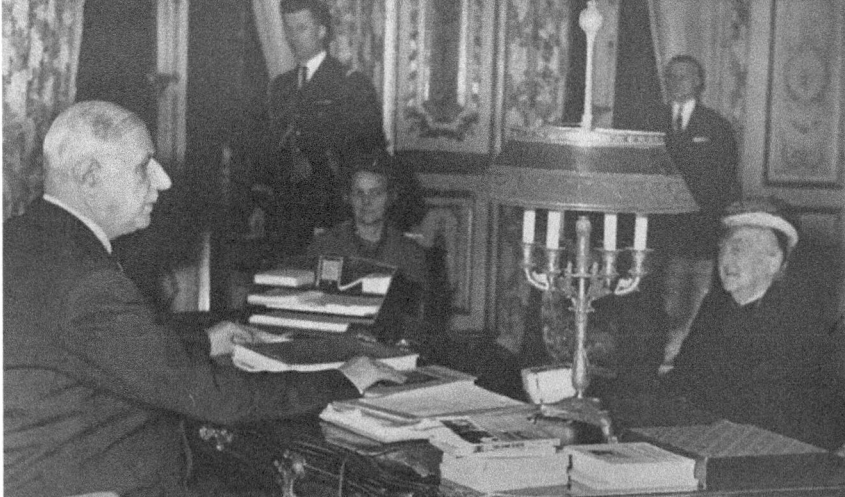

Figure 1.7. Rouault family with General de Gaulle

Although I never met my great-grandfather, I feel privileged to have spent my life surrounded by his art, attending the openings of many exhibitions around the world, and seeing the impact of his art on people who are often encountering his art for the first time. In these days of conflict and division, with many problems in society, Georges Rouault is more relevant than ever in depicting the nature of suffering and what it means to be human.

"Unrefined Impressions"

Dave Reinhardt

Undefined, blocks of color and a path—
The door beckons and ensconces those who enter.
Christ and the clown—two common cast members
haunt the canvas with their pain and with their comfort.
Fishermen along the shores of the lake
look to the Christ for sustenance only He can provide.
The clown looks to the crowd for sustenance he knows they cannot.
Impressions are made and kept in grace,
like the dancer whose form is not fully formed, and whose
face is unrecognizable to all but those who share her frame.
The fire of autumnal colors—embers now of their former flame.
Peasants and paupers overseen by farmers and the Father.
Three figures huddle together, sheltered by the seasons
of life poor and short, stooped by the winter winds.
Lines thick and unrefined, undefined by the shape of a soul,
set within, yet cast without, beyond the pale blue shadow figure.
Lost and found by threads of Passion for those hidden figures,
the God-man looks and sees beyond the scope—true hope.
Self-portrait of a man who seems sadder than the photos
which capture his visage but not his soul.
Lines colored by feelings of despair, an heir unapparent.
Christ of compassion willingly extends his hand to the man
who sees in pictures and brushes his thoughts on canvas.
Seeing anew is the gift he brings to those who come with eyes to see
vistas of the familiar—faint details bestow clarity.
The Story unfolding before the eyes of our spirit.
Indelible impressions of things seen and unseen.

2

Learning to See, Feel, and Say

Rouault's Art as Propaedeutic to Theology

Thomas Hibbs

In Terrence Malick's film *The Tree of Life*, a child says to his mother, "Tell us a story from before we can remember." Children love to hear tales about their birth, their parents' marriage, and their ancestors. The film itself, which is a series of recollections centering on the death of a family member in war, includes the origin story of the entire universe. It probes human questions about suffering, evil, loss, and the presence or absence of God. Early in the film, a character asks, "Where were you? What are we to you?" The film inscribes the drama of one family within the whole of the created order, something that is surprisingly rare even in explicitly theological reflections on human life. Christians tend to concentrate on the exclusively human elements of the cosmos, perhaps in flight from the theory of evolution or befuddled by the vastness of the universe.

Malick's film suggests a visual grammar for recovering a sense of our place within the whole. Moved by its images, story, and artistry, we can learn or relearn how to see, feel, and express mysteries having to do with our relations to neighbor, nature, and God. This is an essential theological task for our time, a task for which the art of Georges Rouault is especially well suited. His art offers precisely this kind of pedagogy in seeing, feeling, and saying. Without such a relearning, the full teaching of the gospel will not resonate in our souls. In the encyclical *Laudato Si'*, Pope Francis puts it this way:

> Human life is grounded in three fundamental and closely intertwined relationships: with God, with our neighbour and with the earth itself. According to the Bible, these three vital relationships have been broken, both outwardly and within us. This rupture is sin. The harmony between the Creator, humanity and

creation as a whole was disrupted by our presuming to take the place of God and refusing to acknowledge our creaturely limitations.[1]

Known in the popular press mostly for its affirmation of global warming, *Laudato Si'* is a theologically rich document. The ecological crisis is a symptom of a much deeper disorder. Francis writes, "If the present ecological crisis is one small sign of the ethical, cultural and spiritual crisis of modernity, we cannot presume to heal our relationship with nature and the environment without healing all fundamental human relationships." At the root of the modern crisis is a mistaken view of human freedom, which Francis, here following his papal predecessors Benedict XVI and John Paul II, calls radical anthropocentrism. We have forgotten that "man is not only a freedom which he creates for himself. Man does not create himself. He is spirit and will, but also nature." According to the anthropocentric or technocratic paradigm, there is "no intrinsic value in lower beings." Diametrically opposed to this view is biocentrism, which sees "no special value in human beings." Our dilemma would be somewhat limited if it had to do with a tendency to opt for one of these options. But it is deeper because we oscillate between the two options, in a "constant schizophrenia." We are lost in the cosmos.[2]

The radically anthropocentric paradigm sees the entire physical world, including the human body, as raw material to be manipulated to satisfy human desire. Such a model has had a huge impact on our visual culture. In his work on the crisis of the visible in contemporary culture, philosopher Jean-Luc Marion argues that in our culture, images typically operate as consumerist idols. In the guise of idols, objects present themselves to us as "proportionate to the expectation of desire," the way in which consumer goods present themselves to us as satisfying whatever desires or preferences we happen to have at the moment. The idol thus satisfies desires, without educating, transforming, or even questioning them.[3] The opposite of the idol is the icon. While Marion's notion of the idol remains quite consistent, his conception of the icon

---

[1]All quotations are from the official English language version of Pope Francis, *Laudato Si': On Care for Our Common Home* (Vatican City: Libreria Editrice Vaticana, 2015), here para. 66. See also Denis Edwards, *The Natural World and God: Theological Explorations* (Adelaide, Australia: ATF, 2017), 102–5.
[2]Francis, *Laudato Si'*, paras. 119, 6, 118.
[3]Jean-Luc Marion, *Crossing the Visible* (Stanford, CA: Stanford University Press, 2003), 51. Marion writes, "The authentic painting would not give itself to be seen in such glory if it had not taken and surprised our scope of expectation."

varies, from a fairly narrow idea connected with traditional religious iconography to a broader notion that covers painting itself. The icon brings "unseen to light" and puts the viewer in question.[4]

Parallel to the crisis of the visible is a crisis of speech, the crumbling connection between word and world. As George Steiner famously put it, the "covenant between signified and signifier is broken."[5] Loss of meaning and belonging results from the demise of the "civilization of the word" and the loss of the "instauration of truth between word and world."[6] Seeing and saying are interconnected; to restore one, we must restore the other. It seems obvious that in order to say something, we would first have to see or know something, but the reverse can be true as well. An expanded vocabulary can help us to see more and better whatever it is that we encounter. Moreover, if our seeing is distorted by disordered desire, we will neither see nor name clearly. What we see or fail to see is often influenced by our passions. We must learn anew how to see, to feel, and to say.

The radical anthropocentric paradigm gives a particular inflection to our incapacity to see, feel, and say. If we tend to think of the external world, perhaps even our own bodies, as raw material at the disposal of the whims of our desires and preferences, that may well distort all sorts of things about nature, others, even ourselves. Another way to articulate the crisis is as a crisis of *homo faber*, the human person as maker. In an illuminating commentary on *Laudato Si'*, Naomi Oreskes, professor of the history of science at Harvard University, identifies the misleading paradigm as "technofideism," which involves a blind faith in technology.[7] The problem is that we have lost our ability to direct technology in an ethical way.[8]

The technocratic disposition focuses on the human capacity to transform nature and thus neglects or repudiates the notion that human persons, in their stance toward nature, are fundamentally receptive to an order not of their own devising. By way of reaction against the consequences of the anthropocentric

---

[4]Marion, *Crossing the Visible*, 42. Marion sees painting as a paradigmatic instance of pure manifestation and thus an ideal subject for phenomenological reflection. Because it is sheer presentation, "the painting becomes for us one of the rare but powerful challenges to mastery."

[5]As quoted and discussed in James Davison Hunter, *To Change the World: The Irony, Tragedy, and Possibility of Christianity in the Late Modern World* (Oxford: Oxford University Press, 2010), 220.

[6]Hunter, *To Change the World*, 205.

[7]Naomi Oreskes, introduction to *Encyclical on Climate Change and Inequality: On Care for Our Common Home* (London: Melville House, 2016), vii-xxiv.

[8]Francis, *Laudato Si'*, para. 112.

model, biocentrism is tempted to see human intervention in nature as dangerous and evil. Pope Francis takes another approach. He highlights the dignity of human persons and the "nobility of the human vocation," which involves a participation "in God's creative action." He advocates for an "aesthetic education." The appreciation and practice of the beautiful fosters the ecological virtues of receptivity, wonder, humility, and gratitude.[9]

The art of Rouault offers precisely such a recovery of the place of human existence within the whole cosmos. One of the striking features of his art is his pairing of words and images, texts and paintings or prints. His art is a pedagogy in seeing, feeling, and saying. In what follows I can give only an introductory exposition of some features of Rouault's art as a kind of propaedeutic to theology in that it prepares us to approach and study theology properly. His art is especially powerful precisely because it is neither purely religious nor purely secular. It mediates between the two in ways that can help us to identify, name, and respond affectively to the disorders and longings of our souls.

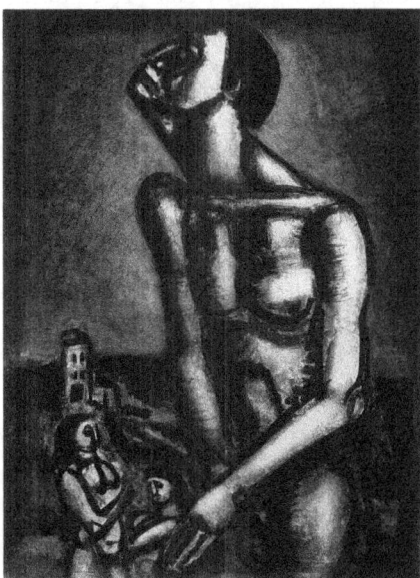

Figure 2.1. Georges Rouault, *Ne sommes-nous pas forçats?* . . . (*Are we not all slaves?* . . .), *Miserere* plate 6, 1926. Aquatint and drypoint with roulette over photogravure, 23 3/8 × 17 3/16

---

[9]Francis, *Laudato Si'*, paras. 65, 131, 220-32. For more on ecology and ethics, see Willis Jenkins, "Environmental Virtues: Charity, Nature, and Divine Friendship in Thomas," in *Ecologies of Grace: Environmental Ethics and Christian Theology* (Oxford: Oxford University Press, 2008), 132-51. Also

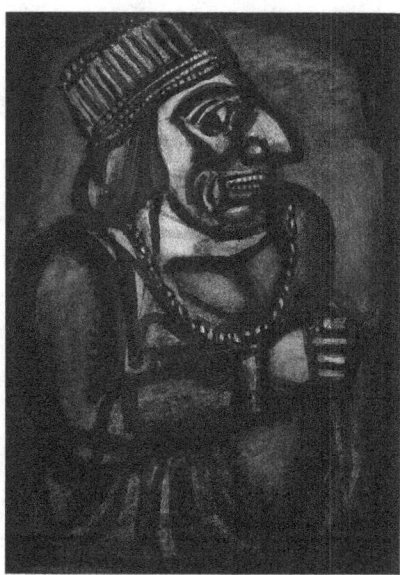

Figure 2.2. Georges Rouault, *nous croyant rois. (believing ourselves to be kings.)*, *Miserere* plate 7, 1923. Heliogravure, with sugar-lift aquatint, scraping, burnishing, and roulette on paper, 23 1/4 × 16 9/16

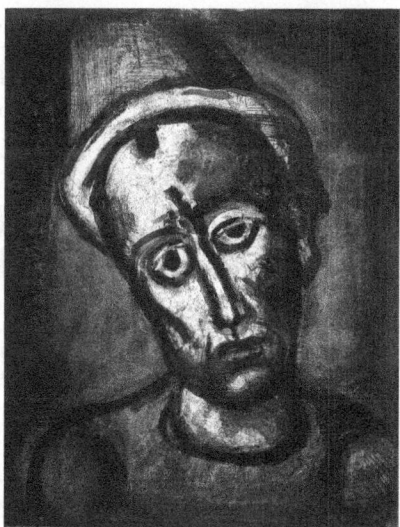

Figure 2.3. Georges Rouault, *Qui ne se grime pas? (Who does not wear a mask?)*, *Miserere* plate 8, 1923. Etching on paper, 22 15/16 × 16 15/16

see Celia Deane-Drummond, *The Ethics of Nature* (Oxford: Wiley-Blackwell, 2004), with a particular emphasis on wisdom (9-28); Elizabeth Johnson, *Ask the Beasts: Darwin and the God of Love* (London: Bloomsbury, 2014), with special attention to humility and joy (272-73); and Jame Schaefer, "The Virtuous Cooperator," *Worldviews: Environment, Culture, Religion* 7 (2003): 171-95.

I begin with the triptych of images in the *Miserere* series: *Are we not all slaves?* . . . (M6; see fig. 2.1), *believing ourselves to be kings* (M7; see fig. 2.2), and *Who does not wear a mask?* (M8; see fig 2.3). The first bears the imprint of sorrow; it is followed by a histrionic figure and a mockery of regal lineage, and the last is a forlorn clown. The contrast between the first and the second statements underscores the gap between who we are and how we conceive of ourselves. The third suggests a deceptive mode of presentation to the external world. It calls to mind the lines from T. S. Eliot's "Love Song of J. Alfred Prufrock": "there will be time to prepare a face to meet the faces that you meet."[10] But the triptych is as much about self-deception (*believing ourselves to be kings*) as it is about deceiving others. The accent on the wearing of masks underscores our manipulation of images to suit our self-aggrandizing desires. We resist self-knowledge. Because of our lack of self-knowledge and our idolatrous relationship to images, we are not rightly disposed to receive what is given in art. We are neither neutral nor ideal viewers. We are prone to the same vices of vanity that Rouault depicts with unflinching honesty in his art. The artist must thus accuse, even offend.[11]

As Susan Michalczyk shows in her essay on Rouault and the aesthetics of shock, Rouault owes much to Charles Baudelaire and his strategy of "dedoublement," the goal of which is to astound and decenter the viewer, who would prefer to occupy a comfortable, detached position at a safe distance from the image. To see ourselves, we will have to acknowledge our guilt and our seemingly insatiable appetite for self-delusion. Early in his career, Rouault focused on certain characters or social types: prostitutes, judges, and clowns. They operate as negative icons, Baudelairean icons, undercutting our consumerist *libido videndi*, the lust of seeing, which leaves viewers at a safe distance from the object under their gaze. The images serve in part to mock our lust, vanity, and addiction to the surface veneer of happiness. One is reminded of the Baudelairean term from Eliot's *The Waste Land*, "hypocrite lecteur" (the hypocrite reader), but in this case Rouault is accusing the *hypocrite spectateur* (the hypocrite viewer).

---

[10]T. S. Eliot, *Collected Poems (1902–1962)* (New York: Ecco, 1991), 4.

[11]See Susan Michalczyk, "The Aesthetics of Shock: Baudelaire, Benjamin, Rouault," in *Mystic Masque: Semblance and Reality in George Rouault, 1971–1958*, ed. Stephen Schloesser (Boston: McMullen Museum of Art, 2008), 193-204; Stephen Schloesser, "1921–1929: Jazz Age Graphic Shock," in Schloesser, *Mystic Masque*, 133-56; and Margaret Miles, "Rouault and the Dynamics of Self-Deception," in Schloesser, *Mystic Masque*, 109-16.

Rouault was never tempted by models of facile transcendence.[12] Some observers have thought him guilty of the opposite vice, that of wallowing in human degradation. Interestingly, the same accusation has been made against Blaise Pascal. But it seems Rouault was a better reader of Pascal than most moderns. He sees that the key insight of Pascal is that the human condition is characterized by a paradoxical combination of wretchedness and greatness. Any judgment of wretchedness presupposes a recognition, however dim and implicit, of some notion of order. As Pascal writes, "All these examples of wretchedness prove his greatness. It is the wretchedness of a dispossessed king."[13] Similarly, in his *Souvenirs Intimes*, Rouault writes, "We are fallen, it is true, but my clowns are really only dispossessed kings; their laugh is familiar to me; it reaches the realm of a million stifled sobs."[14] That we see our condition as wretched presupposes that we recognize some other state as proper to—and better for—us. Thus, we lament in the midst of our misery. Wretchedness, as Pascal tersely puts it, proves greatness. As Jean Grenier writes, Rouault's "prostitutes in their disgrace recall both degraded and real love, while his sad, bewildered clowns evoke by contrast innocent children at play."[15]

Instead of succumbing to vanity, it would be better for us to begin with the humble acknowledgment that we are "vagabonds of misfortune." That is where the *Miserere* begins, with images of Jesus and ordinary human beings. We see Jesus with his head bowed, with the words *Jesus reviled* . . . (M2; see fig. 8.1), followed by another image of Christ, who is described here as *forever scourged* . . . (M3; see fig. 8.2). Immediately after these plates, Rouault offers an image of an ordinary man accompanied by a child. The text for this plate reads, *takes refuge in your heart, vagabond of misfortune* (M4; see fig. 8.3). The man's posture mirrors the image of Christ in the preceding plate. As humans are created in the image and likeness of God, so in the incarnation, Christ takes on our image. As a suffering servant, Christ takes on the image of the poor, the marginalized, and those who wander without hope in a tragic dislocation from self, others, nature, and God. The *Miserere* seeks to shock us into

---

[12]An excellent treatment of Rouault's approach to these matters can be found in William Dryness, *Rouault: A Vision of Suffering and Salvation* (Grand Rapids, MI: Eerdmans, 1971).

[13]Blaise Pascal, *Pensées*, trans. A. J. Krailsheimer (New York: Penguin Classics, 1995), no. 116.

[14]Georges Rouault, *Souvenirs Intimes* (Paris: Frapier, 1926), 14.

[15]Jean Grenier, "Georges Rouault and the Bible," *Preuves* (April 1958), quoted in Pierre Courthion, *Rouault* (London: Thames & Hudson, 1962), 352.

recognition, into knowing for the first time or knowing anew that to which we are oblivious, namely, the significance of how God has become the vagabond of misfortune.

After images of bourgeois female characters (M14-17), for whom wealth and prestige give rise to high self-regard, even to the supposition that they merit a place in heaven, there is a series of images that include a condemned man and a lawyer. Eventually we reach an image of a morgue with piles of skulls surrounding a crucifix (M28; see web 2.1). The accompanying scriptural title here is, *"The one who believes in me, even should he die, will live."* Philosophers and theologians have often detected in the human devotion to wealth and social status a flight from mortality and the fact of our own impending death. Philosophers have sometimes counseled a therapeutic practice of running toward death, not fleeing it. But Rouault is not affirming a Heideggerian being-toward-death or a Stoic indifference in the face of death. Death remains an enemy, the last enemy to be destroyed, as Paul says (1 Cor 15:26). Guided by Rouault's images, we turn, in anxiety and fear and with hesitation, toward death, only to discover that someone is there waiting for us, someone who has embraced desolation and has abandoned himself to the nothingness of death, not out of despair but out of love. In our vanity, we seek to make ourselves into something and only serve to evacuate our lives of meaning. In his fullness, Christ takes the nothingness of sin on himself and embraces the nothingness of death in order to communicate the fullness of life. As philosopher William Desmond puts it: "God is given over to desecration: not as an insulted warlord requiring blood ransom; but as a . . . servant revealing God as there in the instance of death itself, . . . not outside, but within this instance with the most intimate immanence. This intimate immanence is nothing other than generosity . . . for the other as other, for its good as the gift of life itself." This is the logic of the loving "servant who consents to the good by being willing to be as nothing."[16] Christ's emptying of himself, his willingness to take violence into himself without responding with vengeance, his willingness to be in agony until the end of the world, annihilates nihilism.

After a series of images of Christ in the *Miserere*, including his baptism and crucifixion, we encounter an image of an individual turned toward Christ,

---

[16]William Desmond, *God and the Between* (Oxford: Wiley-Blackwell, 2008), 333.

with the words, *Lord, it is you. I recognize you* (M33; see web 2.2). For the first time, instead of alternating images of Christ with those of an ordinary person, they appear together. As Stephen Schloesser notes, Rouault combines two scriptural passages from Christ's appearances to his disciples after the resurrection: the confession of the doubting Thomas and the culmination of the journey to Emmaus, when the disciples recognize Christ in the breaking of the bread.[17] In the next plate, the final plate of the first half of the *Miserere*, Veronica's veil makes its first appearance (M33; see fig. 4.1).[18] As Schloesser notes, the image expresses Rouault's central conviction: "The visible world is the outward expression of unchanging invisible realities—the ongoing passion of Christ and the ongoing compassion of Veronica."[19]

Before turning to the compassion of Veronica, we ought to notice how Rouault here plays with the notion of images as images of other images. One variant of the crisis of the visible is the suspicion that images reflect only other images, never reaching an original or exemplar. From this perspective, the lessons of Plato's cave, with its vision of human persons trapped in an underground world, mistaking images for real things and supposing they are free when they are not, is quite optimistic. Plato presents us with a path out of the cave into a real world, a world ultimately grounded in a transcendent source of illumination. For Plato, we have to begin by grasping an image as an image, and then we can begin an ascent. The modern crisis of the visible is the supposition that there is no exit from images to the real, that each image is but a reflection of another image. For Rouault, the veil of Veronica, whose name means "true image," provides a response to the crisis of the visible.

The veil appears numerous times in the *Miserere*. Sometimes, as in the final image of the first half of the *Miserere*, it is an image by itself. Other times it is an image within an image as it is depicted in a frame hanging on a wall. Ponder for a moment the cascade of images. In the case of *Out of the depths . . .* (M47; see web 2.3), Rouault offers an image within an image, and that image is itself an image of the actual veil, which contains an image of Christ, who is himself

---

[17]Stephen Schloesser, "Notes on the Miserere Plates Exhibited in *Mystic Masque*," in Schloesser, *Mystic Masque*, 171-72.

[18]Veronica's veil is a cloth that some believe bore an image of Jesus' face after Veronica offered it to Jesus to wipe his brow while carrying the cross. This generated a tradition of representing Veronica's veil in iconography and visual art.

[19]Schloesser, "Notes on the Miserere Plates," 172.

the image of the invisible God (Col 1:15). The world that Rouault sees and presents is a world of vanity, a world in which disordered desire, idolatrous seeing, and an inability even to name what is missing or askew in our experience leave us trapped in self-referential images. What if we could encounter an image that leads not endlessly to other images but turns us back on ourselves, offering self-knowledge through an encounter with someone who already knows everything about us and who embraces us with mercy? The compassion of Veronica is an image of, or better a participation in, the very mercy of God.[20]

Bereft of any orientation, human experience threatens to become a house of mirrors, a horrifying carnival of unintelligibility and despair, void of either justice or mercy. Veronica's mercy, embodied in the image of the Crucified, acknowledges injustice and its horrifying cost; it also enables us to recognize our disorders, our deformities of seeing, feeling, and saying.

Miserere, taken from the cry of mercy in Psalm 51, is of course contained in the title of the entire series. We should take mercy broadly, as encompassing but including more than forgiveness. The Latin term *misericordia*, which is often rendered into English as *mercy*, indicates a suffering of the heart over the misfortune of another. Interestingly, there is an instructive parallel between mercy and envy. Both are rooted in sorrow, but envy mourns another's good fortune, especially good fortune that detracts from my own fortune or good name. A culture of envy is rooted in deep but disordered sorrow; paradoxically, it manifests itself not in mourning but in pride and wrath. For Thomas Aquinas, mercy involves not just sympathetic feeling but also, where possible, an active response to the unfortunate condition of another.[21] Merely feeling badly does not constitute the virtue; that requires a willingness to act to alleviate the suffering. It also requires that we see ourselves in the suffering and the destitute.

As is his regular practice, Aquinas talks not just about the virtue but also about the vices and dispositions that derail the practice of the virtue. What

---

[20]Another way to diagnose the affliction is in terms of a contrast between vain fantasy and imagination. Wendell Berry writes, "Fantasy is of the solitary self, and it cannot lead us away from ourselves. It is by imagination that we cross over the differences between ourselves and other beings and thus learn compassion, forbearance, mercy, forgiveness, sympathy, and love. . . . In sex, as in other things, we have liberated fantasy but killed imagination, and so have sealed ourselves in selfishness and loneliness." Berry, *Sex, Economy, Freedom, and Community* (New York: Pantheon, 1993), 143.

[21]Thomas Aquinas, *Summa Theologiae* II-II, question 30, article 1.

most undermines mercy is a false sense of security or self-sufficiency: "The proud are without mercy, because they despise others, and think them wicked, so that they account them as suffering deservedly whatever they suffer."[22] Self-sufficiency is an illusion that supposes we are invulnerable, independent, and without need of mercy. Only through mercy do our feelings, particularly our sorrows, become rightly ordered. Rouault's *Miserere* is a reflection on the manifold miseries, the pervasive sorrows of human life. Only through a right ordering of our passions, particularly our sorrows, can we begin to see and say who we are and identify our place within the whole.

Although almost any of the claims I have made so far could be contested, one might grant them all and still wonder, What has all this to do with the original claim, namely that what we most need is a recovery of our place within the whole?

Here I want to turn to Rouault's late landscape paintings and rely on the commentators who have underscored the importance of these in Rouault's corpus.[23] Here his use of color intensifies, as "gloomy scenes" give way to images of "vibrant light."[24] I suggest that some of these landscapes fulfill what Pope Francis says about creation. "Nature is usually seen as a system which can be studied, understood and controlled." Creation, by contrast, "can only be understood as a gift from the outstretched hand of the Father of all, and as a reality illuminated by the love which calls us together into universal communion."[25] In a remarkable way, the landscapes also address what Francis sees as our tendency to move back and forth between anthropocentrism and biocentrism.

The opening image from Rouault's *Stella Vespertina*, one of his many works with the title *De Profundis*, displays a grave with two mourners, adorned in black and purple cloaks, who appear to be comforting each other. Pierre Courthion notes the "powerful structural lines—verticals and horizontals crossed by diagonals," which "create a curiously impressive, timeless atmosphere."[26]

---

[22]Thomas Aquinas, *Summa Theologiae* II-II, question 30, article 2. For the English translation, see *Summa Theologica, Part II*, vol. 9, QQ. I–XLVI), trans. Fathers of the English Dominican Province (London: Burns, Oates & Washburne, 1917), 393.

[23]Soo Yun Kang, *Rouault in Perspective: Contextual and Theoretical Study of His Art* (Lanham, MD: International Scholars, 2000), 245.

[24]Kang, *Rouault in Perspective*, 245.

[25]Francis, *Laudato Si'*, para. 76.

[26]Courthion, *Rouault*, 294.

The scene of grief is nonetheless imbued with bright sunshine. There is serenity in the midst of loss and grief. The path here is through suffering and
death, not around it.

One of the more noteworthy landscapes is *Autumn Nazareth* (see web 2.4).
Here the shades of blue, green, and brown of the sky, grass, and trees gently
meld into one another and create an ambience of warm harmony. Near the
top of the painting, in yellow and orange with a thick black circumference, is
the sun. Amid this natural setting, there is a road leading to some buildings. In
the foreground, in an opening among the trees, there are six persons, grouped
in three sets of pairs. The human figures are shadowy, "hardly distinguishable
from" their "surroundings."[27] One of the individuals is shrouded in what appears to be a halo, but the halo is subtle and almost indistinct. From the perspective of the contrast between anthropocentrism and biocentrism, this
landscape is hard to categorize. The way the human presence is diminished in
space and size and conformed to the natural shapes make it seem biocentric.
The human does not stand over against the natural or exist independently of
it. Instead, the human is humbled and harmonized with nature. Still, Rouault
seems to offer an alternative to the extremes of anthropocentrism or biocentrism. The painting undercuts any assumption of an antithesis between the
human and the natural. But nature is itself transformed, infused with a striking
beauty and grace.

Aquinas's notion of splendor as a mark of the beautiful may be helpful here.
Jacques Maritain writes that the beautiful has the "splendor of intelligibility:
splendor veri, what Aquinas called the *splendor formae*, said Saint Thomas in
his precise metaphysician's language: for the form . . . is the ontological secret
that they bear within them, their spiritual being, their operating mystery."[28]
Beauty as splendor invites us into the mystery and gratuitousness of being. It
invites us to contemplate nature as a kind of miracle.[29] Such an experience of
beauty has a restorative capacity. Again, as Maritain puts it, the experience of
the beautiful "has the savor of the terrestrial paradise, because it restores, for

---

[27]Stephen Dahme, "'Pilgrim of Art': Artistic Autonomy and Christian Commitment in Rouault's
Late Work," in Schloesser, *Mystic Masque*, 379-87.

[28]Jacques Maritain, *Art and Scholasticism*, trans. James Scanlan (New York: Scribner & Sons, 1930),
28.

[29]Jacques Maritain, *Untrammeled Approaches* (Notre Dame, IN: University of Notre Dame Press,
2017), 213.

a moment, the peace and the simultaneous delight of the intellect and the senses."[30] Landscapes that depict the healing and restoration of our relationships, to one another and to nature, renew a sense of our place within the whole. To be able to see, feel, and articulate our relationships to ourselves, others, nature, and God requires that we be formed as individuals and members of communities in a set of practices that restores our sense of what it means to be a creature, made in the image of God, an image that sin has tarnished and turned into an idol. Rouault's late art fosters the ecological virtues of receptivity, wonder, and gratitude.

The final way in which Rouault's art, especially the late landscapes, provides a kind of propaedeutic to theology is in their eschatological dimension. In these works we see a new heaven and new earth, not an escape from this world but the transfiguration of this world. In that vision, nature itself testifies to the mercy of God, especially on behalf of the poor and the weak. Here is how Francis beautifully puts it toward the end of *Laudato Si'*:

> At the end, we will find ourselves face to face with the infinite beauty of God (cf. *1 Cor* 13:12), and be able to read with admiration and happiness the mystery of the universe, which with us will share in unending plenitude. Even now we are journeying towards the sabbath of eternity, the new Jerusalem, towards our common home in heaven. Jesus says: "I make all things new" (*Rev* 21:5). Eternal life will be a shared experience of awe, in which each creature, resplendently transfigured, will take its rightful place and have something to give those poor men and women who will have been liberated once and for all.[31]

Contemporary artist Makoto Fujimura, who is influenced by Maritain and Rouault, acknowledges that current cultural conditions are not fortuitous for artists. They make it difficult for the beautiful to be directly accessed and presented. Fujimura thus insists that the "hell of the artistic imagination" is the "only real point of departure" for artistic creation today.[32] The new pedagogy will have to accuse as well as attract viewers, since our dispositions and habits

---

[30]Maritain, *Art and Scholasticism*, 28.

[31]Francis, *Laudato Si'*, para. 243.

[32]Makoto Fujimura, *Refractions: A Journey of Faith, Art, Culture* (Colorado Springs: NavPress, 2009), 125. Also see Thomas Hibbs and Makoto Fujimura, *Soliloquies* (Baltimore: Square Halo Books, 2009). I have a much more detailed and expanded treatment of *Laudato Si'*, Rouault, and Fujimura in Thomas Hibbs, *A Theology of Creation: Ecology, Art, and Laudato Si'* (Notre Dame, IN: University of Notre Dame Press, 2023).

create obstacles in our souls to the proper reception of what is given in art. It will proffer hope not through facile transcendence but through a direct encounter with the deprivations and horrors of modern life. It will counter the nihilism of our culture by presenting what Desmond calls the "agapeic servant," who accepts a reduction to nothing out of love.[33] Such agapeic suffering, which takes on the evils and afflictions of this word, traces a path toward beauty, gratitude, and joy, toward a reaffirmation of a new heaven and new earth as our common home.

---

[33]Desmond, *God and the Between,* 333.

How can we fix our eyes on what is unseen?

—See Color Plate 1—

Christina Felten

I have always had lots of questions. Even now I am questioning why I titled this piece with a lengthy question. Asking questions can be uncomfortable and vulnerable. But I love that Rouault normalized questions and doubts and that he was not afraid to push boundaries in his work. Religious art can feel so predictable, and people are often afraid of being offensive or offended, but Rouault made room for contemplation. He was an artist who expressed deep authenticity, even when it brought criticism.

I am moved by Rouault's unconventional use of texture and color. I love the way he paired heavy black lines with bold jewel tones. His portraits convey a depth of emotion that motivated me to attempt the same. I wanted this painting to reflect something of the shadow side of my own faith journey: the confusion and the questions, the fragmentation of my belief system in my early twenties, and the lingering questions I have about God and truth. I wanted to create a portrait that has a mysterious quality that would draw people in. I wanted it to feel tactile and imperfect.

I incorporated printmaking by using some gelli prints as collage elements. I also used a vintage French handwritten letter over the woman's face and intentionally left it flat (actually somewhat wrinkled) and colorless to convey the numbness and apathy that can be experienced when questions are met with religious platitudes.

Artistic Interlude Two

The process of painting this portrait was powerful for me and allowed me to see my questions as valid and to hold space for uncomfortable ideas. While painting, I processed through some of the discomfort I feel with the church. I have so many thoughts and feelings that can feel loud and confusing in my mind, and the church often tells us to stop thinking and just believe, to fix our eyes on things unseen. I feel bewildered by what I see, disillusioned by a church that cannot seem to figure out basic concepts of love, inclusion, and acceptance. It feels dark and scary, considering my history of religious trauma. I had an offset view of God, which skewed and distorted my thinking, and a lot of that had to fall away to make space for authentic faith.

In my portrait, the woman is looking away from the questions that have colored her inner thoughts. There are fragmented parts of her faith that remain, but the beauty that she seeks is masked in gray, shrouded in shadows. She is trying to discover and uncover a new understanding of what God is really like. But she seems peaceful sitting with her doubts and questions. I think we can learn something from her. As Christians, we can be obsessed with certainty and needing to have the answers. But curiosity is a gift. There is so much beauty in the mysterious, and that is what I wanted to convey with this portrait.

As an artist, I have struggled to find my voice in my work. I can be caught up in popular trends and focusing on painting art that sells. But I love that Rouault was not concerned with any of that. He also was not concerned with evangelizing but rather explored ideas that were authentic to his individual faith journey. As he explains, "I carry within myself an infinite depth of suffering and melancholy, which life has only served to develop and of which my paintings, if God allows it, will only be the flowering and imperfect expression."[1]

---

[1] Quoted in William Dyrness, "Seeing Through the Darkness: Georges Rouault's Vision of Christ," *Image* 67 (Winter 2020), https://imagejournal.org/article/seeing-through-the-darkness/.

3

Blessed Are the Poor

A Theology of Poverty in the Art of Rouault

Soo Y. Kang

Georges Rouault spent most of his life in isolation, focused on refining and perfecting his paintings and prints. His public involvement was sparse, and he rarely associated with people other than his family and close friends. Yet he was keenly aware of the affairs of the world. In fact, Rouault made a point of saying that a solitary person can be a humanist, declaring, "I am a silent friend of those who struggle in the deep furrow."[1] He was especially concerned for those who suffer in society, as testified to in his art. Prominent in his oeuvre are images of the poor, which were influenced by the perspective of his spiritual mentor, Léon Bloy. This essay explores the ideas of Bloy that directly shaped Rouault's rendering of the downtrodden.

The subject of suffering, particularly due to poverty, was not foreign to Rouault, who grew up in the industrial, working-class faubourg of Belleville, an enclave of street art and nightlife as well as communist and socialist activities in the late nineteenth and early twentieth centuries.[2] Besides growing up impoverished, his father earning meager wages varnishing pianos for the Pleyel company, Rouault witnessed the destitute in all types of agonizing and unjust situations in his neighborhood. He writes, "In this old quarter, like many others, in silence I took in so much misery, which hollowed out deep

---

[1]"Je suis l'ami silencieux de ceux qui peinent dans le sillon creux." Georges Charensol, *Georges Rouault, l'homme et l'oeuvre* (Paris: Quatre Chemins, 1926), preface. All translations from French to English in this essay are mine.

[2]*Faubourg* refers to a Parisian suburb, the poor, working-class districts that surround Paris.

furrows and wrinkles on the face of the most beautiful girl in the world."[3]
Even after being introduced to refined culture and lofty intellectual discourse
while studying under renowned artist Gustave Moreau at École des Beaux-
Arts from 1892 to 1895, Rouault did not turn away from the dark memories of
Belleville as he captured the unsanitary and unsafe environment of the faubourg in *The brawl on the construction site* (also known as *Night Landscape*) in
1897 (see web 3.1). The two men on the left side of the painting, identified as
butchers by the artist, are fighting just outside the city, where factories still
release toxic fumes after working hours.[4]

Under the influence of Catholic friends whom he met at École de Beaux-
Arts, Rouault came to faith, taking his first Communion in 1895 and even
following a friend in 1901 to join Joris-Karl Huysman's nascent community of
Christian artists and writers associated with a monastery in Ligugé. This community was disbanded soon after, however, due to a law prohibiting all unau-
thorized religious organization.[5] That experience added to Rouault's depression resulting from unpleasant memories of Belleville as well as the
recent death of his mentor Moreau in 1898. His depression was also com-
pounded by constant financial worries, feelings of loneliness, and severe
health issues that snowballed into what Rouault called a "moral crisis," leading
to anger and frustration.[6]

Such sentiments can be discerned in the earlier *Night Landscape*, but after
he moved to Montmartre in 1903 they are fully conveyed through a new mannerism he deemed "outrageous lyricism."[7] This innovative style of stark, independent, choppy brush marks streaming across the entire canvas coincided
with the vanguard movement at the time in Paris, which advocated the formal
aspects of painting—colors and lines—that directly express the thoughts and
feelings of the artist, rather than the traditional illusionistic means of using

---

[3]"Dans ce vieux quartier, comme tant d'autres j'ai souffert en silence de tant de misères qui creusent
sillons et rides profondes sur le visage de la plus belle fille du monde." Georges Rouault, *Soliloques,*
ed. Claude Roulet (Neuchâtel: Ides et Calendes, 1944), 49.

[4]Georges Rouault, *Souvenirs Intimes* (Paris: Frapier, 1926), 50.

[5]The Law of Associations, commonly referred as the Waldeck-Rousseaux Law of 1901, was part of a
series of state attempts to end religious education, which led to the eventual separation of church
and state in France in 1905. See Maurice Larkin, *Church and State After the Dreyfus Affair: The
Separation Issue in France* (London: Macmillan, 1974); John McManners, *Church and State in France
1870–1914* (New York: Harper & Row, 1972).

[6]Charensol, *Georges Rouault,* 23.

[7]Charensol, *Georges Rouault,* 24.

figures and narratives that mimic life. Rouault also readily took on modern subjects such as the spectacles of entertainment and nightlife readily available at Montmartre at the time (e.g., *Sideshow*; see web 3.2). In tune with his contemporaries, Rouault exhibited alongside other avant-garde artist friends, such as Henri Matisse and Albert Marquet, and was soon established as one of the progressive young artists of the time who changed the course of art history. For Rouault, however, his new style was not as much an artistic experiment or a rebellious statement against traditional art as it was a genuine expression of the inner chaos he experienced at the time.

In 1902, while working as the curator at the newly founded Moreau Museum, he came across a novel titled *La Femme pauvre* (*The Poor Woman*), written by Léon Bloy in 1897. This book narrates the story of an impecunious woman named Clotilde whose faith in God grows while she undergoes a series of ordeals. Although Rouault was profoundly touched by the character of the heroine, he did not portray her, painting instead two minor characters of the novel, Monsieur and Madame Poulot, in 1905 (see web 3.3). Corresponding to the book's hideous descriptions of these pestering neighbors of Clotilde, Rouault used his trademark strident brushwork of distinctly marked dashes to delineate unpleasant characteristics. Although Mrs. Poulot was a memorable tormentor of the heroine, the choice is odd considering the focus of the book. The painting, like other works, reflects Rouault's state of mind at the time, still in a dark phase, as he described himself as being "succumbed under the weight of my sadness."[8] While his conversion in the 1890s was genuinely transformative, he could not overcome his inner turmoil at the time. But he shared with a friend in 1904, "I believe in God, I also believe that he will help me to get out of this."[9] As a testament to his faith, he depicted *Head of Christ* in 1905 (see web 3.4), which has the same mannerism of disarrayed drip marks that equally represent Christ's sweat and blood as well as the violence and hostility inflicted on him by soldiers and the angry crowd during his Passion. Rouault meditated on Christ's suffering in the midst of his own depression, loneliness, and poverty, entreating Christ to free him from these burdens. He

---

[8]"Je succombe sous le poids de mes douleurs." Quoted in George Waldemar and Geneviève Nouaille-Rouault, *L'Univers de Rouault* (Paris: Screpel, 1971), 65.

[9]"Je crois en Dieu, je crois aussi qu'il va m'aider à me tirer de là." Quoted in Waldemar and Nouaille-Rouault, *L'Univers de Rouault*, 65.

found it hard to embrace suffering as part of the path toward God, as advocated in the book. Gradually he came to accept this notion through his encounter with Bloy, whom he met in 1904 and conversed with on a consistent
basis over the following decade.

Bloy (1846–1917) was a controversial character.[10] Grounded in the mystical
visions of a friend as well as his own, he saw himself as a latter-day saint in the
line of Jonah who needed to decry the sins of humanity to bring repentance
and salvation to the world. His instrument of remonstrance and adjuration
was writing in various forms, including commentaries, novels, pamphlets, and
private journals.[11] His publications were full of anathemas against almost everyone, particularly the bourgeois and the powerful, who were criticized in
the most violent, invective manner. His explanations were illogical and his
analogies were incompatible. It is no wonder that his writings, for which he
gave up his railway clerk job, were largely ignored, earning neither financial
support nor accolades. He had to beg his friends to meet the needs of his
family—a wife and two daughters—most of his life. Given his unpleasant
verbalization and equally disagreeable temperament, which constantly fluc-
tuated between anger and pity, it is amazing that he was able to convert a small
number of significant people to Catholicism, who remained loyal to him to
the end. Like Rouault, Jacques and Raïssa Maritain were introduced to Bloy
through the reading of *La Femme pauvre* and subsequently became Catholics
through the persuasion of Bloy.[12]

The one appeal of Bloy's otherwise unattractive character was that he was
authentic. However flawed his personality, his devotion to God was unflinching. To him, there was no in-between; if you were a Christian, you had
to be one all the way, giving your entire life to Christ, hence his self-made
epithet, the "pilgrim of the absolute." Bloy criticized the bourgeois for their
mediocrity, unwillingness to take sides, and compromising decision to lead
a middle-class life of comfort and socially acceptable moral standards. He

---

[10]On Bloy, see Albert Béguin, *Léon Bloy. A Study in Impatience* (New York: Sheed & Ward, 1947);
Elfieda Dubois, *Portrait of Léon Bloy* (London: Sheed & Ward, 1951); Emmanuela Polimeni, *Léon
Bloy, the Pauper Prophet 1846–1917* (New York: Philosophical Library, 1951). On his writing, see
Mary Brady, *Thought and Style in the Works of Léon Bloy* (Washington, DC: Catholic University of
America Press, 1946).

[11]See Léon Bloy, *Oeuvres de Léon Bloy*, 15 vols., ed. Joseph Bollery and Jacques Petit (Paris: Bernouard, 1964–1975).

[12]See Raïssa Maritain, *Les Grandes Amitiés*, 10th ed. (Bruges: Desclée de Brouwer, 1965).

advocated avoidance of all obstacles of life that diverted attention from the Lord, including the materialism that gradually took precedence over religion in the nineteenth century, meeting the immediate needs and desires of people and thereby enslaving them for life. To unshackle and wake them up, Bloy reasoned that he had to use colorful, exaggerated language to shock them into attentiveness.

Bloy cursed and reprimanded almost everyone except the poor. The depiction of the unfortunate Clotilde, who is forced by her mother to model for an artist, endures poverty with her husband, and faces harassment from her neighbors, is based on Bloy's own life. Particularly touching is the death of her infant, which was influenced by his own experience of losing two sons. Clotilde also eventually loses her husband. While leading the life of a mendicant, she still rejoices in her faith in God, claiming that her only sadness is not being a saint. While the novel does not evidence a structural flow in terms of character or thematic development and reads more like a composite of painstakingly naturalist descriptions, it nevertheless strikes as genuine, the portrayals being based on real-life circumstances and surroundings. The eventual thesis of the book is that the deprivation of all earthly components of life brings complete and constant relationship with the Lord, an obviously difficult challenge that was not popular with readers. What impressed the Maritains and Rouault was that Bloy actually practiced what he preached in the book as they came to know him intimately over the years.

By 1910, Rouault overcame his previous rage and reached some measure of peace. His marriage in 1908, sales from exhibitions, and regular installments through his contract with Ambroise Vollard brought stability in his life despite his continued anxiety about supporting a growing family. He entered spiritual equanimity, which allowed him to reconsider the misfortunes of his past in a new light. With this change emerged a new subject for his art: the poor. Although he depicted penniless individuals such as prostitutes and clowns in the first decade of the twentieth century, his portrayals focused on the inner agony associated with their means of living. The paintings of the impoverished starting from 1910 characterize them generically, representing them as a group, and they are delineated in a markedly different style: prominent, continuous outlines that compose flat, geometric shapes, inducing stillness and reflecting a sense of composure despite the sad content.

While *Homes of the Wretched* of 1912 manifests squalid homes with people busily attending to their daily work, most paintings unveil a family in migration, such as *The Poor Family* (*Exodus*) of 1911 (see web 3.5). The faces are barely defined, but two parents with three children can be identified, seemingly homeless and looking for solace next to a barren tree and with a church in the background. The drooping and reclined body gestures of the father in the middle and the oldest child speak of despondency and uncertainty about their fate. Despite the minimalist rendering, a slice of family dynamics is sensed in the conversation between the mother and the daughter to the right. Some members of the family are not as depressed as the others, and a child has questions. Overall, there is a somber mood, yet the shades of yellows and blues in subtle brightness are glowing, as if bringing light to the darkness of the situation, implying hope.

The plight of the homeless is more discernible in *The Fugitives—Exodus* of 1911 (see fig 3.1). The stark, black outlines clearly demarcate the hunched bodies of the father and mother, and the latter carries all their meager belongings in one sack, symbolizing the backbreaking burdens of life. While trying to encourage their child, who wants to engage with the parents, the family clearly has no place to go, having left one community on the right and heading to another on the left. They stand for all those who have been temporarily displaced due to the inability to pay rent but also those who suddenly had to leave their homes due to impending invasion or violence. The fugitives are not only physically worn out from the travels but also mentally strained from all the worries. They walk wearily, not knowing what the future holds. Some relief, however, is connoted in the gleaming sky of subtle purplish blues and oranges that seem to lighten slightly the sad and oppressive sight.

While Rouault did not capture specific individuals and rendered the poor in a general manner, he understood every aspect of their lives, having witnessed and experienced their condition himself. Again, although very general, *Faubourg of Toil and Suffering* of 1911 (see web 3.6) depicts a mother with hunched back and reclined head, which indicate her feelings of sadness toward her children. The family is posed before the sea with a sailing boat or a picture of such scenery, revealing perhaps what they wish. In another scene of the same title, children tightly cling to their mother for emotional support and protection.

Rouault composed numerous poems that induced the same sentiments as his paintings. One of them reads:

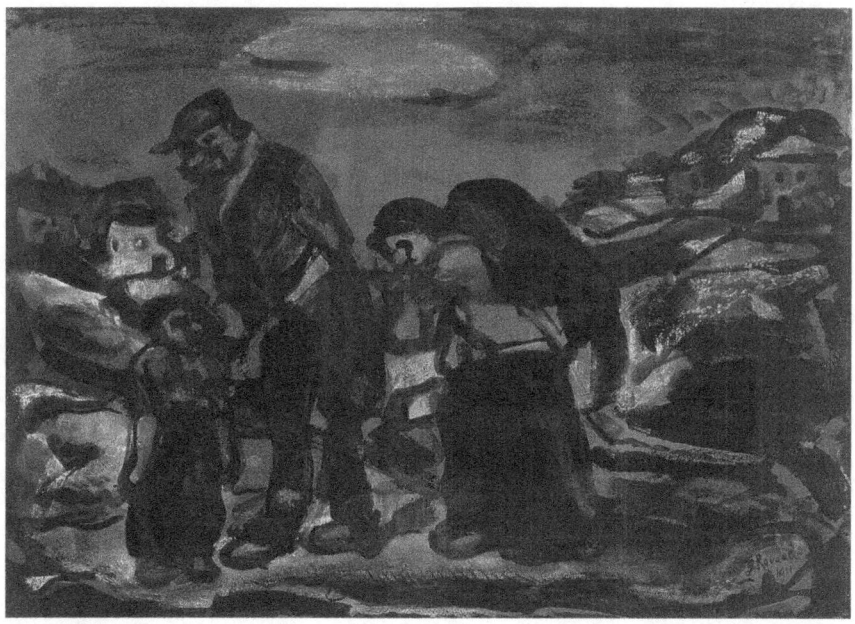

Figure 3.1. Georges Rouault, *Les Fugitifs* (*The Fugitives—Exodus*), 1911. Gouache and pastel on cardboard, 17 3/4 × 24

Sleep my love, said the tender mother

Dream that joyous spring

Follows the harsh winter

Hated by the poor people.

Dream that in this sad quarter

All is beautiful, all is luminous

From the one end to the other of the year

And rats, mice, and cockroaches

Are ancient fairies

Who will resume tomorrow

Their brilliant liveries.

Sleep my love

Like father and mother

You will have misery

But dream that it won't be so.[13]

---

[13]"Dors mon amour, disait la tendre mère/ Rêve que le gai printemps/ Succède au rude hiver/ Haï des pauvres gens./ Rêve qu'en ce triste quartier/ Tout est beau, tout est lumineux/ D'un bout à l'autre de l'année/ Et que rats, souris, cancrelas/ Sont d'antiques fees/ Qui demain reprendront/

Rouault was well aware of the cycle of poverty that locked generations in the same bind. He also created a series of paintings titled *Winter* (see web 3.7), the season indigent folks hate most. The families, as in the *Exodus* series, appear in these landscapes much smaller but still hunched, walking with children and some with heavy burdens on their backs. A calming blend of blues and oranges dominates the land, but the strident black outlines that circumscribe the barren earth and trees speak of their inner emptiness.

That Rouault made the poor a major subject of his art, particularly in the 1910s, demonstrates the influence of Bloy, who decried the inhumane treatment of the destitute in society. In his flamboyant words, he declared that the beggarly did not even own their bodies, just being cast away when dead and unacclaimed.[14] While poverty was the norm in the past, since many were poor prior to the Industrial Revolution, capitalism completed changed the perception of poverty to be something disgraceful and wretched, a failure to be avoided and overcome at all costs. In fact, Bloy claimed:

> Indisputably, Poverty is the most enormous crime, and it alone in any circumstance could never soften the eyes of the fair judge. . . . The destitute were not formally condemned neither to fire, nor to quartering, nor to strappado, nor to skinning, nor to the picket, nor even to the guillotine. . . . Only, the genius tormentor who is called the social Force has known how to bring all this scattered flora of criminal penalties together for them, in a unique sheaf of sovereign tribulation. One has serenely, tacitly excommunicated them from life and one has made them outcasts. Every "man of the world,"—whether he knows is or not—carries in him the absolute contempt for Poverty, and such is the profound secret of HONOR, which is the cornerstone of oligarchies.[15]

Leur brillante livrée./ Dors mon amour./ Comme père et mère/ Tu auras de la misère/ Mais rêve qu'il n'en sera bien" (Rouault, *Soliloques*, 182).

[14] Léon Bloy, *La Femme pauvre*, reprinted in *Oeuvres de Léon Bloy*, 7:49-50.

[15] "Indiscurablement, la Pauvreté est le plus énorme des crimes, et le seul qu'aucune circonstance ne saurait atténuer aux yeux d'un juge équitable. C'est un crime tel que la trahison, l'inceste, le parricide ou le sacrilège paraissent peu de chose, en comparaison, et sollicitent l'attendrissement social. . . . Les indigents ne furent condamnés formellement ni au feu, ni à l'écartèlement, ni à l'estrapade, ni à l'écorchement, ni au pal, ni même à la guillotine. . . . Seulement, le génie tourmenteur qui s'est appelé la Force sociale a su rassembler pour eux, en une gerbe unique de tribulation souveraine, toute cette flore éparse des pénalités criminelles. On les a sereinement, tacitement, excommuniés de la vie et on en a fait des réprouvés. Tout 'home du monde,'—qu'il le sache ou qu'il l'ignore,—pour en soi le mépris absolu de la Pauvreté, et tel est le profond secret de l'HONNEUR, qui est la pierre d'angle des oligarchies." Léon Bloy, *Le Désespéré*, in *Oeuvres de Léon Bloy*, 9:78-150.

Some of Rouault's paintings are titled *Fugitives,* centering on the nomadic predicament of the poor. If they are fleeing from society, their sole crime is poverty.

Bloy wrote extensively on poverty and illustrated his views on it through the case of Clotilde in *La Femme pauvre,* and then theorized it fully in his new publication of 1909, *Le Sang du pauvre* (*The Blood of the Poor*). The destitute are a problem in society, and poverty is a question to be solved. The materialist world has taken the last vestige of humanity from the poor, which is their dignity. Like anyone else, the impoverished have desires beyond the basic necessities. Accordingly to Bloy, these include "the desire to have some bread, to have a little of this good wine which heartens the heart, the desire for flowers and the air of the field, and all that God has created for men, indiscriminately; the desire at least for rest after labor, when the Angelus of the evening rings."[16] Yet Bloy noticed that people were scandalized to observe the penniless indulging in delicacy and luxury. Hence they were no longer considered humans and were effaced from society.

For Rouault, to portray the poor was to render them visible, to acknowledge their existence in the community and draw full attention to them. The poor were one of the few selective subjects that he painted all his life. Clearly, he never forgot them and aimed to restore their dignity through his representations. He shows them with needs, feelings, thoughts, and dreams. The family dynamics of interaction, care, protection, and affection are manifested in his works. Rouault reaffirms their humanity even in their state of deprivation and homelessness.

Bloy takes poverty to another level by declaring it to be a position of divinity, allowing direct access to Christ. This point is already suggested in *The Poor Woman,* where Clotilde realizes that "it is not very far from the sublime, that the Woman truly exists only in the condition without bread, without home, without friends, without husband and without children, and it is only then that she can force her Savior to descend."[17] It is declared more emphatically in *The Blood of the Poor,* which showcases Bloy's own theological

---

[16]"Le désir d'avoir du pain, d'avoir un peu de ce bon vin qui réjouit le coeur, le désir des fleurs et de l'air des champs, de tout de que Dieu a créé pour les hommes, sans distinction; le désir au moins du repos après le labeur, quant sonne l'Angélus du soir." Léon Bloy, *Le Sang du pauvre,* in *Oeuvres de Léon Bloy,* 9:100-101.

[17]"Cela n'est pas très loin du sublime, que la Femme n'existe vraiment qu'à la condition d'être sans pain, sans gîte, sans amis, sans époux et sans enfants, et que c'est comme dela seulement qu'elle peut forcer à descendre son Sauveur" (Bloy, *Oeuvres de Léon Bloy,* 7:268).

apology for poverty. Although the text is loose in logic, he relates the sufferings of the downtrodden to that of Christ, relating, for instance, little children forced to labor in factories to "their older brother in the Garden of Agony."[18] He calls Jesus "the king of the poor," as he was deprived of material possessions and social honor. Jesus is poverty incarnate, he says, and therefore the destitute are privileged to partake in his mystic body sheerly through their suffering. Bloy points to the example of the beggar Lazarus, who has the blessings of God and directly ascends to his kingdom after his death.[19] The poor are the direct recipients of grace, and they represent Christ on the cross. Hence their blood is the blood of Christ, marking their connection and their very existence through the Passion. Poverty is therefore divine, according to Bloy. That does not make it easy; on the contrary, Bloy depicts it as excruciating. Nevertheless, through direct linkage to Christ, the impoverished enter blessedness. Bloy resolutely affirms the Beatitudes: "Blessed are the poor, blessed are the meek, blessed are those who mourn and those who hunger for justice, blessed still are those who are merciful, those whose heart is pure and those who are peaceable. At last blessed are those who suffer persecution. Hey! Undoubtedly."[20]

Although Bloy's expressions are unique, his contentions are not new. Monastic orders in the Middle Ages observed the vow of poverty, seeing material dependence and desires as obstacles to their devotion to God.[21] The figure who lived in absolute poverty was the founder of the mendicant order of Friars Minor, St. Francis of Assisi, who walked barefoot and wore a filthy tunic, denying himself even the bare-minimum necessities of life.[22] St. Francis took seriously Jesus' admonition to the rich man, "If you want to be perfect, go, sell your possessions and give to the poor, and you will have treasure in heaven. Then come, follow me" (Mt 19:21). St. Francis strove to imitate Christ,

---

[18]"À leur grand frère du Jardin de l'Agonie" (Bloy, *Oeuvres de Léon Bloy*, 9:134).

[19]Bloy, *Oeuvres de Léon Bloy*, 9:103.

[20]"Heureux les pauvres, heureux les doux, heureux ceux qui pleurant et ceux qui sont avides de justice, heureux encore ceux qui ont pitié, ceux dont le coeur est pur et ceux qui sont pacifiques. Heureux enfin ceux qui souffrent persécution. Hé! sans doute." Leon Bloy, journal entry, June 8, 1895, in *Oeuvres de Léon Bloy*, 11:189.

[21]See Sidney Turner, "The Vow of Poverty" (PhD diss., Catholic University of America, 1929).

[22]Malcom Lambert, *Franciscan Poverty: The Doctrine of the Absolute Poverty of Christ and the Apostles in the Franciscan Order, 1210–1323* (St. Bonaventura, NY: Franciscan Institute, 1998); Cyprian Lynch, ed., *A Poor Man's Legacy: An Anthology of Franciscan Poverty* (St. Bonaventura, NY: Franciscan Institute, 1988).

whose life exemplified deprivation and renunciation from his humble birth to his crucifixion. The Franciscan Order also sent monks to foreign lands to evangelize without any provision, again following Christ's command. While other leaders assumed poverty as one of the means to reach Christ and perfection, St. Francis considered destitution the absolute way to follow Christ and a primary virtue, along with charity and obedience. He even personified poverty as Lady Poverty, claiming to be married to her, displaying his affection and devotion to her. St. Francis instructed his monks to joyfully embrace this "holy poverty."

To this thirteenth-century saint, there was a direct connection between Christ and poverty, as, like Bloy, he proclaimed to see the image of Jesus in the indigent. St. Francis's statements and advocacy for poverty were primarily aimed at his monks to voluntarily follow this life of mendicancy. However difficult, it is one thing to deliberately choose the life of a mendicant and another to be forced to live penniless, with no way out. While Bloy espoused similar notions to St. Francis, he spoke for the involuntary poor. His examples of Clotilde and others in his books represent those who were born impecunious and struggled with basic needs all their lives. To consider this involuntary poverty as divine, holy, and blessed seems out of touch, except that Bloy experienced that life himself. He applied the same theories and views of the church fathers to the ordinary poor, as he saw them as true recipients of grace and all capable of becoming saints. To him there were no distinctions between them and the mendicant friars, and poverty was all the same, voluntary or involuntary. The same standard and blessedness applied to them all. Especially in the modern era, when even the monks of the mendicant order hardly follow the absolutely poverty of St. Francis and a theologian declares that "poverty is an out-dated virtue," holy poverty is still upheld and practiced by ordinary citizens.[23]

Rouault was familiar with Bloy's understanding of poverty, having read *The Blood of the Poor* and conversed with him on many occasions. A few years after his first paintings of the impoverished, he demonstrates the divine connection in *Christ in the Suburbs* (1920–1924; see web 3.8). Here on a quiet night, two children meet with Christ, who is in close proximity, interacting with them in

---

[23]Ladislas Örsy, "Poverty: The Modern Problem," in *The Way*, supplement 9, "Poverty" (Spring 1970): 8.

the very faubourg where they live. The street is empty and dark, yet they can clearly see each other due to the brilliant moon that shines over them, almost like a divine spotlight. The sacred presence of Christ is a reality in their daily living with its concomitant suffering. Toward the end of his life, Rouault's style changes to Fauve-like colorful visions percolating with optimism and joy.[24] *Old Faubourg* of 1951 (see web 3.9) is no longer sad, and the mother with a child below the sun is bathed in glorious light with analogous colors of green, yellow, and orange patterned all over the surroundings. The early, depressing faubourg scenes of the penniless fugitives next to barren trees have transformed later into brilliant biblical landscapes, many of which display families peacefully strolling adjacent to trees with luscious leaves. As Clotilde says, "One does not enter Paradise tomorrow, nor the day after tomorrow, not in ten years, one enters there 'today,' when one is poor and crucified."[25] Despite suffering, the poor are in paradise as they find home in Christ.

The connection between the oppressed and Christ on the cross is best illustrated in his landmark print series, *Miserere*, which Rouault began in 1922 and was a culmination project that incorporated themes from previous works.[26] The series was conceived as a tribute to his father, who passed away in 1912, and as a response to World War I; hence there are many scenes of death and war. Embedded in the series are his trademark subjects: Christ, the bourgeoise, and the poor. They are all intermixed with no obvious order other than to manifest the relevance of all the figures from different spectra of life to one another. The black ink makes the outlines more emphatic against the white backdrop, creating a contrasting range of neutral colors that render the pictures more dramatic. At the same time, the repetition of the insistent lines makes them more stately, creating an overall sense of stillness and somberness.

Such mood is evident in the familiar faubourg scene that is almost empty in *Street of the Lonely* (M23; see web 3.10). The neighborhood emits a pervasive sense of dejection even with people in it, as seen with *in the old faubourg of Long Suffering* (M10; see web 3.11). Here the touching illustration of

---

[24]Fauvism was a prominent artistic movement in the twentieth century that emphasized strong colors over against more realistic values, such as in the work of André Derain and Henri Matisse.

[25]"On n'entre pas dans le Paradis demain, ni après-demain, ni dans dix ans, on y entre 'aujourd'hui,' quand on est pauvre et crucifié" (Bloy, *Oeuvres de Léon Bloy*, 7:268).

[26]See Holly Flora and Soo Kang, *Georges Rouault's* Miserere et Guerre: *This Anguished World of Shadows*, exhibition catalog (New York: Museum of Biblical Art, 2006).

an affectionate mother and her doting children does not efface the gloominess associated with this district, which is pronouncedly relayed through the gigantic, barren tree in the middle. The homeless are still present in the *Miserere*, as another father with a bundle on his back attempts to cheer up his child in *takes refuge in your heart, vagabond of misfortune* (M4; see fig. 8.3). A woman with a bigger burden on her back is shown in *winter leprosy of the earth* (M24; see web 3.12), echoing the line of his poem quoted above, "the harsh winter, hated by the poor people," since the cold season adds more misery to their lives.[27] How are these figures related to the war? Rouault says that wars usually make the lives of the poor even more unbearable. He laments the miseries of the wars, death, and poverty before the Lord, asking for mercy (*Miserere:* "have mercy on me, O God"), as these scenes of sadness and atrocities are strewn in between the images of Christ, most all of them depicting the Passion. Yet the images of the downtrodden have an additional significance in reference to Christ, with their suffering elevated to the level of Christ's divine persecution.

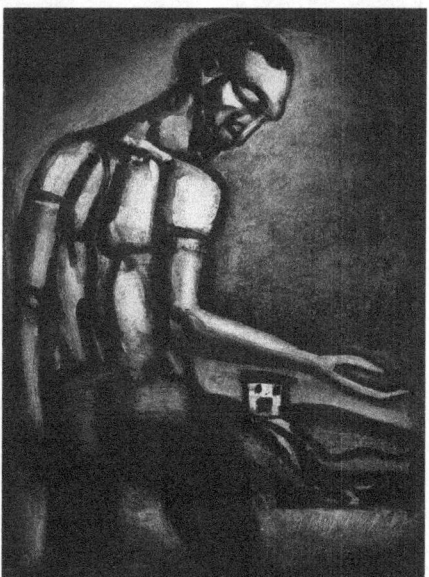

Figure 3.2. Georges Rouault, *En tant d'ordres divers, le beau métier d'ensemencer une terre hostile* (*In so many different realms, the noble work of sowing seed in a hostile earth*), *Miserere* plate 22, 1926. Etching on paper, 23 1/4 × 16 15/16

[27]See his poem translated above.

A hardworking farmer sadly reclines his head in the plate *In so many different realms, the noble work of sowing seed in a hostile earth* (M22; see fig. 3.2). A strange glow surrounds his upper body, mimicking the light and rays around the head of Christ in a similar posture in *"He was oppressed and afflicted, yet he opened not his mouth"* (M21; see fig. 3.3). Both close their eyes and silently bear suffering. Another man sadly shuts his eyes and bends his head down even more in *The hard work of living . . .* (M12; see web 3.13). Like him, Jesus severely lowers his head *forever scourged . . .* (M3; see fig. 8.2). Jesus absorbs all the sins, burdens, and suffering of humanity, and the destitute bear Christ's image through their hardship. In fact, Bloy says that we see the image of Jesus directly through those in severe poverty, and so to forget the impoverished in society is to forget Jesus and the significance of his crucifixion.[28] Poverty, as much as it is taxing, is sacred because it imitates Christ's Passion.

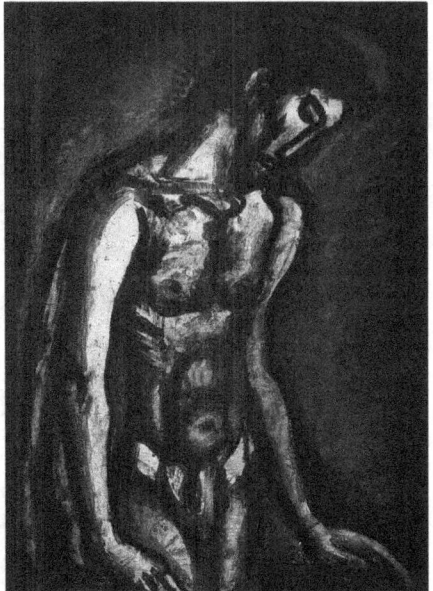

Figure 3.3. Georges Rouault, *"Il a été maltraité et opprimé et il n'a pas ouvert la bouche"* ("He was oppressed and afflicted, yet he opened not his mouth"), *Miserere* plate 21, 1923. Etching on paper, 22 7/8 × 16 3/16

In the *Miserere*, the linkage of poverty to Christ is an ongoing reality, with Christ "eternally scourged" just as the poor continue to suffer. Rouault quotes

---

[28]Leon Bloy, *Dans les ténèbres* of 1918, in *Oeuvres de Léon Bloy*, 9:307-8.

Pascal in *"Jesus will be in agony, until the end of the world . . ."* (M35; see web 3.14). Bloy claims, "I always see Jesus in agony, Jesus on the cross."[29] Similarly, Rouault proclaims, "I believe in such hazardous times only in Jesus on the Cross."[30] Jesus is eternally bearing the sins, sadness, loneliness, and all the negativity of the world until the end of the age. The poor exemplify this mystical substitution through their continued struggles and agonies in life.

All of Rouault's work is rendered in a general manner to encompass varied situations and types. The *Miserere* series is not just about World War I but also representative of all the wars, even those occurring today. His figures in exodus reflect war refugees who leave their possessions and life behind in search of safety, carrying enormous burdens of worry for their loved ones and uncertainties about their future. Rouault's rendering of the impoverished continues to speak and address situations of poverty today, which afflict generation after generation.

What about the theology of poverty? Can it ring true and be relevant today? It is a hard concept to digest, especially in cultures saturated in materialism and consumerism as well as within religious circles that propagate the opposite message that wealth is the blessing of God, not poverty. A temporary financial hardship or relative poverty with limited resources is acceptable and bearable, but not the gruesome, life-taking poverty presented by Bloy and Rouault. Yet departure from abject poverty can lead to less identification with the crucified Christ. The church remembers the sacrifice of Jesus at special moments such as Good Friday, but the daily absorption of his suffering as practiced and represented by Bloy is difficult to find. Without this expression of poverty, however, there is less comprehension of and gratitude for the Passion of Christ, the severity of sin, and the enormous misery Christ bore to effectuate salvation for humanity. When we forget the poor, we forget Christ's suffering.

Rouault understood the impoverished. Like others, he first shunned poverty at all costs, but later through the influence of Bloy he came to accept it not as a disgrace to overcome but as a divine calling to embrace. His depiction of the destitute brings to the fore those whom we avoid and who are

---

[29]"Je vois toujours Jésus en agonie, Jésus en croix." Leon Bloy, journal entry, April 14, 1895, in *Oeuvres de Léon Bloy*, 11:178.

[30]"Je ne crois, dans des temps si hasardeux, qu'à Jésus sur la Croix" (Charensol, *Georges Rouault*, preface).

hidden in this materialistic world.[31] He reminds us that the abject poor, however out of view, still exist, and they are dignified humans with needs, desires, and feelings. Like any human, they are made in the image of God, and as they suffer they bear the image of Jesus on the cross. Rouault painstakingly labored on each work to produce the right line, shape, value, and color for his expression. His art, which is often compared to stained glass, projects a sense of glow. Even in the somber scenes of the impoverished in the 1910s, the figures subtly glimmer. They carry a sense of the divine, because blessed indeed are the poor.

---

[31]This is not far from the theological trend called "the preferential option for the poor," which advocates foremost consideration for the poor, just as Jesus preferentially did; see Daniel Groody and Gustavo Gutiérrez, *The Preferential Option for the Poor Beyond Theology* (Notre Dame, IN: University of Notre Dame Press, 2014).

Saint Isidore

—See Color Plate 2—

Bryn Gillette

My painting *Saint Isidore* had just been finished when I was invited to participate in the symposium on the art of Georges Rouault at Gordon-Conwell Theological Seminary. It began as a live painting at a symposium of the Charlotte Institute of Faith and Work called Work and Worship on April 9, 2022, at New City Church and was later finished in my studio. While this work was not a conscious response to the legacy of Rouault, the more I came to understand him as a man and artist, the more I found the echoes of his legacy in my own work.

Rouault has been described as a prophetic painter, repeating the use of symbolic characters in his work to carry the weight of meaning: the clown, the prostitute, and the judge. The plower has equally been a repeated symbol in my life ever since my mentor, Bruce Herman, challenged me to "serve the work." When I was a nineteen-year-old college student, Bruce pointed out that my artistic talent was like a fertile field in which I was haphazardly casting seeds and getting easy results, but that I would never know the full intention of God's assignment in my life as an artist unless I plowed up the entire field of my capacity, planted deeply, waited and tended the work through the long season. Then and only then would I see the full harvest. The plower has now followed me through more than twenty years of painting, prayer, and raising a family while pursuing the full harvest of God's work in my life. It first appeared while deeply engaged in hours of daily painting during my MFA (master of fine arts) studies. It showed up again years later during a prophetic live painting session in a church service on Easter Sunday, only to have my nearly three-year-old daughter give her life to Christ that night. It has shown up more since then, most recently with the new Saint Isidore iteration. I was moved to find that Rouault was also deeply shaped by his allegiance to his mentor Moreau, and much of his life and career carried the ripples of his mentor's legacy and impact, just as mine has carried the impact of Bruce Herman.

There is also a similar subject matter in Rouault's work and my own related to the poor, the downtrodden, and the oppressed. A large part of my artistic journey has been as an artistic ambassador of the impoverished nation of Haiti, visually advocating for their restoration and depicting the suffering citizens in their dual reality of beauty and brokenness. The plower shares these same themes but also incorporates the hope of divine collaboration at work in our lives. Saint Isidore was fabled to be able to plow three times faster than his contemporaries due to an angelic presence pushing him from behind. I think it is the hope of kingdom-hearted artists to have divine momentum taking our work "infinitely beyond anything we might ask or imagine," as expressed in Ephesians 3. The very fact that we are still looking and marveling at the work of Rouault a century later and describing him as one of the most influential Christian artists of the twentieth century demonstrates God's pushing at the back of his work. Rouault, like Saint Isidore, has accomplished more in his authentic and gritty work than anyone could have accomplished alone with his humble tools. He has lifted the poor and the broken to a place of beautified transcendence that causes the viewer to grieve and ache in hope for the restoration of all things.

4

The Healing Poetics of Georges Rouault

Veils of Veronica

Joel Klepac

More than twenty years ago, after finishing a bachelor's degree in fine art painting and discovering Georges Rouault through William Dyrness's work *Rouault: A Vision of Suffering and Salvation*, my wife and I moved to Romania to work with at-risk children.[1] After a year we decided to start a family and shortly thereafter rejoiced over a positive pregnancy test. At that time, we had daily meetings with children living on the streets as we played soccer and ate meals together.

When we announced the pregnancy, Iulian and Bogdan said right away, "Let's take bets on whether it is a boy or a girl." They both decided it was a boy, and I was on the girl side of the bet. "I'll bet you a pizza you are going to have a boy," said Iulian.

The pregnancy was miscarried some weeks later. I felt desolate. Our best friends were all traveling at the time, and we were an ocean away from family. With my youthful sense of invincibility shattered, I was devastated seeing the limp body of my first son. A week or so later, I needed to face the boys on the street again and tell them what happened. Iulian put his head down looked at my feet and said, "So was it a boy or a girl?" Telling him it was a boy, he immediately responded, "I guess you owe me a pizza, then."

Several weeks later Iulian and Bogdan came to cash in on the bet. I flopped the pizza box on the floor of our new and still empty apartment. They asked about his name, how old he was, and what he looked like. They probed with

---

[1]William Dyrness, *Rouault: A Vision of Suffering and Salvation* (Grand Rapids, MI: Eerdmans, 1971).

the natural comfort you might ask about someone's shoes. Their comfort with death allowed me to be reconciled to my own grieving places in a way nothing else had. The place of suffering was transformed into a place of communion and belonging. My suffering parts were welcome and held safely in that room.

Rouault, in his artistry, enters the unfurnished apartment of human suffering with the boldness these boys had, comfortably sitting and staying. Rouault's instinct to psychologically explore suffering places with compassionate vision finds resonance with the story of Veronica, who is believed to have reached for the suffering face of Christ. The thin cloth between her hands and his face became a relic that healed wherever it went.[2] So too, Rouault's canvases become face cloths, imbued with psycho-spiritual healing elements similar to those found in current psychotherapy and in Byzantine or Eastern Orthodox spirituality.

Images depicting the holy face or veil of Veronica appear throughout Rouault's body of work as both standalone images and background images, begging the viewer to consider the historical mythos and character of Veronica (see web 4.1).[3] In the *Miserere*, the title of plate 33 connects her actions to the image itself: *and Veronica with the soft linen still walks along the road . . .* (see fig. 4.1). For Rouault, Veronica was the archetype for the artist's compassionate vision.

The term *poetics* indicates an aesthetic lens through which an artist, poet, or philosopher interprets the world. Rouault's poetics was a system that integrated his faith with his aesthetic sensibilities, an agapeic vision made material with oils on canvas; this created a concretization of compassion, just as Veronica's veil came to bear the image of the suffering servant. *Veronica* means "true image," which resonates with Rouault's determination to see rightly and with compassion the true nature of his subjects: Christ and all people as made in the image of God.

Rouault's work has been seen through the lens of the Christian vision of salvation.[4] Salvation in the Eastern Orthodox sense is understood not

---

[2]Vladimir Lossky and Leonid Ouspensky, *The Meaning of Icons*, trans. G. E. H. Palmer and E. Kadloubovsky (Yonkers, NY: St. Vladimir's Seminary Press, 1982), 69.

[3]James F. Keenan, "Et Veronique au tendre lin passe encore sur le chemin," in *Mystic Masque: Semblance and Reality in Georges Rouault, 1871–1958*, ed. Stephen Schloesser (Boston: McMullen Museum of Art, 2008), 437.

[4]Dyrness, *Rouault: A Vision*. See also Susan A. Michalczyk, "The Aesthetics of Shock: Baudelaire, Benjamin, Rouault," in Schloesser, *Mystic Masque*, 201.

primarily as a rescue from hell but rather the process of theosis, which empha-
sizes integration, reconciliation, and healing.[5] Rouault was aware of the poetics of the Eastern Orthodox iconographic tradition, which also has the
purpose of facilitating salvation, spiritual healing, or theosis.[6]

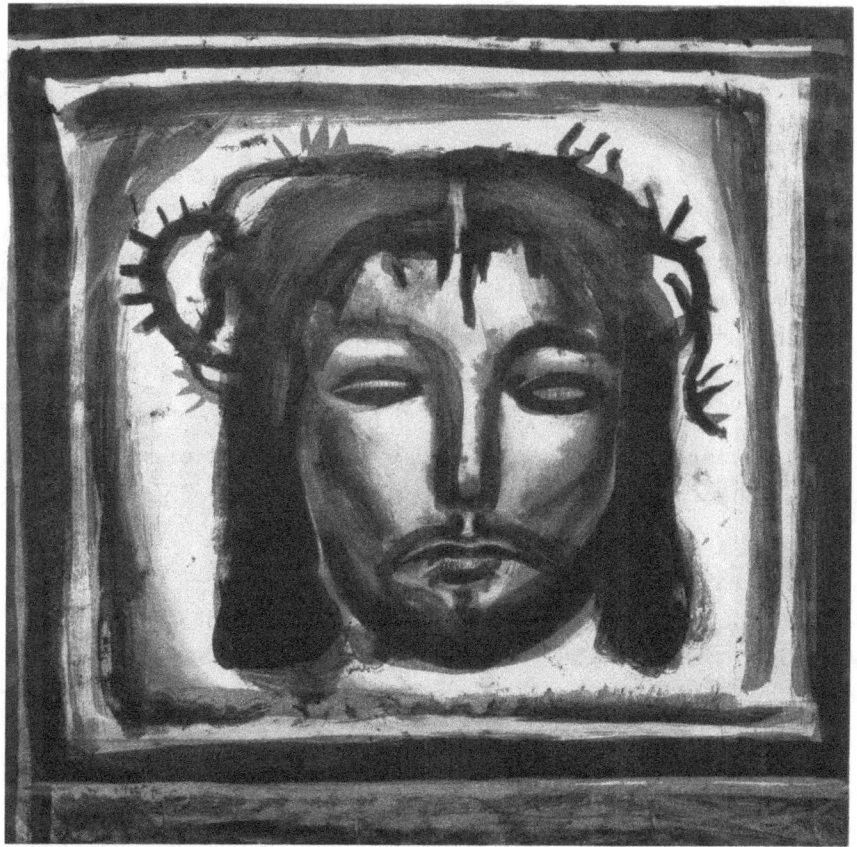

Figure 4.1. Georges Rouault, *et Véronique au tendre lin passe encore sur le chemin . . . (and Veronica with the soft linen still walks along the road . . .), Miserere* plate 33, 1922. Etching on paper, 17 1/4 x 16 15/16

---

[5]Dumitru Stăniloae, *Orthodox Spirituality: A Practical Guide for the Faithful and a Definitive Manual for the Scholar* (Waymart, PA: St. Tikhon's Seminary Press, 2002), 118. The verses commonly refer-
enced include 2 Pet 1:4 and Eph 4:13.
[6]Dyrness, *Rouault: A Vision*, 185.

Similar to how Veronica was blind to the future healing potential of the sweat cloth she used to wipe the face of Christ, Rouault probably never imagined that his work would have such deep correspondences with ancient and current healing methodologies (or *poetics* as used in this chapter). Rouault's body of work is inadvertently a collection of healing relics, a veil of a certain kind, in connection with his poetics. While Rouault was not concerned about mental health in the modern sense, his poetics took him into psycho-spiritual territories shared with both Eastern iconographers and current psychotherapy.

The poetics of the Eastern Orthodox icon stand as a precedent for a visual poetics of healing through image making, and the internal family systems psychotherapy model can be used as a companion to this healing poetics. This essay explores the shared territory of the poetics of Rouault, Eastern Orthodox iconographic spirituality, and the internal family systems model of psychotherapy. At the nexus of these three is not only a deeper appreciation for the genius of Rouault but also an outline of poetics for the artist, therapist, and anyone who wants to participate more intentionally in the healing work of restoring the lost and exiled elements among us and within us.

The veil of Veronica, an image of the holy face, has a history associated with supernatural healing.[7] The validity of these claims is not my concern here but rather psycho-spiritual healing, how one may be reconciled and experience emotional and psychological integration through the practice of engaging with holy images. In the Eastern Christian tradition, psychological healing can be understood within the theological concept of theosis, the gradual process of having all aspects of one's being brought into the divine life.[8]

Icons have a healing poetics within the sacramental design of church life, where healing is understood as part of salvation or theosis. Byzantine liturgies, sacraments, and icons all exist for the life and healing of the world: for theosis, reconciliation, and integration.[9] The multisensory, sacramental design works to heal our vision of God, ourselves, and our neighbors, and

---

[7]Lossky and Ouspensky, *Meaning of Icons,* 72.

[8]See Stăniloae, *Orthodox Spirituality.*

[9]George Morelli, "Healing the Infirmity of Sin: A Spiritual Nutshell," Antiochian Orthodox Christian Archdiocese of North America, 2009, http://ww1.antiochian.org/content/healing-infirmity-sin-spiritual-nutshell.

this in turn shifts how we live and relate to ourselves, our neighbors, and the rest of the world. Rouault is in a long tradition of image-making healers, connecting vision and healing as does the icon of the transfiguration, to be explored next.

BYZANTINE HEALING POETICS AS AGAPEIC VISION: TRANSFIGURATION

Rouault's poetics can be understood as his compassionate interpretive lens, much like Byzantine icons. Eastern Orthodox theologian and philosopher David Bentley Hart writes, "A truly Christian aesthetics might bestow . . . the eye illumined by charity, the eye whose own light can make visible what otherwise would be forever hidden."[10] The use of gold leaf, flattened space, and visual hierarchy in Byzantine iconography helps to uncloud one's vision in order to see spiritual realities that might otherwise be undisclosed. Rouault likewise unclouds the viewer's vision by means of his poetics, coaxing a deeper vision from paint and canvas.

Rouault's guiding interpretive lens was to create images that penetrated below the mask with "immeasurable pity" for the subject, which was another vision of "myself, ourselves, almost all of us."[11] Rouault never painted an objectified enemy but only the manifestations of his own experience and his treatment of his subjects with compassionate understanding. Rouault once encountered a clown traveling in a caravan, and he remarked on the significance of this moment: "A star had clutched my heart, and from that I was able to derive an entire system of poetics. . . . We are all of us clowns . . . we all wear a 'spangled costume,' but if we are caught by surprise, the way I caught that old clown, oh then; who would dare to claim he is not moved deeply by immeasurable pity?"[12]

The clown encounter was Rouault's Mount Tabor, transfiguring his vision, removing the scales, and making way for a "favorable furrow" to work the land of the human soul.[13] Rouault's visual references to the narrative of Veronica

---

[10]David Bentley Hart, *Theological Territories: A David Bentley Hart Digest* (Notre Dame, IN: University of Notre Dame Press, 2020), 269.

[11]Quoted in Dyrness, *Rouault: A Vision*, 149.

[12]Quoted in Frank Getlin and Dorothy Getlin, *Georges Rouault's Miserere* (Milwaukee: Bruce, 1964), 43.

[13]Dyrness, *Rouault: A Vision*, 149.

are a shorthand for this kind of unveiling vision, as she, by her compassionate action, inadvertently created an image that reveals Christ beneath the mask of the tortured criminal.

Veronica's image fits well in the systems of desert spirituality that see the healing power of cleansed vision. The Byzantine icon of the transfiguration is an icon undergirding the Orthodox spirituality of illumination, along with purification and deification.[14] Icons heal by peeling away scales from the viewer's eyes, just like the breaking of bread reveals that the stranger on the road to Emmaus was in fact the risen Christ (Lk 24:13-35). Rouault creates images depicting the reality beneath the masks, and just as the disciples see Christ's eternal glory in the transfiguration icon, Rouault sees Christ, the divine image, beneath the distressing masks as the true image of his characters. This kind of seeing can be referred to as agapeic vision, always seeing with eyes of compassion the image of God in the other.

BYZANTINE HEALING POETICS AS APATHEIA: TRINITY AND CRUCIFIXION

Apatheia, or dispassion, undergirds this iconographic tradition, which St. Evagrius Ponticus describes as "only a relatively permanent state of deep calm, arising from the full and harmonious integration of the emotional life, under the influence of love. . . . Apatheia and agape, divine love, are but two aspects of a single reality. In fact, the offspring of apatheia is agape."[15]

The aesthetic manifestation of apatheia can be seen in the Byzantine icons of Christ, with the preference for showing abiding calm and compassion versus momentary feelings. Equanimity over emotionality, apatheia is the eternal, essential nature of things rather than fleeting states. Vladimir Lossky and Leonid Ouspensky explain how this lies at the heart of iconography:

> [When the iconographer] reaches a state in which his usual dispersed condition, "thoughts and feelings coming from the fallen nature" is, with the help of the Holy Spirit, replaced by a state of concentrated prayer (read: apatheia). . . . Corresponding with this state of the saint, his whole image in the

---

[14]Staniloae, *Orthodox Spirituality*; see also Lossky and Ouspensky, *Meaning of Icons*, 35.

[15]Evagrius Ponticus, *The Praktikos and Chapters on Prayer*, trans. John E. Bamberger (Mulgrave, VIC: Cistercian Publications, 1970), 85.

icon, his face and other details, all lose the sensory aspect of corruptible flesh and become spiritualised.[16]

Apatheia is the remainder when emotions, appetites, or passions are set aside, enabling a vision of the unclouded truth of things. Oliver Clement discusses this transfiguring vision: "It is, therefore, essential to let the 'heart-spirit' settle like calm water. Then it becomes a tranquil lake in which the sky is reflected, in which the face of Christ can be seen and thereby the true face of one's neighbor also."[17] Settling the turbulence of the inner life leads to a true vision of God and neighbor. Both in the patristic writings and in internal family systems therapy as discussed below, a subtraction process of setting aside passions results not in a void but rather, in the words of St. Isaac the Syrian, a "luminous love."[18] When one's vision is unblocked by the removal of the scales—the passions, appetites, emotions, or attachments—one is able to truly see behind the distressing mask to the divine image underneath and to acquire love of neighbor. Rouault, speaking of the conception of his poetics, remarks, "Who would dare to claim he is not moved deeply by immeasurable pity" in the face of the suffering human under the clown mask?[19] This transfiguring vision for Rouault leaves him with compassion for what he sees.

The icon of the Old Testament Holy Trinity by Andrei Rublev carries a deep calm, integration, and mutual love: apatheia. From this perfect calm and contentment, without necessity, without passion, God creates the universe out of the overflow of love, joy, communion, and calm, without compulsion or necessity; he creates out of agape and apatheia.[20] Likewise, divine love is the foundation of all God creates.

This divine love—agape and apatheia—is displayed in the Eastern Christian iconographic depiction of the crucifixion. The crucifixion is an act done not of necessity or compulsion but out of the overflow of the agape of the Holy Trinity

---

[16]Lossky and Ouspensky, *Meaning of Icons*, 38.

[17]Olivier Clément, *The Roots of Christian Mysticism: Texts from the Patristic Era with Commentary* (Hyde Park, NY: New City, 2013), 167.

[18]Hilarion Alfeyev, *The Spiritual World of Isaac the Syrian* (Collegeville, MN: Cistercian Publications, 2000), 33.

[19]Quoted in Dyrness, *Rouault: A Vision*, 149.

[20]For an excellent discussion of these terms, see David Bentley Hart, *The Hidden and the Manifest: Essays in Theology and Metaphysics* (Grand Rapids, MI: Eerdmans, 2017), 41-55.

(Mt 16:21-23). Byzantine poetics offer the idea of healing vision purified by dis-passion, which clears the way for divine love for all humanity. The whole life of the Eastern Church in its liturgical cycle and spiritual practices, including icons, is designed for the purification of the passions to make way for apatheia.[21]

The "immeasurable pity" of Rouault is the antithesis of fear-driven crit-icism and judgment, which are common passions. James Keenan writes, "Like [Léon] Bloy, Rouault painted his prostitutes in the unbecoming light of reality, but unlike Bloy, he does not judge them morally."[22] Instead of seeing the mask, his pity penetrates with x-ray vision to the suffering divine image. Fearful criticism is peeled back (apatheia), making way for compassionate vision to see the truer reality of the hidden divine image.

Rouault's painting, in the spirit of Veronica's luminous love, creates can-vases that make the viewer see the divine image under the distressing mask. Maritain writes of Rouault, "What he sees and knows with a strange pity, and what he makes us see, is the miserable affliction and the lamentable meanness of our times, not just the affliction of the body, but the affliction of the soul, the bestiality and the self-satisfied vainglory of the rich and the worldly, the crushing weariness of the poor, the frailty of us all."[23] Further elaborating what Rouault "makes us see," Marchiori writes, "Hurried interpreters of Rouault's art have missed its true religious point, which lies in his penetrating search for character. But it is a search always dominated by a feeling of compassion to-wards humble people and by a protest against injustice and hypocrisy."[24] Rouault set aside judgment toward the people he depicted, a movement of apatheia. This apatheia, and its offspring, agapeic vision, aligns with the healing dynamics in the poetics of Byzantine icons.

BYZANTINE HEALING POETICS AS PRESENCE: THE HOLY FACE

Veronica's veil is often considered the original icon, the icon of icons and im-portant for its apologetic role in defending the use of icons in the East.[25] The

---

[21]Phillip Sherrard, *The Sacred in Life and Art* (Limni, Greece: Denise Harvey, 2004), 68.

[22]Keenan, "Et Veronique au tendre," 445.

[23]Jacques Maritain, "Georges Rouault," *Cahiers Jacques Maritain*, no. 12 (November 1985): 24, quoted in Bernanrd Doering, "Lacrimae Rerum—Tears at the Heart of Things: Jacques Maritain and Georges Rouault," in *Truth Matters: Essays in Honor of Jacques Maritain*, ed. John G. Trapani (Washington, DC: Catholic University of America Press, 2004), 214.

[24]Giuseppe Marchiori, *Rouault* (New York: Reynal, 1965), 10.

[25]Lossky and Ouspensky, *Meaning of Icons*, 72.

image itself is a convergence of multiple layers of incarnation, a materialization of the divine. Christ's incarnate compassion makes God visible in the flesh. Veronica's embodied compassion makes Christ's face a visible image, the face made without hands. Veronica's veil is an image of the incarnation in material form, which makes the viewer aware of the eternal presence of the compassion of Christ and in church tradition transmits healing through its presence. In an encounter with the icon, one may sense communion in suffering, while isolation is healed by presence.

Rouault's graphic work is an art of presence as his compassionate gaze seeks the true image in the face of other subjects. The image of the face of Christ conveys divine presence. This is both a strategy of Rouault and the poetics of the icon. Theologian and psychologist James Loder writes, "The primal experience of the face as actual presence and its significance as symbolic expression provides a prototype for the convicting presence of God."[26] In a sense, to be compassionately present to the suffering and to have that loving presence accepted is to be reconciled. One is saved from exile by receiving the presence of the beloved. Through loving presence to the suffering of humanity, Rouault's work becomes a healing instrument, like the veil of Veronica. Or, as John of Damascus said, "I have seen the human image of God, and my soul is saved."[27] As in the author's interpretation of *The Holy Face* (plate 3), the viewer becomes the subject and the recipient of the compassionate gaze: seeing and seen, beholding and beheld. Byzantine iconographic poetics and Rouault's poetics share a recovery of agapeic vision, state of apatheia, and the immediacy of compassionate presence ready for reconciliation.

THE HEALING POETICS OF INTERNAL FAMILY SYSTEMS THERAPY AND GEORGES ROUAULT

Several salient features of one form of evidence-based psychotherapy, internal family systems therapy, lend to a natural conversation between Rouault's poetics and Eastern Orthodox mystics.[28] By examining healing features of the

---

[26]James E. Loder, *The Logic of the Spirit: Human Development in Theological Perspective* (San Francisco: Jossey-Bass, 1998), 100.

[27]Quoted in Lossky and Ouspensky, *Meaning of Icons*, 34.

[28]Richard C. Schwartz and Martha Sweezy, *Internal Family Systems Therapy* (New York: Guilford, 2019).

internal family systems therapy model in comparison with Rouault's poetics, it becomes clear that Rouault's poetics generates important conditions for psycho-spiritual healing.

Richard Schwartz, the founder of internal family systems therapy, began to notice while working with disordered eating clients that they spoke of "a part that binges" and a "part that purges."[29] Eventually, he worked with these parts with the same methodology he used in working with families, getting each part to be understood and seen by the others, finding out what each needed, negotiating new ways of getting needs met, and so on. He learned to ask certain parts to step aside while the target part had the floor. When he asked for enough parts to make space, he eventually discovered that the same spiritual qualities emerged even with the most traumatized individuals. An entity seen by clients as "not a part" emerged that had spiritual qualities such as compassion, curiosity, calm, connectedness, creativity, clarity, courage, and confidence. When asked what this was, his clients would say, "Well that is just my self." For lack of a more natural term, he called it "Self," while others may call it higher self, wise self, true self, or perhaps "being in the Spirit." This discovery of Self made him question his lifelong atheism. For him, it was a spiritual awakening to discover these spiritual qualities at the core of every client without having to teach it, grow it, train it, or somehow implant it. Calm compassion was just there waiting to be uncovered, just as agape in the Eastern Orthodox tradition was found after the process of apatheia.

Internal family systems therapy is a synthesis of the multiplicity of mind, family systems theory, and spirituality.[30] Schwartz's discovery of a compassionate, calm core within even the most traumatized clients became for him a spiritual awakening, and this finding became an indispensable feature of the treatment modality.

Multiplicity of mind has been articulated and used in therapies such as gestalt, Jungian, ego state therapy, and psychosynthesis, and is supported by the neuroscience research of Dan Seigel and others.[31] Just as with the disordered eating clients mentioned above, we can recognize that one part of us

[29]Schwartz and Sweezy, *Internal Family Systems Therapy*, 10.
[30]Schwartz and Sweezy, *Internal Family Systems Therapy*, 39-43.
[31]Daniel Siegel and Richard Schwartz, *The Myth of Unitary Self: A Dialogue on the Multiplicity of Mind*, DVD (Eau Claire, WI: PESI, 2015).

would like to do one thing while another part would like to do another in any given situation. This phenomenon is called "multiplicity of mind" and is common to all people.

Family systems theory says the social, family, and inner dynamics explored in internal family systems therapy share similar systemic dynamics that can be addressed to bring balance. Within each layer of a system, there tend to be protective parts, preventative maintenance parts, parts that put out hot emotions, and parts that get exiled and shut out, voices that seem too dangerous to listen to if the system is to survive.

Internal Family Systems Healing Poetics: Agapeic Vision

Internal family systems therapy provides a methodology for reasonably assuring that a client is only approached when there is significant "Self-energy" present, or, in the language of spirituality, agape or luminous love.[32] In practice, the therapist is taught to recognize their own state, checking for qualities of this calm, compassion, and curiosity, as well as learning to check for when the client has a base level of compassion for their own parts. One only enters the inner territory if compassion and calm are adequately present.

Rouault's *Miserere* series mimics this progression of entering with compassion by starting in the first three plates with images of Christ, reinforcing that the following plates are to be viewed in light of this image of God identifying with all forms of suffering. In short, he indicates that all distressing masks to come hide a "forever scourged" divine presence. In doing so, Rouault sets aside his own judgment of the characters, seeing with agapeic vision in the same way the internal family systems therapist must only approach a client with calm compassion or "Self-energy," love that sees Christ within the sufferer.

One feature of internal family systems therapy is the depathologizing of distressing aspects of human thoughts and behaviors.[33] For example, many clients enter the therapy room ashamed of a suicidal part, an angry part, or an acting-out part. In the internal family systems therapy process, the therapist and eventually the client befriend each part. The suicidal part becomes understood perhaps as attempting to protect from suffering forever or may serve to wake the client out of a depressive slump. The angry part is often the only part

---

[32]Schwartz and Sweezy, *Internal Family Systems Therapy*, 43-54.
[33]Schwartz and Sweezy, *Internal Family Systems Therapy*, ix.

to stand up for the client's dignity when the inner system wants to make peace at all costs and sacrifice authenticity. An acting-out part may have the intention of bringing relief from the exhaustion of overworking parts dominating the system.

The internal family systems therapy process builds on the assumption that even distressing parts of the client have a positive intention, and that approaching them with compassion and curiosity allows the therapist and client to see this intention; in addition, the client can find a compassionate posture toward their own distressing parts. The angry part now can be appreciated and integrated. New ways to stand up for the client can be negotiated. Rather than raging, perhaps the angry part becomes a signal to the client to speak up in an appropriate way to meet particular needs. The therapist does not lose sight of the client's core Self and relies on that to become the healing agent in the process.

From a posture similar to an internal family systems therapist, Rouault gazes at diverse and distressing characters but seems to hold the assumption that the surface is but a mask of the divine. His images bear a material residue of this type of healing vision. Rouault's poetics, driven by agapeic vision, aligns with core aspects of healing from the internal family systems perspective. Like Veronica's veil, his paintings are imbued with healing properties.

INTERNAL FAMILY SYSTEMS HEALING POETICS: APATHEIA-AGAPE

The condition of both therapist and client finding calm, compassion, and curiosity (Self-led state or Self-energy) allows for deeper work with more vulnerable parts. This state, or Self-energy, corresponds with agape found through the process of apatheia described above. The more vulnerable parts are typically the disowned parts: the shame, guilt, or other intense feelings it did not seem safe for the system to acknowledge. Internal family systems therapy refers to them as "exiles."[34] The compassionate vision of Rouault has an acute sensitivity toward exiled characters: outcast, poor, and suffering victims of every variety. In line with Rouault's statements regarding the suffering clown, he approaches all subjects with deep, personal identification. "Are we not all clowns?" And by extension, are we not all castaways, refugees, and the

---

[34]Schwartz and Sweezy, *Internal Family Systems Therapy*, 160-72.

vulnerable?[35] Rouault seems to portray both the outer historical character and the inner aspect of himself, and he invites viewers to consider how this may be true for themselves. This becomes a psycho-spiritual invitation that begs the viewer, "Can you recognize yourself, and can you have pity?"

Holding compassion toward difficult characters who are often considered detestable is paramount in internal family systems therapy, and Rouault finds a way as well as with the works *Woman from a chic district believes that she has a reserved seat in Heaven* (M16), *while his lawyer, in hollow phrases, proclaims his complete innocence* (M19), and *believing ourselves kings* (M7; see fig. 2.2). Internal family systems therapy seeks to see these kinds of characters with compassion and finds them trying to protect in some way by their often-obnoxious behavior. Rouault starts with pity for the desperate show of righteousness in the evident injustice. Many artists have depicted despicable characters in a way that leaves the viewer with contempt.[36] However, Rouault's depictions of his disreputable characters leave one with empathy and personal insight rather than contempt. He somehow achieves depictions that both acknowledge the distressing state of the character—a masked state—and see past it to the luminous essence underneath, apatheia enabling agapeic vision.

While internal family systems therapy has a specific procedure, it is understood that as long as the therapist can stay in enough of a Self-led state, with compassion and curiosity, the healing work is happening regardless of following specific steps.[37] Calm, compassion, and curiosity are the ground of healing work. Without this, following all the steps will be futile and even dangerous to client progress. Throughout Rouault's body of work, he creates and refines pieces out of his poetics of agapeic vision resonant with the state of Self-energy in internal family systems therapy. Rouault carries these internal family systems therapy conditions for healing as well as presenting the heart of Veronica being moved with compassion toward the face of Christ under every distressing disguise.

INTERNAL FAMILY SYSTEMS HEALING POETICS: PRESENCE

Many have wondered how they could feel desperately alone while in the midst of many people, even friends or spouses. Internal family systems therapy offers

---

[35]Dyrness, *Rouault: A Vision*, 149-50.
[36]Consider Honoré Daumier's *Gargantua* (1831).
[37]Schwartz and Sweezy, *Internal Family Systems Therapy*, 122.

a paradigm that understands that while one may relate to others from manager or firefighter parts, there may also by exiled parts that hold feelings of aloneness, exile, or abandonment. One of the important contributions of internal family systems therapy is a methodology for descending past the managerial, protective parts through patient dialogue with those parts and to move on to those exiled parts hidden away. One may imagine plate 23 (*Street of the Lonely*; see web 3.10) or plate 26 (*in the land of thirst and fear*; see web 4.2) of the *Miserere* as embodying the feelings of some exiles. Internal family systems therapy offers a safe way to get to these kinds of psychological spaces where vulnerable and exiled parts dwell.

Healing in internal family systems therapy happens when the therapist, led by agapeic vision, empowers and guides the client to find their own spiritual core of agapeic vision to rightly see their own parts with calm and compassion, allowing this core Self of the client to be present to the exiled part. The exiled part, in the presence of agape, can be witnessed, seen, and heard for all the painful feelings it has been carrying. Often this part feels acknowledged for the first time. Beliefs picked up from key historical moments, such as, "I learned I was worthless," now are revised and released in the presence of the contradicting compassion that expels such beliefs. Healing in internal family systems therapy is eventually unexiling the exile, bringing this vulnerable part back into communion with the other parts.

This healing process mirrors the descent of Christ into hell and return with the captives. Rouault's *The one who believes in me, even should he die, will live* (M28; see web 2.1) conjures a descent into hell with skulls in a crypt, and this is followed by *Sing Matins, the day is reborn* (M29). When Thomas appears in plate 32, it is as if he is seeking evidence for this descent into death and hell (see web 2.2). Christ is present to Thomas even in his doubt, allowing the tenderness of being examined so that Thomas may see evidence of Christ's presence in the suffering of the world and even in Hades. This is followed by another Veronica image in plate 33: *and Veronica with the soft linen still walks along the road . . .* (see fig. 4.1). One could alter this slightly to describe Rouault's project, "And Rouault with his soft canvases still goes his way . . ." as we see his agapeic vision enter the depths of human suffering. It is as if Rouault is going with his own linen to touch the face of Christ found in every exile of society and by implication every psychological exile within the human mind.

Rouault's poetics guides him through the passageways of Hades in a way similar to the internal family systems therapy healing process. He offers a psychological presence to the viewer's exiled parts and leads the viewer back to the full sunshine of singing Matins. The *Miserere* series leads the viewer on a healing journey parallel to the healing process of internal family systems therapy. Rouault's work, then, becomes a healing veil of Veronica by becoming psychologically present to exiles, enabling a kind of resurrection with Christ into healing.

CONCLUSION

By looking at the poetics of Georges Rouault in the light of Byzantine icons and internal family systems therapy, salient correspondences arise, allowing one to see Rouault's body of work fulfilling a function similar to the veil of Veronica. Agapeic vision is the ground of psycho-spiritual healing. Apatheia sets free agapeic vision, which enables us to seek, find, and restore social exiles as well as the exiles of our inner systems.

In the works of Rouault, we find a luminous example of agapeic vision in material form, an incarnation of divine love. His genius is not that he treats subjects that are distressing but that he could do so while maintaining a vision of the utter dignity of the subject. "Are we not all clowns?" he says in his basic psychological identification with his subjects. To love despite the distressing disguise of another person is a rehearsal for loving and reconciling the distressing disguise in one's self and vice versa.

Rouault's work, like Veronica's veil, is an embodiment of his agapeic vision, which removes the scales from our eyes, enables our own agapeic vision, awakens us to our true core of luminous love, and invites us to be present with compassion to every part of ourselves and the world. His graphic works, all of which in a sense act as veils of Veronica, remain an open invitation to healing, an open door to anyone with eyes to see and willingness to be found by his agapeic vision. One could ask how the dogged pursuit of agapeic vision, apatheia, and presence could transform any vocation into instruments of theosis, into veils of Veronica. As David Bentley Hart writes:

> A truly Christian aesthetics might bestow on those who seek to adopt it: the eye illumined by charity, the eye whose own light can make visible what otherwise would be forever hidden. To see the fullness of divine love, the greatness

of the extremes that the shape of the divine life encompasses, in the very brokenness and desolation of a murdered slave is to have entered into an order of
vision that can never simply take leave of the despised and rejected in its haste
to find the loveliness and serenity and nobility of which they seem to have been
utterly deprived. It is a way of seeing things powerful enough still to descry the
glory of God amid that darkness, and still to rejoice in it. It can find the delight
of love even among those who have been driven far from the light of this present
world because it cannot now lose sight of the divine image that no extremity of
ruin can extinguish.[38]

---

[38]Hart, *Theological Territories*, 269.

To Carry Across

—See Color Plate 4—

Josh Jensen

The piece I created in response to Georges Rouault is an attempt to pay homage to his legacy while using elements of my own work and history in several key ways. Through much of my training during college earning a bachelor in fine arts, I focused on self-portraits that had a psychological undercurrent. This work was an important bridge to what has become my dual career as a psychotherapist and an artist. My work as an artist has always had psychological components, and likewise my work as a therapist has always valued creativity to form deep connections intellectually, emotionally, and socially. Although I have not painted a portrait in over fifteen years, this project was a return to old roots, as I have been particularly drawn to Rouault's portraits of Christ, clowns, and prostitutes. Although my work has been largely abstract for the last several years, I believe that all abstract art is some form of a self-portrait: when a piece is not created out of what is seen with the eyes, the artist's inspiration must come from within. For this reason, I did not use a specific reference when I created *To Carry Across*. Instead, it was an accumulation of action-response steps that pulled the piece toward the noticeable qualities of a face and then pushed against the realism through abstracting those shapes, colors, and proportions.

I also wanted to modernize the material that was used for this project. My piece is painted on raw canvas, also known as unprimed canvas. This technique is achieved through staining the fabric with acrylic paint in addition to painting on top of the surface. The effect is a watercolored/

stained-glass appearance due to the way the paint bleeds and stains the fabric. Rouault's work was often compared to stained glass because of his prominent line work and rich, glowing colors that seem to illuminate their surroundings. He achieved his aesthetic with oil paint and charcoal since acrylic-paint technology was not available during his lifetime. We cannot know for sure, but I suspect that if Rouault lived during our twenty-first century, he may have opted to use these acrylic materials and techniques since they resonate so strongly with his aesthetic.

My color choices were also very intentional. I started with an ochre yellow base that was quite popular in Rouault's time. From there, I added more vibrant, contemporary tones and a brighter light value that resonate more with a modern audience. I believe that color is similar to language in that we have tones that speak to our zeitgeist. Preferences for some tones over others come and go the same way words can be worn out while others come into vogue. As an artist (and therapist) I want to live well in the space and time that I am placed, and I can achieve this best when using language and colors that resonate most strongly with my contemporary audience.

Where many have praised Rouault for his bold social commentary by depicting the downtrodden, outcast, and persecuted, I also resonate with the deep emotional component of his subjects. His portrayals not only convey the spirt of the subject matter; they also evoke a deep sense of tenderness, compassion, and sadness. This same essence was what I hoped to convey in my piece. I always appreciate feedback about my work in all its forms, but I have personally found the most meaningful thing someone can say is that my work has a mysterious, emotional quality, something that evokes a deep resonance within them. Although I value and enjoy the cerebral world, I believe what matters most is our attachments to other humans and the deep emotional ties that can be created.

5

Art in Community

Rouault, Walter Brueggemann, and Postindustrial Imagination

Pamela Rossi-Keen

Georges Rouault first fascinated me in graduate school, where my interests converged at the nexus of art, Christian theology, and contemporary life. My interest at the time was purely academic,[1] but decades later it has morphed into application of theory. In this chapter I will share both this academic and applied work as I suggest that the community artists I now lead can learn from Rouault in the way he embodied what Walter Brueggemann calls the prophetic imagination. I will tell you here about my community, spend time with Brueggemann and Rouault, and then revisit my community.

BACKGROUND

The Genesis Collective in Beaver County, Pennsylvania, is a diverse group of artists and advocates who support artists and their work, connect the public with art and creativity, and come alongside community development work that is already happening and enhance it through art and media.[2] This manifests in many different ways. We organize commissions, seek grants, host exhibits, install public art, work with community stakeholders, provide technical and business education to artists, and do anything that fits within the bucket of our mission.

---

[1]See Pamela Rossi-Keen, "Peering Through the Window: Divergent Treatments of Evil in the Works of Olivier Messiaen and Georges Rouault," in *Considering Evil and Human Wickedness*, ed. Daniel Keen and Pamela Rossi-Keen (Oxford: Interdisciplinary, 2004), 67-81, www.yumpu.com/en/document/read/6627874/daniel-e-keen-pamela-rossi-keen-inter-disciplinarynet.
[2]To learn more about the Genesis Collective, visit www.gcollective.org.

Beaver County is largely suburban and rural but has a few small cities sprinkled in the mix. It is a twenty-minute drive away from Pittsburgh in an area literally built by the steel industry and then abandoned overnight.[3] The trauma wrought by industrial dreams and industrial abandonment cannot be overstated. Beaver County is now the site of the largest petrochemical investment in the nation, and the trauma response of generations of residents has been a bizarre type of shoulder shrugging—after all, what could we do?—and hope that industry will emerge as our economic and community savior once again.

The Genesis Collective emerged in the midst of the isolation of the dual pandemics of racial unrest and Covid-19.[4] I facilitated conversation among artists who were part of an art competition that asked participants to respond in creative work to the current pandemic climate. What was more jarring than I expected is that they *did* respond. They were *able* to do so. Their pieces were varied in medium, style, and concept. There was a piece that showed the plight of Black women bearing the weight of the world on their shoulders, and the world was on fire. There was a piece that celebrated first responders in the artist's community. There was a piece filled with anger at the perennial sins of racism. There was one that celebrated human resourcefulness in wild primary colors. One sculpture showed children playing telephone, displaying innocence, hope, and sweetness. All these pieces showed us ourselves and pointed to something more than our scenario.[5]

What struck me about this result was that when I finished the Zoom calls set up for these conversations between the artists and me, I was moving from a place of volition, imagination, and hope to a place of stagnation, where nobody really knew what to do. We could stay at home, we could march, we could at the time hope for a vaccine, but we were paralyzed by the realities that George Floyd had been murdered by one called to serve and protect, and we

---

[3]For a firsthand account of this period, see Paul Hertneky, *Rust Belt Boy: Stories of an American Childhood* (Peterborough, NH: Bauhan, 2016).

[4]The Genesis Collective was funded as part of a joint response from the Pittsburgh philanthropic community called Arts Equity Reimagined: Covid-19 Action Working Group. This group provided funds to many arts initiatives throughout Pittsburgh and surrounding areas for one year. You can read more about this work and the working group's participants by visiting Art Equity Reimagined, https://artsreimagined.org.

[5]To find out more about these pieces and this work, see "Exploring COVID-19 Impacts Through Visual Art," New Sun Rising, accessed March 22, 2024, www.newsunrising.org/virtual-gallery -exploring-covid-19-impacts/.

lived in desperate fear of a deadly virus that we could neither see nor avoid.[6] There was little space in which to move and little vision for what could be next. But among the artists I found both movement and vision. Armed with this discrepancy, in a region where artists create in their basements in the off hours of their days as an unpaid hobby, I began to organize the prophets. A couple of journalists quoted me in media pieces as calling artists the "canaries in the coal mine."[7] I mean this not in the sense that they have the grim task of going first to their death but rather in the sense that they tell us what is really happening that others are unable to discern.

The concept of the artist as a prophet for their community is not new. The masters of Renaissance Florence delved into politics and philosophy, chiseling and painting subversive messages into their great works.[8] Francisco Goya, Jacques-Louis David, and Ferdinand Delacroix tackled politics and war head-on in their paintings of national atrocities and hopes.[9] Giuseppe Verdi composed a rallying cry for a united Italy and inserted it into the opera *Nabucco*.[10] And Pittsburgh native Andy Warhol held a mirror up to the developed world and showed us, in our frenzy, where we were and where we were heading at a level akin to Jean-François Lyotard's *Postmodern Condition*.[11] While the reader may be familiar with artists serving as prophets, it will serve us well to establish an understanding of what a prophet is and how a prophet functions within a community. For that, we turn to theology.

---

[6]The first vaccines were administered only six months after Covid-19 was declared a pandemic.

[7]To read these pieces, see Abby Mackey, "The Genesis Collective Gives Beaver County Artists a Voice," *Pittsburgh Post-Gazette*, August 11, 2022, www.post-gazette.com/life/goodness/2022/08/11 /genesis-collective-beaver-art-mural/stories/202207240005. See also Liam Watters, "Creative Lift Off: How The Genesis Collective Is Shaping an Arts Community in Beaver County," Pittsburgh Foundation, August 1, 2022, https://pittsburghfoundation.org/creative-lift-off.

[8]See, for instance, the statue of the biblical hero David sculpted by Donatello in the mid-fifteenth century. Sculpted in the round, David is suggestive of the artist's own sexuality as well as political phenomena in Medici Florence around the time of the statue's making. See Laurie Schneider, "Donatello's Bronze David," *The Art Bulletin* 55, no. 2 (1973): 213-16, https://doi.org/10.2307/3049095.

[9]See, for example, Francisco Goya's *The Third of May 1808*, Jacques-Louis David's *The Death of Marat*, and Ferdinand Delecroix's *Liberty Leading the People*.

[10]I refer here to the piece "Va, pensiero," in *Nabucco*, 1842.

[11]Note, for example, Warhol's repetitive tiles in pieces that showed us in garish colors our preoccupation with media, immediacy, and celebrity in works such as those celebrating contemporary cultural icons Marilyn Monroe and Jacqueline Kennedy Onassis. Jean-François Lyotard's concise work *The Postmodern Condition: A Report on Knowledge*, trans. Geoff Bennington (Minneapolis: University of Minnesota Press, 2010), produced for the Conseil des universités du Québec, is an oddly prescient look at our evolving concept of truth, reality, and knowledge.

WALTER BRUEGGEMANN'S PROPHETIC IMAGINATION

Theologian Walter Brueggemann created a compelling way of understanding biblical prophets. He writes, "The task of prophetic ministry is to nurture, nourish, and evoke a consciousness and perception alternative to the consciousness and perception of the dominant culture around us."[12] What exactly does that mean? In ancient Israel, prophets spoke the truth. Often it was a hard truth at a time when monarchs and groups of people thought all was well. The prophetic task in this ancient semi-theocratic civilization was to express the divine displeasure of God and to bring about something unconventional, to act in such a way as to draw attention and provoke change in thought and action, or simply to share a new thing that would emerge. Often, the prophetic message is something that throws people off their game and leads them away from what they take for granted as the way things are or will be.[13] They are tripped up by the prophetic. In his seminal work *The Prophetic Imagination*, Brueggemann takes the reader on a sweeping tour of major themes in the biblical prophets as well as extrapolating on the role of the prophet within a contemporary cultural context. Here I will summarize his ideas before turning attention to Rouault and then to a contemporary example close to my own heart.

Toward the end of Brueggemann's powerful tome, he writes a note on the ministry of the prophet: "I have tried to say that prophetic ministry does not consist of spectacular acts of social crusading or of abrasive measures of indignation. Rather, prophetic ministry consists of offering an alternative perception of reality and in letting people see their own history in the light of God's freedom and his will for justice." The prophet speaks into the calcified, well-behaved rhetoric of empire, which is the reigning order, without a real vision or hope for how it can be otherwise. Empire asks us to pretend things are all right, and as long as we can sustain this pretense, there will be no serious criticism. The economy of empire is crafted to keep people satiated so that they do not notice their pain. The status quo of any culture is preserved through numbness.[14]

---

[12]Walter Brueggemann, *The Prophetic Imagination*, 40th anniversary ed. (Minneapolis: Fortress, 2018), 3.

[13]The Old Testament is full of these. Daniel, Joseph, Samuel, Isaiah, and Amos are a few such examples.

[14]Brueggemann, *Prophetic Imagination*, 116-17, 11, 35.

But, says Brueggemann, confronting the status quo cannot take place through a direct hit or it will land like a foam bullet. It will not achieve its goals. The prophet cannot scold or reprimand. What is required is the expansiveness of imagination wherein the prophet engages the possibility and promise of something new. The consciousness of empire "leads people to despair about the power to move toward new life," and "our culture is competent to implement almost anything and to imagine almost nothing." Thus, says Brueggemann, "Every totalitarian regime is frightened of the artist."[15]

How does the artist engage this numbness and offer something different? Pure imagination is not as catalytic as we might hope. The prophet brings people out of this numbness through the engagement of pain and symbols. After all, turning our collective eye toward suffering is the role of the prophet. Brueggemann writes, "Passion as the capacity and readiness to care, to suffer, to die, and to feel is the enemy of imperial reality," and so the prophet's job is to lead people to *engage* their experience of suffering. This is central to the prophetic consciousness. The prophet must make perennial issues of suffering "audible and visible" to produce hope. The prophet refuses to be satiated by imperial prescriptions. She creates hope through speech. She *makes something*, and suggests an alternative community. Making something metabolizes despair into energy.[16]

The way to understand the despair of a community with integrity is through solidarity with the marginalized. Brueggemann cites the prophetic life of Jesus when he addresses this point. "(Jesus) has, in fact, dismantled the dominant culture and nullified its claims. The way of his ultimate criticism is his decisive solidarity with marginal people and the accompanying vulnerability required by that solidarity."[17] When we feel the pain of the marginalized, it "means an end to all social arrangements that nullified pain by a remarkable depth of numbness." It is in fact a revolution to stand *with*.[18]

---

[15] Brueggemann, *Prophetic Imagination*, xxix, 46, 59-60, 40.

[16] Brueggemann, *Prophetic Imagination*, 77.

[17] Brueggemann, *Prophetic Imagination*, 35, 41, xxix, 91, 69, 67, 9, 77, 82.

[18] Brueggemann, *Prophetic Imagination*, 91, 95. At the time of this writing, there are protests around the world against the killing of an Iranian woman, Mahsa Amini, for wearing her hijab improperly. An art collective in New York City, Anonymous Artists for Iran, unfurled red banners through the center of the Solomon R. Guggenheim Museum. The banners bear the likeness of Amini. To read more about this installation, see "Artists Make New York's Guggenheim Site of Protest Against Killing of Mahsa Amini," Art Forum, October 24, 2022, www.artforum.com/news/artists-make-new-york-s-guggenheim-site-of-protest-against-killing-of-mahsa-amini-89476.

In summary, we have empire, the dominant cultural force that numbs those under its thumb. We have the despairing masses, who see no alternative to that which is. But we also have the prophet, whose job it is to spark imagination through indirect means and solidarity with those whom the empire marginalizes. But what is the *act*? How is this solidarity and confrontation performed? It is accomplished, says Brueggemann, through the use of symbols. "Hope requires a very careful symbolization," and the symbols should be a deeply rooted vocabulary of the community. These symbols are primal memories. The prophet "mine(s) the memory of this people" and educates, using "tools of hope."[19]

The symbols, deployed in this sideways manner, confront the ways things are through surprise. This is reminiscent of the primal community identity and calls the community to apply the symbols to a hopeful and purposeful future. These symbols bring to the public an expression of the fears that are suppressed and unnamed under empire. In this solidarity—this weeping *with*—there is the potential for newness.

Brueggemann draws our eye again to Jesus, who "gives signs; he promises alternatives." He "practiced in the most radical form the main elements of prophetic ministry and imagination. On the one hand, he practiced criticism of the deathly world around him. The dismantling was fully wrought in his crucifixion, in which he himself embodied the thing dismantled. On the other hand, he practiced the energizing of the new future given by God."[20] Indeed, in the metaphysical realm of cosmic possibility, the crucifixion is theater for *us*.[21] The symbol of the sacrifice was ancient, even then, but it was not, in the context of all possible worlds, required. It was chosen.

Such a practice of hope requires careful symbolization and "can't be expressed too fully" or it will be co-opted by the managers of empire. Brueggemann gives a circumspect view of biblical prophets, but he recognizes the artist as fitting this role. He writes that the *imagination* must come before the *implementation*.[22]

---

[19]Brueggemann, *Prophetic Imagination*, 64.

[20]Brueggemann, *Prophetic Imagination*, 95, 116.

[21]I owe this—what would become to me profound—revelation to philosopher Vladimir Marchenkov of Ohio University's School of Interdisciplinary Arts. In this declaration lies the very kernel from which the whole of a theology and philosophy of creation, theology proper, and human identity would unfurl.

[22]Brueggemann, *Prophetic Imagination*, 64, 40.

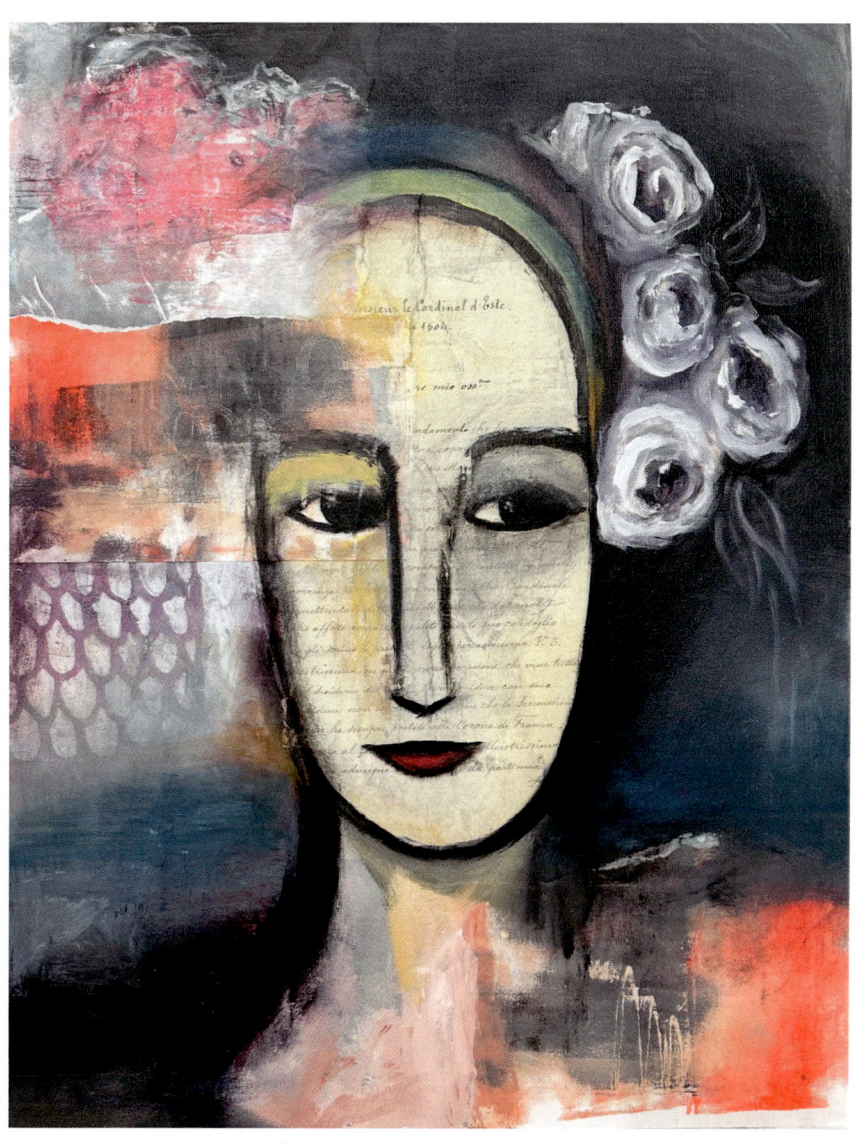

CHRISTINA **FELTEN**

How can we fix our eyes on what is unseen?, 2022

Mixed media on canvas, 18 × 24

PLATE 1

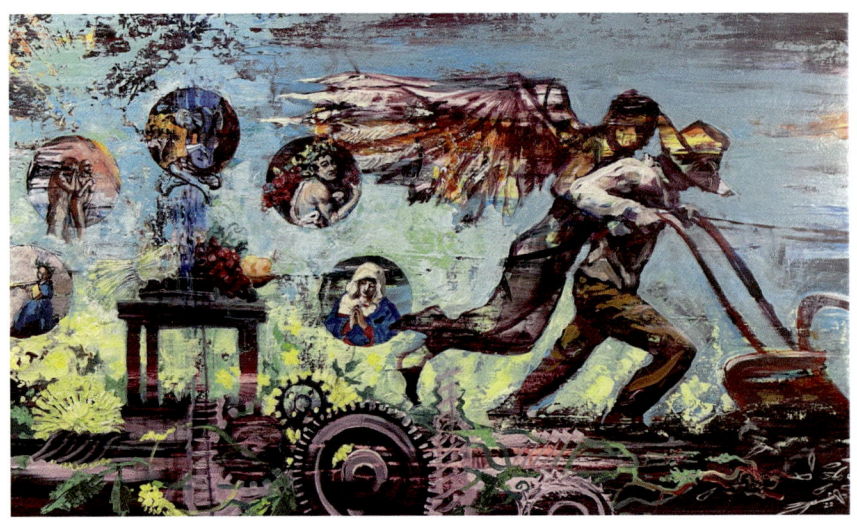

BRYN **GILLETTE**

Saint Isidore, 2021

PLATE 2

Acrylic and pen on wood panel, 36 × 22 ¼

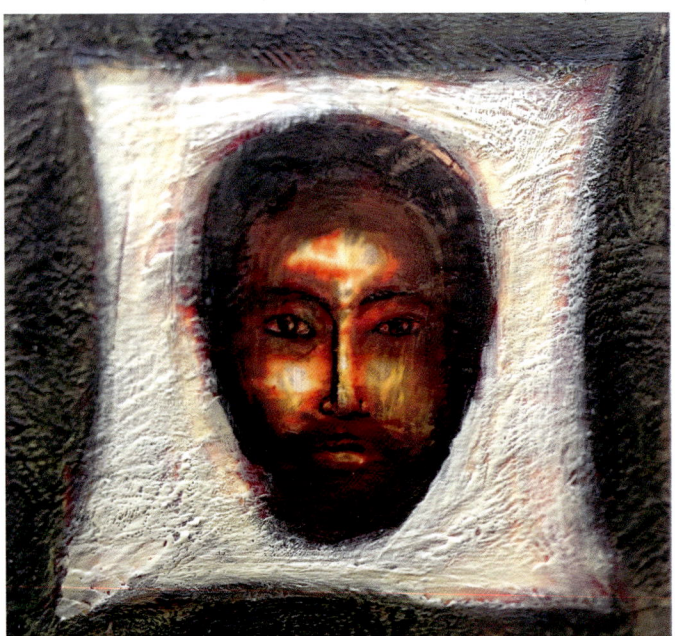

JOEL **KLEPAC**

The Holy Face, 2020

PLATE 3

Encaustic on wood panel, 19 ½ × 19 ½

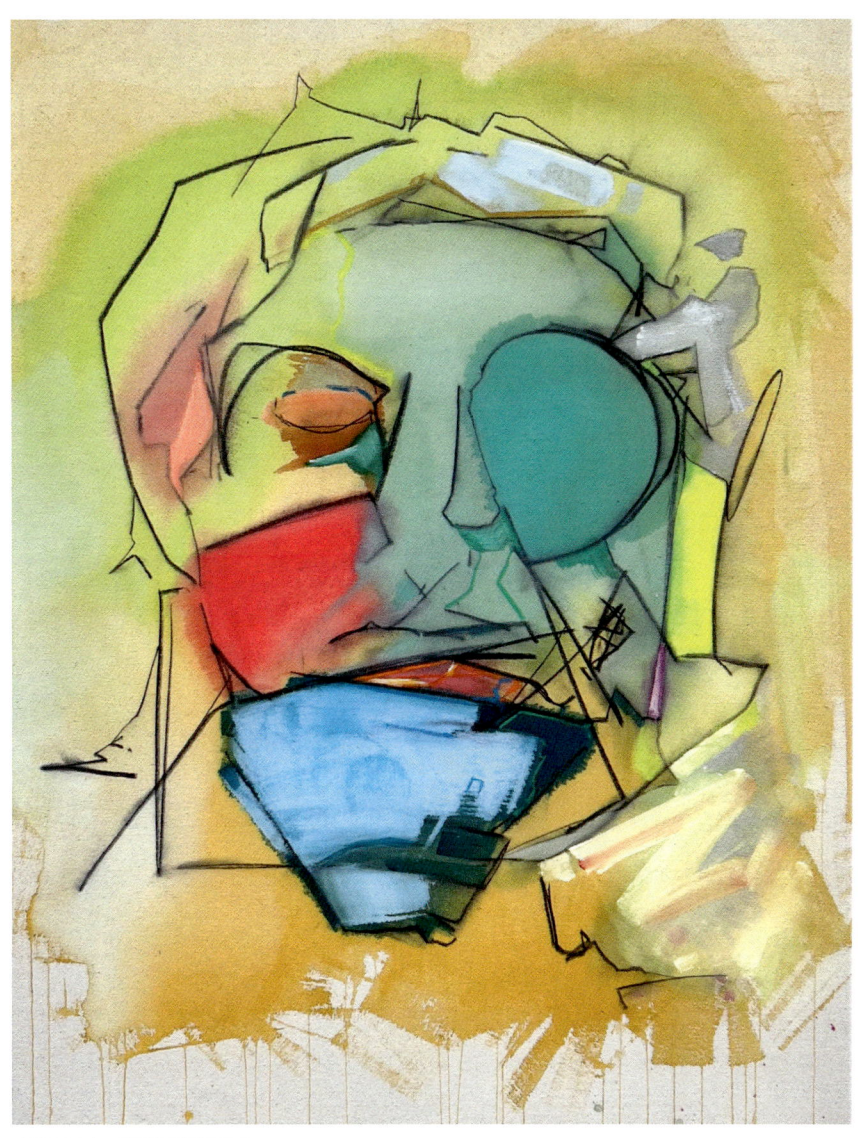

JOSH **JENSEN**

To Carry Across, 2023

Mixed media on canvas, 31 × 41 × 2 ½

PLATE 4

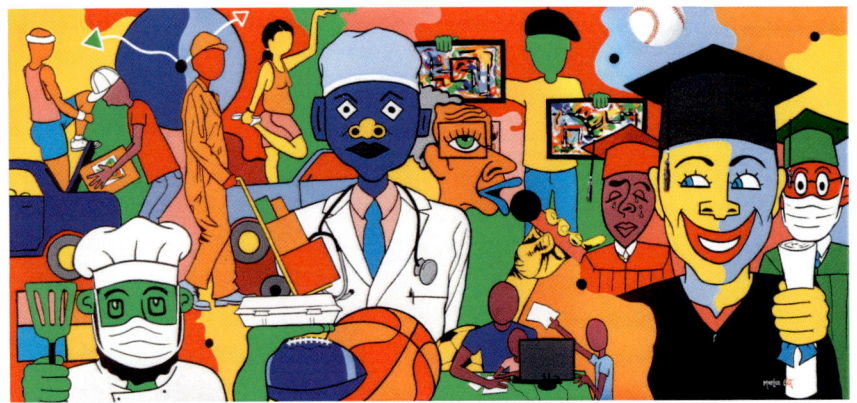

MARLON **GIST**

Navigating COVID-19, 2020   PLATE 5

Acrylic on canvas, 24 × 48

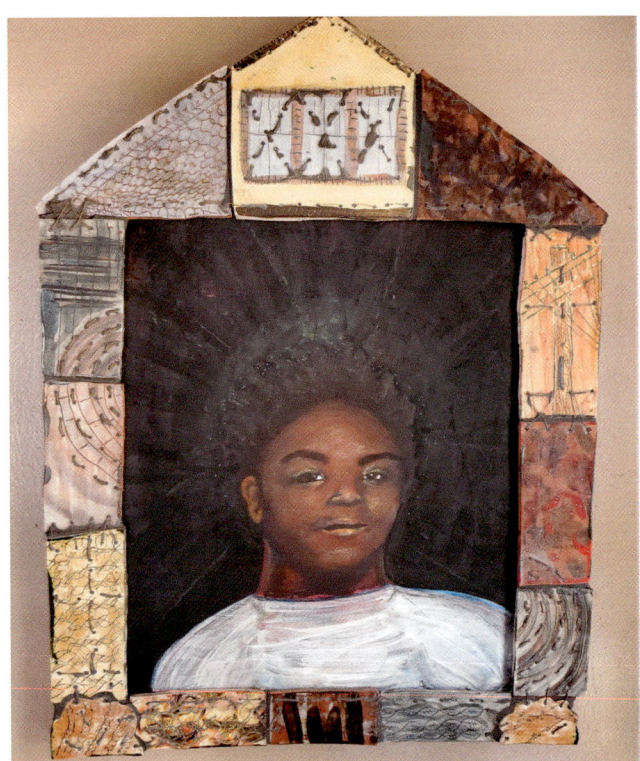

HELMS **JARRELL**

Beloved, 2017   PLATE 6

Ceramic, metal, acrylic, and collage on wood panel, 23 × 31

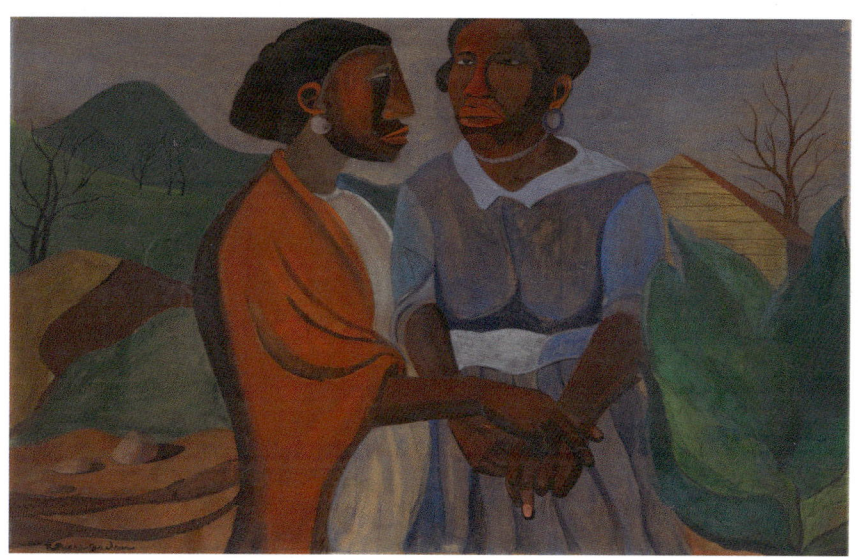

ROMARE **BEARDEN**

The Visitation, 1941

Gouache, ink, and pencil on colored paper, 30 ½ × 46 ½

PLATE 7

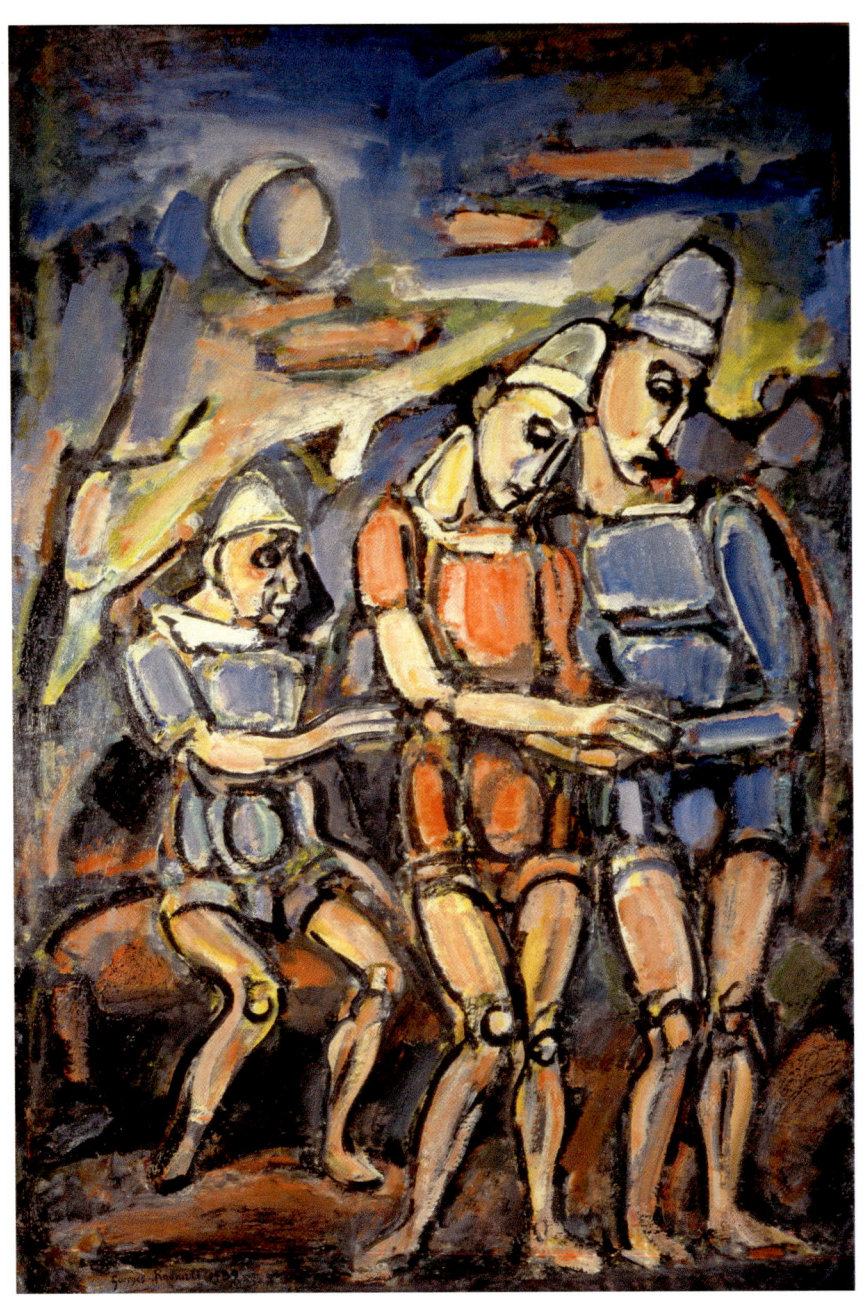

GEORGES **ROUAULT**

The Wounded Clown, 1939

Oil on paper on masonite, 72 × 47

PLATE 8

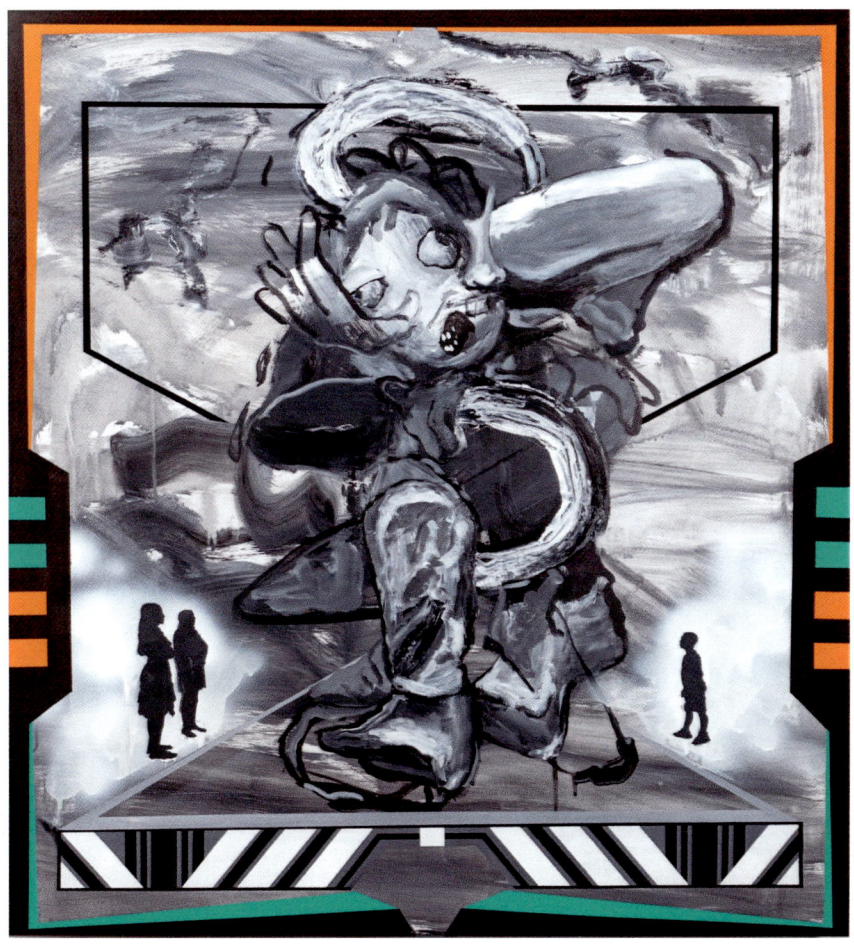

RYAN **LAUTERIO**

Alphabet Soup, 2022   PLATE 9

Acrylic, flashe, and spray paint on wood panel, 32 × 36 × 3

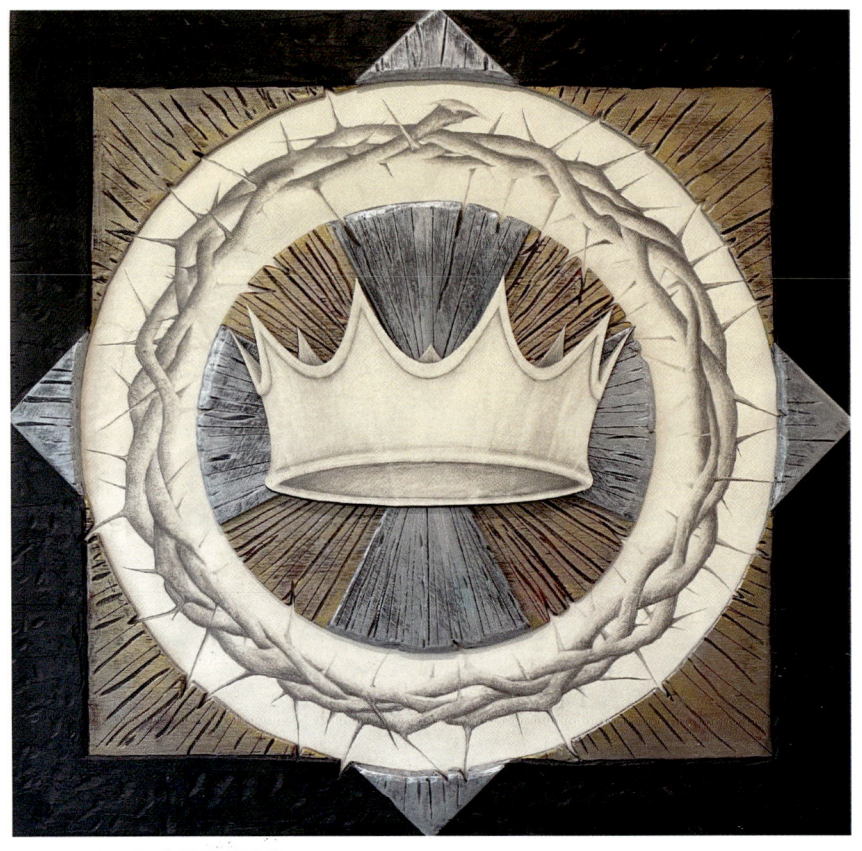

MELANIE **SPINKS**

Crown, 2022
Mixed media, 40 × 40

ROUAULT AS PROPHET

How does Brueggemann's work relate to that of Rouault and his leaden lines, luminous color, portrayal of prostitutes, to his Catholic conviction and his uncategorizable style? Frankly, Rouault provides a solid model of Brueggemann's prophet and a model for contemporary community artists. Any Rouault enthusiast is familiar with Rouault's teen apprenticeship in stained glass. In every style in which he worked, structural elements of the lead, the glass, and the absolute vivacity of the color and form seem never to have left him but rather find differing emphases throughout his career. We know, too, of his deep connection with his Catholic community of intellectuals: Léon Bloy, Joris-Karl Huysmann, and Jacques and Raïssa Maritain.[23] It was within the context of this community that Bloy's emphasis on the great chain of being and the communion of saints, the sacramental nature of poverty and of suffering, and medieval symbolism weighed on the consciousness of Rouault.[24] While Rouault was not verbose about theology, theology certainly invigorates his work.[25]

We see Rouault move into an avant-garde style in the first decade of the twentieth century. While these works were relatively few, some of his most famous images of these early works are of Parisian prostitutes. Much has been said of the generic abstraction of his style: the hideous color choices, the heavy lines that erase distinguishable features and create instead a monolithic category of the dangerous and diseased outcasts. One scholar attributes this portrayal to his simultaneous intrigue and revulsion.[26] I wonder, though, whether there is more here that is reflective of Rouault's compassion for the abject of society, his concern for the suffering, and his frustration with societal ills that harm the inherent dignity of human life. It seems that, in this reading, we have a prophetic move: we see the artist aligning with Brueggemann's prophet, making suffering and pain visible. "Look here," says Rouault. He does not shame the women by showing their faces. He gives the viewer the energy

---

[23]To explore these relationships further, see sources listed in the bibliography by Soo Yun Kang, Raïssa Maritain, Jacques Maritain, and William Dyrness.

[24]Léon Bloy, *La Femme pouvre*, trans. I. J. Collins (South Bend, IN: St. Augustine's, 2015).

[25]William Dyrness, *Rouault: A Vision of Suffering and Salvation* (Grand Rapids, MI: Eerdmans, 1971), 68.

[26]Soo Yun Kang, *Rouault in Perspective: Contextual and Theoretical Study of His Art* (Lanham, MD: International Scholars, 2000), 53.

of their abjection: frenetic lines, garish color, and frankness of their reality, like we see in *Girl in the Mirror* (see web 5.1).[27]

We see a similar martyred appearance in his clowns from around the same period. Soo Yun Kang writes, "These clowns directly confront the viewers with their torment, as if to charge the onlookers as the guilty accomplices responsible for their suffering. They exhibit themselves as the sacrificial victims of society."[28] Naturally, we see these ideas in Rouault's sacred subjects, but that is too easy. What we are looking for here is the prophetic community artist who draws materials from his community: the portrayer of the bedraggled, the dignity of the mundane, and the hope of something that transcends a scenario.[29] Given the influence of Bloy on Rouault's thinking during this period, this reading is a legitimate one.[30] I ask the viewer to see subliminally what we see blatantly in the artist's later works such as *The Old King* (see web 5.2) and *Blue Pierrots with Bouquet* (see web 5.3): the symbolism of color, even if it is *via negativa*. There is a medieval sense that the color is the way spiritual reality penetrates the physical world and leads to a redemptive and loving God. The grotesque prostitutes, the morose clowns, the depraved judges: all will be well.[31] Raïssa Mairitain writes, "One feels he is perpetually watching over the evangelical values of human life.'"[32] We see in Rouault's work the dignity of all members of society, even as that dignity is victimized by powerful forces, which the artist judges in relief against the foundation of the Christian faith, a faith shaped in his tight community of mutual influence and encouragement.

Profile of Beaver County

Where I live, this prophetic practice is a requirement. Beaver County, Pennsylvania, is the home of the steel industry of the early twentieth century. Its nearest city, Pittsburgh, whose football team is named for this industry, boasts the nexus of three rivers, which were thoroughfares for the steel industry, both its materials and its refuse. This unique geography made Beaver County a

---

[27]Dyrness, *Rouault: A Vision*, 89.

[28]Kang, *Rouault in Perspective*, 89, 91.

[29]Dyrness, *Rouault: A Vision*, 139.

[30]Dyrness devotes the chapter "The Religious Reaction of Léon Bloy" to the discussion of this relationship. Bloy's concept of the sacrosanct nature of suffering finds resonance with Rouault. See *Rouault: A Vision*, 32-45.

[31]Dyrness, *Rouault: A Vision*, 90.

[32]Quoted in Dyrness, *Rouault: A Vision*, 71.

unique opportunity for immigrants and industry. J&L Steel built the towns in which we live, including the neighborhoods and homes. These neighborhoods were segregated by language and ethnicity of immigrants in order to avoid large-scale organizing and unionizing of workers. This move of the empire eventually failed, as Aliquippa, my city, was the home of our nation's first labor strike of steel workers.[33] This industry was the locus around which all of life moved. It supported and organized masses of immigrant families, including mine, for several generations. Then, in a period spanning a few months, it left. In one year, over fifty thousand jobs simply vanished.[34] Those with accumulated resources left. Those who could not, many of whom were Black workers and their families, remained. What remains in Aliquippa and other river towns of our region is a sense that the glory days were here with industry—with empire—and we are at empire's mercy. Nobody says that out loud. But these are the deeply held, subliminal symbologies of our culture. In the wake of steel's exodus, poverty and its sisters moved in: broken families, drug use, rising crime, and poor educational offerings and outcomes.

Nearly ten years ago, a new industry crept in. I say *crept* because it came in through a back door, through massive tax breaks and secrecy, and set up shop again along the river.[35] Shell Oil rerouted our roads, plowed under our trees, and promised economic thriving that has not materialized.[36] Environmentalists are horrified.[37] We the people were largely quiet, because this is our

---

[33]The University of Pittsburgh maintains a repository of files pertaining to the initiative to organize. See "Guide to the Beaver Valley Labor History Society Collection, 1909–1981," USL Digital Collections, University of Pittsburgh, October 28, 2022, https://digital.library.pitt.edu/islandora/object/pitt%3AUS-PPiU-ais198108/viewer.

[34]Interviews with residents and historian Paul Hertneky that fill out the points here can be found in the film *Boom & Bust: A Journey from Beaver County to the Gulf Coast* by Christopher Padgett for RiverWise, 2022. The film is not yet publicly available, but a resource page can be found at https://boomandbust.movie.

[35]Robert J. Vickers, "Analysis: Gov. Tom Corbett's Plan to Give Tax Break for Shell Refinery Raises Questions About Jobs," PennLive, June 21, 2012, www.pennlive.com/midstate/2012/06/analysis_gov_tom_corbetts_plan.html.

[36]See Eric de Place and Molly Kiick, "A Cautionary Tale of Petrochemicals from Pennsylvania," Ohio River Valley Institute, November 30, 2021, https://ohiorivervalleyinstitute.org/author/molly-kiick/; Tom Sanzillo and Kathy Hipple, "IEEFA Report: Financial Risks Loom for Shell's Pennsylvania Petrochemicals Complex," Institute for Energy Economics and Financial Analysis, June 4, 2020, https://ieefa.org/articles/ieefa-report-financial-risks-loom-shells-pennsylvania-petrochemicals-complex; Kristina Marusic, "These Are the New Titans of Plastic," *Sierra: The Magazine of the Sierra Club*, September 15, 2022, www.sierraclub.org/sierra/2022-3-fall/feature/these-are-new-titans-plastic-shell-pennsylvania-fracking.

[37]See the Breathe Project, for example, at https://breatheproject.org/.

story: powerlessness at the hand of industry and identity formation within industry. What else could there be?

PROPHETIC ART

It is time for the prophets. If Rouault could tap into the symbols of stained glass throughout his career—its theology of transcendent light, of material containers for beauty, the beauty of the divine reflected in the material, no matter how garish the material—maybe artists here can do that too. Maybe they can give the public a glimpse of reality and of hope. I want to feature a few examples of this work.

First is a painting called *Navigating COVID-19* by Aliquippa artist Marlon Gist (see plate 5). Gist wanted to use what emerged from Covid and the murder of George Floyd and what followed to paint a picture of resilience. He chose to focus on stark reality but also to show what was hopeful in the moment. Gist is quite proficient at many different styles, but what seems to get the most traction for him is this starkly graphic, flat work. In obvious ways, it shares color—though not the luminosity—and bold outlines with the work of Rouault. Gist tells a story here of the hopeful within the mundane. As a worldwide community, we were confused, fearful, and sick. With this piece, though, Gist communicates that the frontline workers are excellent humans and people are going outside to get in shape. It is terrible, but we are juggling jobs and children and school. We are moving through the paces of our lives. In reality, we are resilient and industrious.

The eye of Ambridge photographer and activist Erin Ninehouser misses nothing. Her output is so vast that it was difficult to choose just one piece, so I will feature three. First, in the wake of Floyd's murder, Beaver County towns saw many protests. In *Together*, Erin captures in the foreground two elderly African American citizens, perhaps too enfeebled to march but showing a move of solidarity from another era, reprising it for this racial justice rally (see fig. 5.1). We know the raised fist of Black power, and we know this town. We know the symbols of age, and we see yet another march. This is an image of generational transfer, of seeking justice, of local unrest and aspiration. Ninehouser encourages us to maintain that generational chain not through proselytizing but through hallowing the grit of the mundane.

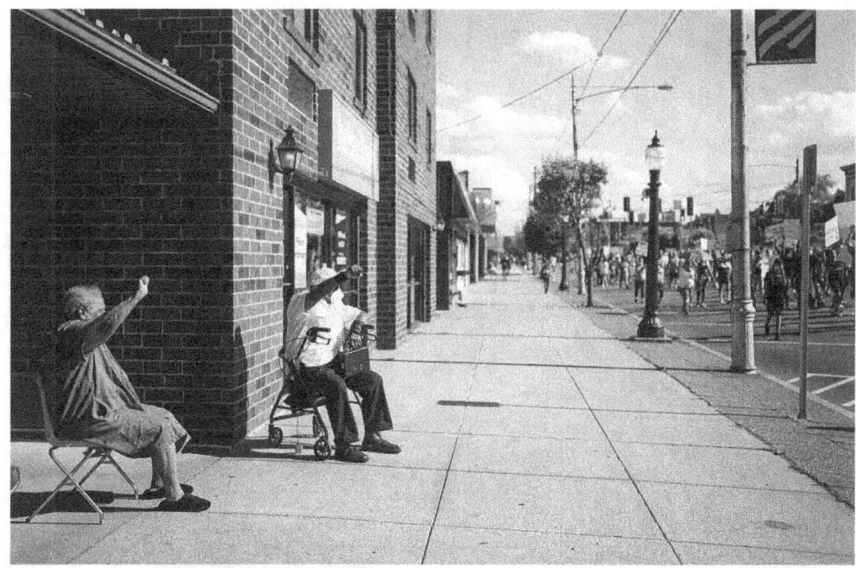

Figure 5.1. Erin Ninehouser, *Together*, 2020. Photograph

Ninehouser captured *Not One More* at an antidrug rally (see fig. 5.2). She gives us a close-up of an older woman who lost her son to opioid addiction. What are our symbols? They are clear signs of age in her weathered hands, class markers of clothes and jewelry choices, a marker of her cause on her bracelet, and yet, though the symbol of her aged hands betrays a wealth of experiences, there is the hope of the flame, small and central, juxtaposing her grief.

Finally, Ninehouser takes on nature and industry in *Rig in the Fog* (see fig. 5.3). Our rivers have long been blighted with rotting industrial equipment and edifices. Truly, one hardly notices the rivers on large swaths of the riverfront. But here Ninehouser catches the secret moment when the fog and the light betray where we are: our nearly British gloomy skies, the moment in the morning when the sun catches the mist on the water's surface. Even the industrial remnants left bobbing in the water cannot rival the beauty of the moody water and trees and sky, the essentially Beaver County moment, where the viewer is hushed by the beauty and hopeful as the remnant of human industry is subsumed by the elements working together.

The final piece of prophetic art was a collaboration between the Genesis Collective, the City of Aliquippa, Aliquippa Impact (a youth development

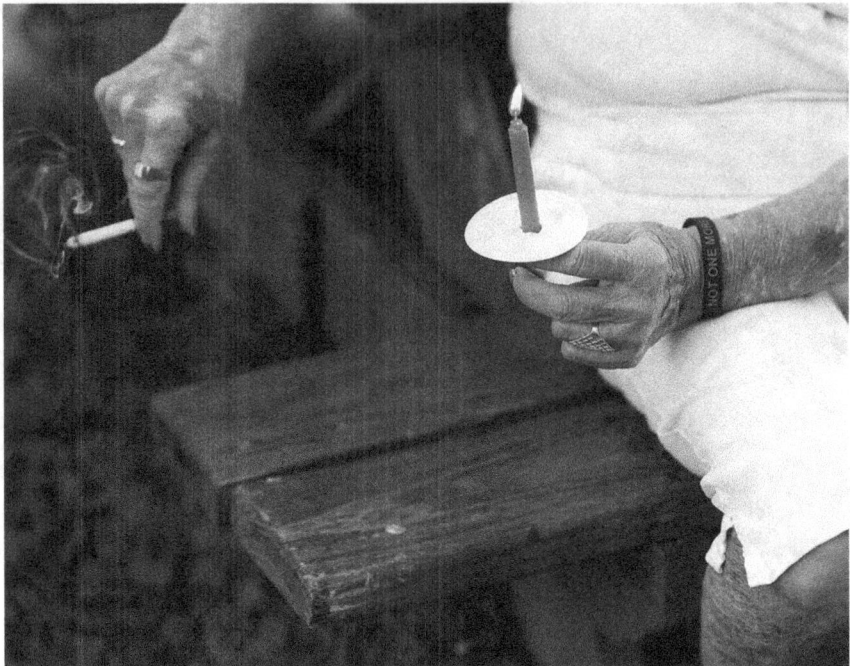

Figure 5.2. Erin Ninehouser, *Not One More*, 2017. Photograph

organization), and the Inside Out Project, which is an international temporary portrait installation project started by the photographer JR.[38] We taught the children, the most at risk in our region, to take portraits of fellow citizens. We turned a crumbling wall in a vacant field on a gutted street into a phenomenon. A film by community filmmaker Christopher Padgett titled *Our Beauty, Our Place: Public Art in Beaver County, Pennsylvania* captured the reaction of the youth as they beam with pride and claim their identity as creators, and it recorded the mayor of Aliquippa speaking hope and optimism to the children gathered there.[39] Throughout this work, we watched the residents come out and eat lunch in front of the wall, we heard them tell stories and *dream* into the future, and we saw the prophetic manifestation in real time.

[38]See Inside Out Project at www.insideoutproject.net/en/.

[39]Christopher Padgett, *Our Beauty, Our Place: Public Art in Beaver County, PA*, Genesis Collective, September 3, 2021, https://youtu.be/pVA3tC86ins. Padgett's work can be found at humancity creative.com and the Genesis Collective's YouTube channel, https://www.youtube.com/channel /UC3W4ZotND5-yot8eMULljYQ.

Figure 5.3. Erin Ninehouser, *Rig in the Fog*, 2016. Photograph

These artists are a few of the storytellers within an identity formed by location, shared experience, and shared conviction. For some, this comes from the deep-seated belief that human beings are image bearers of the glorious God. Others may not be sure of this point, but they know deep down that we are all creators of beauty, communities, and life. They set forth a vision out of the motive of mutual care. As Rouault's band of ponderous creatives did for him, the creators of the Genesis Collective form a network of creators who encourage and appreciate each other. Together we hold to the tenets that we are creators and we have a sacrosanct worth. The pain that rivals this reality is captured and morphed into beauty and hope through the raw material of art. We are trying, imperfectly, to foster a prophetic imagination with tangible impact.

I like that Rouault does this with such nuance that the viewer of his paintings must do a double take. His images are artistically interesting. Even when they seem harsh, they can be considered aesthetically beautiful. But for Rouault, it is not propagandistic; rather, it is suggestive. Like Ninehouser's evocative photography, Rouault's work gives us concept and composition, subject and design. But we see something deeper too. We find human subjects and their experience: their pain, their sacred bodies, their sorrow, and delight of color and form that draws the viewer into the experience of the subject. We find a deeper reality of identity and reciprocity between the viewer and the subject, and this pulls us into a hopeful yearning. Rouault's work provides a template and a catalyst for creators and communities like Beaver County and pained people everywhere. The prophet has spoken.

Beloved

—See Color Plate 6—

Helms Jarrell

Art-making and creating are contemplative practices for me. I am often trying to figure out how I weave together what I believe with how I behave. The weaving and threading together start to take shape in two-dimensional format, on canvas with metal, ceramic, thread, paper, and paint in the context of daily life, where I am rooted on the west side of Charlotte, North Carolina, and practice intentional community, living in solidarity with people who are in poverty. I am trying to think about how we mesh the gospel of hope and a living Christ with the living, material makeup of the community, the ways in which we embody Christ in daily life.

I moved to west Charlotte in 2005. My neighborhood, Enderly Park, has been generationally poor and divested from municipal funds and governmental support for a long time. We are dealing with a lot of the backlash of these issues in the neighborhood. I moved here because I truly believe the poor will inherit the kingdom of God, and if I want to be connected to God, I need to be deeply connected to the poor.

Over the course of time in the neighborhood, we developed a thriving youth group. During the time of many police brutality reports, and especially when Trayvon Martin was killed, our youth group members were expressing concern: "This could be me! This boy carrying Skittles and wearing a hood could have been me, and I could have been harmed." There was so much rhetoric in the media using the language of "thugs," blaming Black children for the brutality that was happening. I wanted to tell the truth about the real story of our youth, so I created a series of saint icons using photographs of youth members and mixed-media techniques. The art gallery where these saints are located is my house, a place where the youth gather and enter freely. This was my first practice of mixed media, trying to translate how I was thinking, what I was reflecting on, and telling the truth to these children and youth who I love.

I saved one person, "Beloved," until last because our relationship with each other is very tender to me. As time moved on, neighbors were experiencing housing instability in new ways. The experience of frequent housing transition had been commonplace for decades, but now people were not able to come back to the neighborhood after transitioning from a home because prices had gone up and homeownership had changed. Due to real estate speculation combined with rental housing changing hands to high-cost investment properties, longtime residents have been displaced and cannot return to the neighborhood.

I was concerned about Beloved. Was he going to be displaced from the neighborhood? During the creation of this piece, I was thinking about how I weave together and build Beloved a house. In the piece, I used whatever resources I had on hand. There is raw material, ceramic, dark mortar, wire, paper, paint, and symbols that represent Beloved. When you get up close, you can see layers of paint and paper, the texture, lines, rigidness, and grit, which are in concert with Rouault's work. This portrait has been sitting in our home for quite a while because the tender-to-me art pieces are harder to give away. I have shown this piece in a few places, though, and I have asked the curators to label it "For sale in exchange for a house for Beloved."

The reason I think this painting is in concert with Rouault is the similarities in darkness I see in Rouault's work as well as his imagery of clowns. Beloved is the most darkly complected person in our youth group, and there were a lot of times that this feature was made fun of. There is quite a bit of colorism happening within our youth group, but I find Beloved's skin tone to be beautiful and also very difficult to depict. I started with a dark background because I wanted to figure out how to bring the light out and honor the darkness of his skin tone. I hope that by doing so I am proclaiming to the youth who make fun of him that his skin tone is really quite beautiful. Rouault also used dark colors, especially black, to amplify the light, and the contrast of dark and light is a prominent feature of his work.

Rouault's use of clowns is both symbolic and a result of his encounters with real clowns. Similarly, through the making of *Beloved*, I was thinking about how I might take a subject that not everyone would see as honored or sacred and name him as such. I was asking, "How do I honor the ordinary? How do I sanctify, tell the truth, tell the sacredness of this human being who some might call a thug?" This is one way that I see *Beloved* in harmony with Rouault's work.

There continue to be threads of integration and coherence that are weaving their way through. After creating *Beloved*, I started to create reliquaries: sacred containers inside of which are belongings of saints. I created reliquaries for the evicted, a series of sacred vessels made from evicted belongings, in honor of people who have been evicted. Right now, I am reflecting on what is at the root of these issues and how I tell the truth of that story. The pieces I am currently making are taking the shape of trees, using thread, ceramic, textile, paint, and other objects to reflect on the seeds we plant and what is at the root.

Sometimes I want to press every bit of meaning out of my work. This practice leaves me feeling very heavy. There are times when I just want to play. I love the movement between play, telling the truth, playing some more, making marks, and letting marks remain even when you do not want them to be there and allowing that to be. This method is also in concert with the artwork of Rouault, whose work has an unpolished, experimental quality.

When I presented him with the portrait of himself, Beloved was very nonchalant. He likes to pretend he does not have any responses. He has never said anything ugly about it, which lets me know that he really finds it to be something special and tender. He always wants to look macho, so he is not going to let on about something that is vulnerable to him. In a way, I am relieved our interplay is this way. I present him with something vulnerable and deeply loving, and he responds in a similar way.

6

Romare Bearden, Georges Rouault, and the Art of Empathy

James Romaine

This essay sets side by side the work of two great twentieth-century artists, Georges Rouault and Romare Bearden. While the aim is to describe parallels rather than draw direct connections or firm conclusions, if we allow Rouault and Bearden's art to converse, an enriching dialogue emerges. Both Rouault and Bearden conceived of their respective artistic projects as an effort to connect on a deeply human level with their viewers, making empathy one of their art's central and shared themes. Bearden's *The Visitation* (see plate 7) and Rouault's *The Wounded Clown* (see plate 8) depict scenes in which figures offer each other physical, emotional, and spiritual support. Furthermore, both artists developed visual methods of depicting these motifs that encourage the viewer's own sense of empathy.

Born in 1871, Rouault was forty years older than Bearden. The French modernist was seemingly unaware of the younger artist's work. Like that of many African American artists, Bearden's art was and still is largely unknown in France.[1] Born in 1911, Bearden had numerous opportunities to see Rouault's art. Rouault's prominence made him both an inspiration for younger artists such as Bearden and a point of reference for critics trying to champion modernist art in America. Even in Bearden's lifetime, critics suggested associations between his art and that of the French modernist. Carl Van Vechten, a prominent figure in the Harlem Renaissance, called Bearden "the Negro Rouault."[2]

---

[1]Bearden was included in some group exhibitions in France: Galerie John Devoluy, Paris, October 19–November 21, 1945; *Introduction a la Peinture Moderne Americaine*, Galerie Maeght, Paris, November 6, 1947–January 11, 1948.

[2]Sharon F. Patton, "Memory and Metaphor: The Art of Romare Bearden, 1940–1987," in *Memory and Metaphor: The Art of Romare Bearden, 1940–1987* (New York: Oxford University Press, 1991), 27.

Although scholars have repeatedly cited Rouault as a model for Bearden, these references have usually been vague.[3] Generally speaking, they have been confined to a mention that the evolution of Bearden's method, around 1945, was in part influenced by a Rouault retrospective held that same year at the Museum of Modern Art. There is less certainty, however, when we try to press the question further and ask, Which specific works by Bearden evidence direct influence of which specific works by Rouault? While more definitive connections remain elusive, this essay examines a spiritual and artistic kinship between these two artists.

INTRODUCING BEARDEN

In the context of this collection of essays, there is no need to introduce Rouault; however, a brief survey of Bearden's life and work maps the contexts in which he encountered Rouault's art. Bearden was born in Charlotte, North Carolina, in 1911. When he was a child, his family moved to the Harlem community of New York City as part of a mass exodus of African Americans from the South in what has been called the Great Migration. Bearden created his first mature paintings between 1939 and 1942, exemplified by works such as *The Visitation* and *Factory Workers*. These paintings evidence a realist visual language, which was popular among American artists who wished to employ their work as a means of advancing social issues. This first period of Bearden's artistic career was abruptly ended by his military service in World War II.

Following the war, Bearden returned to New York. From October 8-27, 1945, he had a one-person exhibition titled "The Passion of Christ" at the Samuel Kootz Gallery.[4] The paintings in that exhibition, such as *Golgatha* (see web 6.1)

That Van Vechten would employ Rouault as point of reference for praising Bearden speaks to the prominence Rouault had at this time.

[3]For the most in-depth comparison between Bearden and Rouault, see Patton, "Memory and Metaphor," and Sharon F. Patton, "A Divine Presence in the Art of Romare Bearden," *Prism* 15 (1992): 29-32. Other mentions of Rouault in the Bearden literature include Mary Schmidt Campbell, *An American Odyssey: The Life and Work of Romare Bearden* (New York: Oxford University Press, 2018); Ruth Fine, ed., *The Art of Romare Bearden* (Washington, DC: National Gallery of Art, 2003); Pepe Karmel, "The Negro Artist's Dilemma: Bearden, Picasso, and Pop Art," in *Romare Bearden, American Modernist*, ed. Ruth Fine and Jaqueline Francis (Washington, DC: National Gallery of Art, 2011), 249-68; Kymberly N. Pinder, "Deep Waters: Rebirth, Transcendence, and Abstraction in Romare Bearden's Passion of Christ," in Fine and Francis, *Romare Bearden, American Modernist*, 145-61; and Myron Schwartzman, *Romare Bearden: His Life and Art* (New York: Harry N. Abrams, 1990).

[4]Bearden had previously exhibited works from the "The Passion of Christ" in the G Place Gallery in Washington, DC.

and *Christ Taken by Soldiers*, radically depart from Bearden's early works in both their motifs and methods. His art now evidenced a study of European modernism, including both cubism and Fauvism. For "The Passion of Christ," Bearden created paintings in both watercolor and oil. These cubist-inspired compositions visualize Christ's arrest, crucifixion, and resurrection. While this body of work was titled, presumably by the artist, "The Passion of Christ," Bearden also depicts other motifs from the life of Christ such as the annunciation, Madonna and child, and adoration of the magi.

In discussing Bearden's motif selection, Kymberly N. Pinder proposes that he turned to the Bible for archetypal narratives that evoked universal experiences of joy, suffering, struggle, and triumph.[5] To bring these epic narratives into a contemporary context, Bearden consciously departed from his previous social-realist visual language and adopted more distinctly modernist methods.

Bearden's investigation of modernist designs was motivated by two central concerns of his artistic project. The first was to create art that directly addressed the twentieth-century viewer. The second was to develop a creative project that had universal resonance. By abstracting his subject, Bearden aimed to speak across boundaries of race and nationality. This departure in both motif and method from his early works was an effort by Bearden to expand his art's moral range, to expand his art beyond his personal experiences to universal values. Bearden reflected on his artistic project, saying, "I am trying to find out what there is in me that is common to, or touches, other men."[6]

While "The Passion of Christ" was a point of connection between Bearden and Rouault, it also reveals a key difference in their art. In *He Is Arisen* (see web 6.2), Bearden employs a Christian motif to visualize universal themes. In *The Wounded Clown*, Rouault also employs what he regarded as a universal motif of the comedic performer to visualize Christian themes. Bearden's exhibition at the Samuel Kootz Gallery was a success. *He Is Arisen* was acquired by the Museum of Modern Art, which was the first museum purchase of his work. And Kootz's support led to one occasion when Bearden and Rouault's careers intersected. Both artists were included in an exhibition titled "Modern Religious Paintings" at the New York branch of the renowned Durand-Ruel

---

[5]Pinder, "Deep Waters."
[6]Carroll Greene, *Romare Bearden: The Prevalence of Ritual* (New York: Museum of Modern Art, 1971), 7.

Galleries.[7] Bearden showed a work titled *The Annunciation*, and Rouault was represented by *Christ in Profile*. Edward Alden Jewell reviewed this exhibition for *The New York Times*.[8]

Although Bearden continued to explore this artistic direction until 1947 or 1948, he ultimately found that he could not develop his own distinct artistic voice by imitating European modernism.[9] In 1950 Bearden moved from New York to Paris for two years. He frequented museums and galleries and met with many artists including Pablo Picasso, Georges Braque, Fernand Léger, and Constantin Brancusi (there is no record of him meeting Rouault).[10] Perhaps overwhelmed by his environment, Bearden produced no art of his own while in Paris. Bearden returned to New York in 1952, and the next decade of his work was a period of artistic searching, which included a period of abstraction, until his development of a collage method in 1963 and 1964.

Almost two decades after his well-received but ultimately abandoned investigation into modernist art's moral potential, Bearden found his artistic voice. He began to develop the collage technique for which he became best known. In works such as *Prevalence of Ritual: Baptism* (see web 6.3), he collaged fragments of images cut from magazines and books. Collages such as *The Dove* (see web 6.4) have established Bearden among the most important American artists of the turbulent decades of the 1960s and 1970s. His place in art history rests securely on several accomplishments.

First, there is no visual artist who more profoundly bears witness to the complexities and contradictions of African American life during the period of the civil rights movement. Bearden heroized contemporary experiences by visualizing them as motifs in which African American figures are archetypal models of humanity. Additionally, Bearden developed a method of visual construction, characterized by an improvisational pictorial structure composed of fragmented imagery, that advanced the art of collage into the era of mass media.

---

[7]January 9–February 2, 1946. Since this exhibition was in New York, Rouault may have not been aware of it or seen Bearden's work.

[8]Edward Alden Jewell, "Religious Art Seen in Modern Display: 24 Painters Show Works in an Exhibition to Aid Grosvenor Neighborhood House Avery's Bare Style," *New York Times*, January 9, 1946.

[9]Bearden exhibited twice more at the Samuel Kootz Gallery, in 1946 and 1947, but these shows did not include works with Christian motifs. See Patton, "Memory and Metaphor."

[10]Schwartzman, *Romare Bearden: His Life and Art*, 163.

Even this brief survey of the motifs, themes, and methods of Bearden's art evidences the iconographic breadth and stylistic diversity of his art. A viewer encountering *The Visitation, Golgotha,* and *Prevalence of Ritual: Baptism* might be forgiven for wondering whether these works are in fact by different artists. Nevertheless, there is a thematic unity to Bearden's work. His creativity remained motivated by an empathy he felt for humanity and a compulsion to give this empathy visual form.

Furthermore, Bearden's five-decade career was unified across a complex evolution of visual and creative methods by a continual return to sacred motifs and themes. Some of Bearden's works, such as *The Visitation* and *Golgotha,* depict biblical narratives. Other works, such as *Prevalence of Ritual: Baptism,* visualize the power and purpose of faith within the African American community. This work's title, *Prevalence of Ritual: Baptism,* suggests a complex network of visual, conceptual, and spiritual references organized around the term *ritual.* This work evidences how Bearden regarded art-making as a creative and spiritual ritual. A *ritual* is a practice that creatively, culturally, and spiritually binds people together. Through ritual, people can be connected across distances and differences of time, geography, culture. Ultimately, not only as a depiction of ritual but also a visual realization of ritual, Bearden's art connects humanity across these boundaries. Even *The Dove*'s visualization of modern city life employs a slippage between the ordinary and the sacred. Bearden was well aware of the use of the dove in Christian art as a motif evoking the presence of God in our midst.

Bearden's repeated engagement with Christian motifs and themes accomplished two things. First, he employed these to tell contemporary truths and to give moral weight to his own experiences. Second, Bearden's art revitalized the history of Christianity and the visual arts by demonstrating its relevance to the challenges of the modern world. In developing this twofold exchange between Christianity and contemporary experience, Bearden joined a rich and diverse company of artists, including Rouault.

Bearden employed these Christian motifs and themes as metaphors for the human condition. He articulated the purpose of his art as a "need to redefine the image of man in the terms of the [African American] experience, I know best. . . . What I've attempted to do is establish a world through art in which the validity of my [African American] experience would live and make its own logic."[11] Bearden understood that picturing a reality or an experience was a means of establishing its validity and right to exist. By insisting that African American images and experiences be visually expressed and celebrated, Bearden's art morally paralleled the civil rights movement's demand for racial equality.

To achieve that sense of purpose, Christian themes and motifs were means by which Bearden could visually validate his own experiences and address personal, social, and universal questions. Although he did not embrace an active religious practice, Bearden's art was motivated and guided by a potent spiritual sensibility and clear sense of moral purpose. The seriousness of this moral purpose could only find expression in the most profound motifs. These motifs were wells of significance, wells dug deep into the history of art from which Bearden could draw a multiplicity of references. Biblical motifs are present, even frequent, throughout Bearden's work. As these Christian subjects recurred across every period of his art except for his venture into abstraction, they became a unifying element in a career marked by stylistic diversity.

ENCOUNTERING ROUAULT

As Bearden drew from this deep well of the history of Christianity and the visual arts, Rouault's art became a consequential point of reference. It is unknown when Bearden first became aware of Rouault's art. Given Rouault's renown, it is possible that Bearden first saw reproductions of his art in contemporary publications such as a 1939 illustrated book titled *Passion*.[12] In 1945, Rouault had a one-person exhibition at Museum of Modern Art in New York, which is when we can more firmly establish a connection between Rouault's art and Bearden's creative project. This exhibition, as well as Bearden's study of other European modernists, is credited with the previously described transformation of Bearden's visual language from a form of modernist realism to a method characterized by the pictorial fracturing of the motif.

Only eight years later, Museum of Modern Art held a second Rouault retrospective. That he had two one-person exhibitions at Museum of Modern Art in such a short span of time speaks to the midcentury prominence Rouault's

---

[11]Patton, "Memory and Metaphor," 38.
[12]Pinder, "Deep Waters."

art enjoyed. Bearden mentions visiting this 1953 exhibition in a letter to Carl Holty.[13]

In fact, Bearden had many opportunities to see Rouault's art. The central place the French artist had in the original conception of modern art is demonstrated by the fact that Rouault's work was featured in no fewer than sixty-seven Museum of Modern Art exhibitions between 1930 and 1988. This included three one-person shows as well as the intriguingly titled 1951 show *Modern Bible Illustration*.[14] The 1945 exhibition was described, in the museum's press release, as "the largest retrospective of the work of Georges Rouault ever held in this country," with "all the periods of the painter's work . . . represented."[15]

Perhaps striking is the degree to which the catalog essay, written by James Thrall Soby, foregrounds and praises Rouault's Catholicism. Soby not only credits Rouault's faith as foundational to his art but also goes on to critically examine what that meant. Discussing Rouault's artistic conviction, Soby writes, "But wherein does a religious painter differ from a painter of religious subjects? In broad terms the answer is self-evidently a matter of heartfelt conviction as opposed to surface interest."[16] Soby identifies the spiritual integrity of Rouault's art not in the motifs but rather in the empathetic motivations and methods evidenced in Rouault's creative project. Rouault's paintings may or may not always depict the sacred, but they invariably inspire the sacred that resides within the viewer.

THE WOUNDED CLOWN

Having briefly introduced Bearden and documented some opportunities he had to see Rouault's art, we now turn our attention to examinations of specific paintings by Rouault (*The Wounded Clown*) and Bearden (*The Visitation*) to identify how these works visualize the theme of empathy in both the motifs they depict and the methods they developed.

---

[13]Fine, *Art of Romare Bearden.*

[14]Since all the works in this exhibition were from the museum's own print collection, Bearden was not included. *He Is Arisen*, then already in the Museum of Modern Art's collection, is a watercolor and ink on paper and was therefore outside the exhibition's parameters. No catalog was published for this show.

[15]Museum of Modern Art press release, 1945.

[16]James Thrall Soby, *Georges Rouault: Paintings and Prints* (New York: Museum of Modern Art, 1945), 10.

Two of the works exhibited in Rouault's 1945 Museum of Modern Art show shared the title *The Wounded Clown*. One was an oil painting on paper and masonite from 1939. That work, then in a private collection, is now in the collection of the Currier Museum of Art in Manchester, New Hampshire. The second work was a wool tapestry that has a similar composition to the later painting but in reverse. The preparatory model for this tapestry was an oil on paper mounted on canvas that is now in the collection of the Centre Pompidou in Paris.[17]

Discussing this motif, Rouault said, "*The Wounded Clown* may be just as religious as certain compositions with a biblical title."[18] His treatment of this motif, as we find it in all three works, evidences an aesthetic of empathy. Rouault depicts three figures. The central figure is the title character, the wounded clown. His companions assist him as they journey through a moonlit landscape. There is no specific narrative here and no explanation of how or in what way the clown has been wounded.

There is a crescent moon in the composition's upper left. This moon accomplishes several things in Rouault's painting. First, it situates the moment depicted in time and place. While Rouault's narrative remains deliberately ambiguous, the moon establishes that these figures are outdoors and that it is night. Second, the moon sets a certain mysterious, if not also melancholic, mood. Third and perhaps most significantly, the crescent moon evokes the Passion of Christ.[19] In *The Wounded Clown*, this crescent moon gives a sacred context and interpretation to this tragic yet ordinary moment. If the crescent moon is a symbol of Christ, perhaps we could read this composition as Christ compassionately looking down from above onto the world of suffering below.

The motifs of grief and injustice, so prevalent in Rouault's art, might initially make viewers want to look away or move on. But the authenticity of his treatment of these motifs draws the viewer back and urges them to look again.

---

[17] This work was not included in the 1945 Museum of Modern Art exhibition.

[18] "Georges Rouault, Le clown blessé [1932]," Centre Pompidou, accessed March 18, 2024, www .centrepompidou.fr/en/ressources/oeuvre/cKazzn.

[19] The crescent moon, often paired with an eclipsed sun, has been part of the visual iconography of the Christ's Passion since at least the sixth century. The scriptural basis for these motifs is descriptions in the Gospels of Matthew, Mark, and Luke of darkness enveloping the land at the crucifixion. However, the passing away and reappearance of moon might also remind the viewer of Christ's death and resurrection. Bearden knew this symbolism and included a crescent moon in *He Is Arisen*.

Rouault's method of empathy is designed to implicate the viewer. The act of reading this image joins and intertwines the viewer with the motif.

Rouault's *The Wounded Clown* is not only empathetic in the motif it depicts; it is also empathetic in the method it employs. By describing *The Wounded Clown* as empathetic in its method, I mean that Rouault has gone beyond merely illustrating, for a detached viewer, a scene portraying a moment of empathy. Rouault has created a work of art in which the visual elements we encounter in the gallery, such as form and color, become actors themselves in a drama in which initially disparate elements develop authentic, empathetic relationships. In the act of reading this work—studying its real composition rather than only observing its depicted motif—the viewer's imagination becomes an active participant in Rouault's theater of empathy.

This work evidences an aesthetic combination of bold colors circumvented by black lines, which is prevalent in Rouault's work. Since both of these features contribute to Rouault's visualization of empathy, we can examine each in turn.

Rouault's use of color is both depictive and nondepictive. There are at least two historical precedents or contexts for this use of simultaneously depictive and nondepictive colors. The first of these was the stained-glass windows of cathedrals. The second artistic context was Fauvism, a movement of early European modernism in which Rouault had participated. Rouault gave this color technique a theological purpose. This aesthetic method supported Rouault's project of visualizing the spiritual union of two realities. One of these realities was a temporal, visible, and broken world. The other equally real world was eternal, invisible, and redeemed. In Rouault's *The Wounded Clown*, these two realities coexist. Rouault's depictive and nondepictive forms of color visualize the world and the world to come. His art is a vision of a present moment of suffering seen through the glow of eternal glory.

Rouault's areas of color are compositionally organized by black lines. Again, there are historical and modernist precedents for Rouault's practice. These bold lines recall the lead binding in medieval stained-glass windows. They also have connections to a method called cloisonnism, which had been developed by Émile Bernard and further popularized by Paul Gauguin. In a work such as *The Wounded Clown*, however, these lines both individualize the forms and unite them. Two forms share one line. This is an empathetic aesthetic. The parts are not consumed by the whole, but they find meaning and purpose in relationship with each other. Looking at these lines abstractly, they create a design that unites the whole image. This design is neither depictive nor pictorial. Rather than creating an illusion, this design interconnects the image's visual elements.

In *The Wounded Clown*, one place where we can see Rouault's empathetic aesthetic clearly is in the way the two tallest clowns, including the wounded clown, embrace each other. Because only two of their arms are visible, their torsos might be interpreted as one single form. Standing shoulder to shoulder, these two figures presumably each have one arm holding the other in the back. But we can view the two clasped hands in front as if they might belong to a single person. This brilliant compositional move on Rouault's part, inducing the viewer to read the two clowns as one figure, realizes the work's empathetic theme.

THE VISITATION

Having studied *The Wounded Clown* as an example of an empathetic aesthetic, we turn now to consider how Bearden also visualizes empathy. Depicting a biblical narrative in a modern context, *The Visitation* is among the best paintings from Bearden's work prior to his development of collage. One has a sense in this work that Bearden is invested with a need to visualize empathy. Although *The Visitation* is painted in gouache—a type of watercolor—on paper, at 2.5 feet high and nearly 4 feet long, it is a large work. This is a scale that establishes a relationship with the viewer and reinforces the motif's gravitas.

The painting depicts a mostly empty landscape occupied by two women. The bleak landscape in which the women stand evokes the difficulties of their lives. This terrain is populated by some barren trees, a few rocks, a wooden structure, and a large leafy plant at the far right. The landscape and the wooden structure evoke the rural American South; the hills rising into mountains recall North Carolina's terrain. The barrenness of landscape contrasts with the pregnant women.

Although *The Visitation* predates any documented connections between Bearden and Rouault, this painting suggests that Bearden had some knowledge of a modernist approach to using color as a formal or compositional device. *The Visitation* is painted in earth tones of browns, greens, and reds. The simplicity of Bearden's forms supports the complexity of his color application. Red and green are complementary colors. In *The Visitation*, Bearden unifies these contrasting colors using a similar value and surface texture. Bearden applied gouache to brown paper in a method that creates a soft surface and unifies the broad forms of color.

The two women are the composition's focal point. Bearden employs the heavy forms of their bodies to visualize a strength of inner spirit. These large figures stand close to the picture plane, which is suggested by how they are cut off by the painting's top and bottom edge. Because of their closeness to the picture plane, the women have an authority that projects out of the image and toward the viewer. The women's powerful visual presence, which is created both by the size of the work and their size within the image, advances a central theme in Bearden's art, which is the triumph of African Americans, especially women, over adversity. While the two women's presence dominates the composition, the forms of their bodies and the features of their faces have been both simplified and exaggerated. The sharp profile of the woman at left recalls an African mask. This further complicates the relationship between the image we see and the subject suggested by the title.

Bearden's title recalls a narrative from the Bible: the virgin Mary's visit to her cousin Elizabeth during their miraculous pregnancies as recounted in the Gospel of Luke. Having entered the scene from the left, Mary wears a red mantel. She greets Elizabeth with a gesture of blessing, and their hands converge over Elizabeth's body. Perhaps this is in response to her declaration, "When the sound of your greeting came to my ears, the baby in my womb leaped for joy" (Lk 1:44 ESV). Bearden's reference to this biblical narrative is relevant to his work's theme of visualizing the women as heroic because the Bible describes both Elizabeth and Mary as women of faith and perseverance. Although we do not know the contemporary women in Bearden's picture, his casting them as Elizabeth and Mary communicates that they have a similar strength of character. Nevertheless, the more we look at Bearden's painting, the less it seems to depict Mary and Elizabeth with scriptural accuracy.

Drawing on his memory and imagination of the American South, Bearden depicts Mary and Elizabeth as African American women dressed in modern clothing. While these women are not portraits of any specific persons, they were inspired by women in Bearden's life. He reinterprets the biblical narrative through the examples of his own family's strong matriarchs. By imagining contemporary life as a biblical narrative, Bearden visualizes a strength of inner spirit and heroizes ordinary people's daily experiences. In *The Visitation*, Bearden combines memory and imagination to create an image that is simultaneously personal and universal.

The women in Bearden's painting visualize the presence of powerful figures supporting each other, and their interconnecting hands visualize a singleness of common purpose. As with Rouault's *The Wounded Clown*, the composition of the hands has a significant role in Bearden's aesthetic of empathy.

CONCLUSION

Romare Bearden and Georges Rouault might seem an unlikely couple. They were from different generations, different countries, different cultural and religious backgrounds. Nevertheless, they shared something that was deeper than their differences: a love of humanity. Both artists saw this human condition as equally tragic and beautiful, and both artists believed that art could tip the balance of history in favor of grace, and possibly redemption, by awakening within the viewer an empathy for the motif and the people depicted.

Rouault and Bearden created art with motifs that addressed spiritual and social inequities, but they depicted those motifs in ways that visualized the possibility of triumph over adversity. Their art, in both methods and motifs, presents the viewer with an empathetic aesthetic, an approach to seeing and acting that is characterized by faith, compassion, humility, creativity, mercy, justice, and care for others. This makes their art vital to our own moment, in which empathy is needed more than ever.

"Paint the Mind"

Derrell Young

I sat and I pondered what to tell you.
I wish I could paint a beautiful utopia
but life is hard and sometimes its frame
contains scratches.
I thought about pointing out the melodic song
of the caged bird,
but her wings are caged
from a third of her freedom.
And the taste of freedom drips in shadows
of those that retreat from confronting
the battle of the mind.
So they stay seated on the sidelines of life.
To be honest with you, life can paint with you
but the picture depends on the brushes you choose
to paint your view,
emotions or truth.
Emotions depict alluring scenery
until it snares you into its fickle highs and lows.
Truth remains constant but doesn't have the prettiest view
yet produces freedom.
I would urge you to allow your mind to roam free
with creativity and if your frame obtains scratches
it doesn't take away from the painting of the mind,
because your mind is beautiful.
Stand for what you believe in
and never take a seat for deceit.
You have the authority to be free
because life is in what you see.
From the mind paint a beautiful picture of free.

7

Georges Rouault and the Irony of Religious Responses to Modern Art

William A. Dyrness

It may seem strange to use the example of Georges Rouault to open up the whole question of religious responses to modernity and to modern art in particular, but this painter's work embodies precisely the irony represented by this conflicted response. On the one hand, Rouault is rightly considered the archetypal Catholic modern artist of the twentieth century. This was certainly the view of most people in France and even North America during the midcentury apex of his popularity. Furthermore, recently we have learned about his profound influence on other modern artists who identified as Catholics (or even more broadly religious). On the other hand, church authorities up until the time of Rouault's death in 1958, almost without exception, refused to acknowledge his work as properly religious. It is this irony I wish to explore and apply more generally.

I

Georges Rouault and his close friend Jacques Maritain were both important players in the cultural renewal in France, which grew out of a revival of Catholic faith during the early twentieth century and responded to the stark materialism and realism of the time. This revival had far-reaching influence on French culture; indeed, revival artists and writers sparked innovations in the visual arts and literature that influenced subsequent developments in modern culture.[1] Rouault studied with Gustave Moreau at the prestigious École des

---

[1] Here I draw on William Dyrness, "Rouault and Maritain and the Shaping of a Catholic Modernity" (paper presented at The Artist as Truth Teller symposium on Georges Rouault, Institute Catholique de Paris, June 17, 2022, publication forthcoming).

Beaux-Arts in the 1890s, and it was during this period that he sought Dominican priest Father Vallee for instruction and preparation for formal affili-
ation with the Catholic Church. Moreau, despite his unusual Catholic beliefs,
was as much spiritual mentor as teacher for Rouault, and Rouault absorbed
Moreau's symbolism. He later recalled Moreau's faith: "Do you believe in God,
I am asked? I only believe in God. In fact I do not believe in what I touch nor
in what I see. I only believe in what I cannot see, only in what moves me. . . .
Only my internal sense seems to me eternal and indubitably certain."[2] Between 1900 and 1905, Rouault was deeply affected by his encounter with nov-
elists Joris-Karl Huysmans and Léon Bloy, who were both central in the
emerging Catholic revival. Rouault even joined Huysmans's short-lived monastic experiment in Ligugé, and he was deeply moved by reading Bloy's
novels *Le Désespéré* and *La Femme pauvre*.[3] Together Huysmans and Bloy
provided the spiritual impulse that Rouault needed, especially the connection
of their radical faith in God with the necessity of suffering.

But it was friendship with Jacques and Raïssa Maritain that helped to so-
lidify the role of Rouault's spirituality in his artistry. He met this couple in 1905
in the home of Léon Bloy, whose influence led to the Maritains' baptism the
following year. The Maritains had been awakened from their materialist
slumbers by the vitalism of Henri Bergson, who taught that art and poetry
offered unmediated access to reality.[4] All three fell under the spell of Bloy,
who Jacques said represented "the tenderness of a deeply Christian friendship,
of a certain trembling misericordia, that seizes one confronted with a soul
marked by the love of God."[5] Rouault exhibited with Fauvist artists in 1905,
a benchmark in the development of modern styles, showing a work based on
Bloy's novel *La Femme pauvre* (*The Poor Woman*) titled *Les Poulots* (see
web 3.3), which was meant as a tribute to his friend.[6] Bloy, despite defining his

---

[2]George Rouault and André Suarès, "Moreau," *L'Art et les Artistes* (April 1926): 240.
[3]*The Desperate Man* (1887) and *The Poor Woman* (1897).
[4]David Schultenover calls the Jewish Bergson perhaps the important figure in the Catholic revival.
   See Schultenover, ed., *The Reception of Pragmatism in France and the Rise of Catholic Modernism,
   1890–1914* (Washington, DC: Catholic University of America Press, 2009), 52.
[5]A statement he made in 1927; see preface to *Lettres de Léon Bloy*, vol. 3 of *Oeuvres Completes*, 1022,
   quoted in Nora Possenti-Ghiglia, *Cahiers Jacques Maritain* (Kolbsheim, France: Cercle d'Etudes
   Jacques et Raïssa Maritain, 1985), 7-8.
[6]"Les Fauves" is French for "wild beasts" and described a group of early twentieth-century modern
   artists with an emphasis on strong colors.

characters in such a style, was horrified by the painter's deformed portrayal of the couple in his novel. Though surprising to the artist, Bloy's response to Rouault's brooding characters was typical of religious responses to his work. Indeed, this response was consistent with the larger public's incomprehension of modern art and the dismissive response on both sides of the Atlantic. President Roosevelt famously likened Marcel Duchamp's *Nude Descending a Staircase* in the 1913 Armory Show to an "explosion in a shingle factory."[7]

In 1920 Jacques Maritain, influenced by his association with Rouault, published his most influential work, *Art and Scholasticism*, which offered the first theological interpretation of these new styles. Stephen Schloesser argues that Maritain, influenced by his friendship with Jean Cocteau, helped define the idea of the avant-garde and even gave it religious importance. Maritain believed artists were able to bring to light deeper, spiritual realities, which can be shown in a contemporary sensibility that he defined as tradition assuming a modern form. It is artists who see these realities first. Thus, the modern notion of the avant-garde was born: artists lead, the public follows. According to Schloesser, *Art and Scholasticism* reconciled Catholicism with modernity, and for many people, Rouault came to embody this reconciliation. Though realist in method, he employed deformation in a symbolist sense, to get at what was truly real, a move that allowed him to open up the wound of postwar Europe to religious scrutiny. As his friend Maritain put it in a 1924 review: "There is in Rouault a purity that is almost Jansenist . . . a profound religious sentiment . . . that leads him to see the Lamb of God in all the abandoned, and rejected."[8] This led critic Gaston Varene to see in Rouault's postwar work a liberated modernity, even "a cry of the heart which rises up to God," which he compared unfavorably to the religious work of Maurice Denis as "prayers learned by rote."[9]

Try as they might, many Catholic authorities and even art lovers could not see prayers in Rouault's work. Even the Dominicans in the early incarnations of the journal *L'Art Sacré* referred to modern art as antireligious, disparaging the work of Rouault as "full of extremes and brutality." There is a further irony here as well, for the postwar version of the journal, and Father Couturier in

---

[7]Stephen Scholesser, *Jazz Age Catholicism: Mystic Modernism in Postwar Paris, 1919–1933* (Toronto: University of Toronto Press, 2005), 143. For what follows, see 143-51.
[8]Quoted in Schloesser, *Jazz Age Catholicism*, 252.
[9]Schloesser, *Jazz Age Catholicism*, 230-31.

particular, came to celebrate Rouault as the century's most famous Catholic artists.[10] But continued distaste was the common religious response to modern art and literary styles.

As Sheila Nowinski points out, the 1950 papal encyclical *Humani Generis* had a reactionary cultural influence—Henri de Lubac was barred from teaching in Lyon, and Maritain himself was threatened. Two of Rouault's prints from the *Miserere* were rejected from the 1950 jubilee art exhibit when officials decided that in Rouault, as in Georges Bernanos and Graham Greene, "human wretchedness carried the day."[11]

In 1952, the Pontifical Commission on Sacred Art issued instructions reiterating the church's rejection of modern art and architecture. The focus there was on the "deviation" evident in modern styles, insisting that "sacred art, which originated within Christian society, possesses its own ends, from which it can never diverge," and it must not allow "deformations and debasement of some art, which at times are even in open contradiction to Christian grace."[12] Meanwhile, Rouault—motivated by gospel values and in contrast to these church officials—came to *focus* on the marginal and abandoned, and to see through them to Christ (e.g., *The Abandoned*; see web 7.1).

Catholic teaching radically changed in the 1960s, especially during the Second Vatican Council and the issuance in 1963 of the Constitution on the Sacred Liturgy (*Sacrosanctum Concilium*). There one hears echoes of Maritain: art by its nature reflects the beauty of God. "The Church has not adopted any particular style of art as her very own; she has admitted fashions from every period according to the natural talents and circumstances of peoples and the needs of the various rites."[13] Even the art of our own period should be given

---

[10]See Aiden Nichols, "The Dominicans and the Journal *L'Art Sacré*," *New Blackfriars* (January 2007): 33-34. Though Father M. A. Couturier, who would later become Rouault's defender, did come to his defense already in 1938, noting the problem was with the clergy who refused to commission the painter to do any work. See Couturier, "Rouault et le publique ecclésiastique," *L'Art Sacré* (September 1938): 245-47.

[11]Stephen Schloesser, "1939–1958: Perpetual Pelegrinas," in *Mystic Masque: Semblance and Reality in Georges Rouault, 1871–1958*, ed. Stephen Schloesser (Boston: McMullen Museum of Art, 2008), 351. See reference to Paul VI bringing Rouault to the United Nations at 351-32. See also Sheila Nowinski, "Creating Rouault's Legacy: 1945–1965," in Schloesser, *Mystic Masque*, 399-409, esp. 403. On John XXIII, see 405.

[12]The Pontifical Commission on Sacred Art, "Documents: 1952 Instructions on Sacred Art," *The Furrow* 6, no. 6 (June 1955): 369.

[13]Pope Paul VI, *Sacrosanctum Concilium*, 1963.

"free scope." This focus on permission led Thomas Merton to suggest that even the landscapes of Paul Cezanne and Claude Monet, or the portraits of Amedeo Modigliani, can display the beauty of God.[14] During this time Pope John XXIII opened a room in the Vatican Museum to modern artists and to Rouault in particular. A few years later, Pope Paul VI gave Rouault his own room in the museum and brought one of Rouault's paintings of the crucifixion to the United Nations when he declared, "No more war" (see web 7.2).[15] Nowinski goes so far as to argue, "Without Rouault, it seems unlikely that the Catholic Church could have been imagined as an institution that valued the 'modern.'"[16]

Though the recognition of church authorities came late, Rouault, Maritain, and those they influenced had already done their work. Out of the glare of church officials, they were busy proposing a new kind of sacred art, one that suited the anguish and violence of their century. This deep irony forms a pattern that helps us understand religious responses to modern art.

II

It is unfair to single out the Catholic Church for its hostility to modern styles. This feeling was widely shared by religious thought leaders during the first half of the twentieth century. There were exceptions on the Protestant side just as there were on the part of Catholics. In fact, contemporary theological discussions around modern art owe a tremendous debt to the leadership of Alfred Barr and his midcentury work at the Museum of Modern Art in New York. Barr, a pastor's son and a faithful Presbyterian elder his whole life, recognized the spiritual component of modern art. In his 1943 book that sought to introduce modern art to a uncomprehending public, he argued that "artists are the sensitive antennae of society" and that a work of art is "a symbol, a visible symbol of the human spirit in its search for truth, freedom and perfection."[17] In 1954, Barr became head of the Commission on Art for the National Council of Churches, and later he cofounded the Society for Arts, Religion and Contemporary Culture along with theologian Paul Tillich and major New York

---

[14]"Sacred Art and Sacred Furnishings," in *The Documents of Vatican II*, by Walter M. Abbott, SJ (New York: Guild, 1966), 175; Thomas Merton, "The Vatican Council and Sacred Art," *The Merton Seasonal* 35, no. 3 (Fall 2010): 3-5, https://merton.org/ITMS/Seasonal/35/35-3Merton.pdf.

[15]Pope Paul VI had read and admired Maritain's *Art and Scholasticism* in his earlier years.

[16]Nowinski, "Creating Rouault's Legacy," 405-6.

[17]Alfred Barr, *What Is Modern Painting?* (New York: Museum of Modern Art, 1943), 3.

artists, including Robert Motherwell and Ad Reinhardt. This group did much to promote a mutually enriching conversation between religion and the arts at least among mainline Protestants.[18]

Among more conservative Protestants, however, suspicion of modern culture continued to hold sway, right up until Hans Rookmaaker's important book *Modern Art and the Death of a Culture*.[19] Rookmaaker, professor of art history at the Free University of Amsterdam, presented a scholarly—if decidedly declinist—narrative of the rise of modern art, beginning with the impressionists and descending through the symbolists to Dada and Marcel Duchamp. These modernists, Rookmaaker argued, represented a rejection of religious faith, one that led to the elimination of human values. This argument resonated not only with the turmoil of the 1960s—the Vietnam War, the death-of-God movement, and the unrest of the civil rights movements—but also with the fundamentalist cultural suspicions of modernity more generally.

This part of the story is well-known, but I want to turn here to some important voices that have not been made a part of the conversation: G. K. Chesterton, C. S. Lewis, and the Orthodox response to modern art as represented by Paul Evdokimov. These leaders inherited a deep-seated revulsion against the materialism and reductive scientism of the previous century, but, unlike Maritain, they were unable to see the religious potential opened by modern styles of art, or indeed the possible contribution of their own religious traditions to the development of modern art.[20] They held to universalist and essentialist views of religion that occluded the diversity and pluralism of the modern world, and what follows is a small sketch of the concomitant issues.

Though a Catholic, G. K. Chesterton (1874–1936) exercised huge influence on the English-speaking Protestant world. Coming to maturity at the turn of the twentieth century, he directed his fin-de-siècle wrath against George Bernard Shaw and Henrik Ibsen. He thought that their realism without idealism constructed on an underlying determinism left people adrift in a sea of

---

[18]See Jonathan A. Anderson and William A. Dyrness, *Modern Art and the Life of a Culture: The Religious Impulses of Modernism* (Downers Grove, IL: InterVarsity Press, 2016), 271-76.

[19]Hans Rookmaaker, *Modern Art and the Death of a Culture* (Downers Grove, IL: InterVarsity Press, 1970).

[20]It is important to recall, as Steven Schloesser saw, that the work of Maritain in the 1920s was both modern and antimodern at the same time. Maritain himself would write an important book, *Antimoderne* (Paris: Ed. De la Revue des Jeunes, 1922), in which he lamented the modern turn away from medieval ontology toward a modern, psychologically driven intellect.

uncertainty.[21] Interestingly, it was Chesterton's reaction against modern culture that led him to embrace Christianity. In *Orthodoxy* (1908), Chesterton argues that tradition, best embodied in Catholic Christianity, is the only reasonable basis for reform and human freedom. In many respects he shared the wider religious suspicions directed against the whole complex of ideas associated with Charles Darwin and the related materialism, but he was unique in frequently directing his critiques against modern art in particular—despite the fact that (or because) his only advanced education was at an art school. A very brief tour of his writings offers a profile of this antipathy toward modern art forms.[22]

In *Alarms and Discursions* (1911), Chesterton discusses the origin of realism, which he associates with a collection of things that have lost their center but which people celebrate as great art and the way things really are. Christianity had provided that center, but its influence has dissipated: "Modern art and science practically mean having the million monsters and being unable to control them; and I will venture to call that disruption and decay."[23] The disruption and decay Chesterton has in mind resulted in the proliferation of means to solve an ever-growing set of individually chosen ends. Modernity, he writes in *What's Wrong with the World* (1910), replaces ancient universal things with specialist things; religion has been taken over by specialist trades: "The romance of ritual and colored emblem has been taken over by the narrowest of all trades, modern art (the sort called art for art's sake), and men are in the modern practice informed that they may use all symbols so long as they mean nothing by them." Everything "has been sundered from everything and everything has grown cold. . . . The world is one wild divorce court."[24] This judgment is evident in his assessment of the impressionists, who portrayed a world with no backbone.[25] In *Alarms and Discursions*, he laments the loss of the human "chorus" in modern forms. The human chorus, by which he means

---

[21]See Jay P. Corrin, *G. K. Chesterton and Hilaire Belloc: The Battle Against Christendom* (Athens: Ohio University Press, 1981), 7-8. For what follows, see 9.

[22]Here we are fortunate to have an electronic version of many of Chesterton's writings that is searchable. See *The G. K. Chesterton Collection: 50 Books* (N.p.: Catholic Way, 2014).

[23]G. K. Chesterton, *Alarms and Discursions* (New York: Dodd, Mead, 1911), 14.

[24]G. K. Chesterton, *What's Wrong with the World* (New York: Dodd, Mead, 1910), 151-152.

[25]This is reported by Colin Gunton in *The One, the Three and the Many* (Cambridge: Cambridge University Press, 1993), 192. To support Chesterton's observation, he notes, "Some analyses of late modernity appear to confirm the judgment that a loss of substantiality is at the heart of the matter."

the larger vision of human life, can illumine a dark story. By contrast, modern art has to be "intense," which means "saying only one thing at a time, and saying it wrong."[26] The celebration of facts—of reality—in modern art has pushed out the larger human story.

Like many religious leaders, Chesterton reacted against the esoteric character of modern styles, which he thought displayed an intentional disdain for public embrace. In *All Things Considered* (1915), he contrasts Michelangelo with James Whistler, whom he views as a typical modern artist. While the public frescos of Michelangelo are meant to strike the "popular judgment," Whistler's pictures "are elusive, fugitive; they fly even from praise," showing how modern artists have "a positive bias against the populace."[27] In his excursus on the place of comedy among common folk, he notes that in modern art we hear only the voices of pain. None of these should be silenced, he notes, but in modern art they are the only voices we hear: "They are the voices of men, but not the voice of man [*sic*]."[28] Such judgments reveal Chesterton's democratic bias and his distaste for aristocracy of any kind, but they also show his inability to see the spiritual potential in the proliferating "specialist trades" that would dominate the art world of the twentieth century.

Though different in many ways, C. S. Lewis (1898–1963) instinctively shared Chesterton's resistance to modern art styles, and Chesterton's book *The Everlasting Man* was influential in Lewis's conversion to Christianity. Arguably no twentieth-century writer has had a greater cultural influence on contemporary believers from many different communions than this Oxford professor. Furthermore, one can argue that no one has done more, especially in his Narnia series, to help Christians integrate imagination, faith, and apologetics. Aesthetics, Lewis consistently claimed, pertains to the longing and search for another world, is an innate feature of humanity, and represents the key to our capacity for God. But here our central problem emerges. Though aesthetics is critical to human flourishing, Lewis believes modern aesthetics makes no contribution to this, a fact revealed by the lack of his engagement with modern visual artists and styles. He admits to leaving parts of culture

---

[26]Chesterton, *Alarms and Discursions*, 291.
[27]G. K. Chesterton, *All Things Considered* (New York: John Lane, 1910), 238.
[28]G. K. Chesterton, *Varied Types* (New York: Dodd, Mead, 1903), 88. This is in his discussion of French dramatist Edmond Rostand.

aside to focus on particular kinds of literature simply because "I know them best," but this is also connected to his problems with modern art.[29]

Lewis thinks modern culture is the product of a long historical drift, part of what he terms the "whole tradition of educated infidelity . . . one phase in that general rebellion against God which began in the eighteenth century."[30] Like Chesterton, he focuses on modernity's preference for the particular over the universal. As Wesley Kort describes this, modern culture fails for Lewis "because it has broken experiences and entities into separate, unrelated components, objective facts and subjective understandings and evaluations of them."[31] As a result, all meanings are private, despite the fact that values are always relational and shared. For Lewis, culture is always shared, and though Christianity has had positive internal relations with human cultures— especially in the medieval period—it necessarily has contrary relations with modern Western culture with its narcissism, materialism, and fact/value split. In *Pilgrim's Regress* (1933), Lewis locates Enlightenment rationalism, modern art, romantic art, nihilism, and hedonism on the map of modernity; Pilgrim tries them all and finds them wanting.[32] Modern art, then, can only reflect this defective development. In one of the few comments he makes on visual art, Lewis reflects on this captivity: "It was only in the nineteenth century that we became aware of the full dignity of art. We began to 'take it seriously.' . . . But the result seems to have been a dislocation of the aesthetic life in which little is left for us but high-minded works which fewer and fewer people want to read, or hear or see."[33]

It is important to remember the deep influence of the Great War on Lewis, as on Chesterton. Early in his life, as Alister McGrath points out, Lewis made a "treaty with reality," setting boundaries around reality so it would not disturb him: reality was passive, he was active. Interestingly, again it was Bergson who

---

[29]C. S. Lewis, "Christianity and Culture," in *Christian Reflections*, ed. Walter Hooper (Grand Rapids, MI: Eerdmans, 1967), 23. From this essay it is clear that for Lewis culture means "high culture," in which he argues the New Testament is uninterested. Though this essay is an early expression of Lewis's thinking, Hooper argues that it remains a consistent refrain.

[30]Quoted in Steven Logan, "Literary Theorist," in *The Cambridge Companion to C. S. Lewis*, ed. Rob MacSwain and Michael Ward (Cambridge: Cambridge University Press, 2010), 31.

[31]Wesley Kort, *C. S. Lewis: Then and Now* (Oxford: Oxford University Press, 2001), 77; see also 79. For what follows, see 82-87.

[32]Alister McGrath, *C. S. Lewis: A Life* (Carol Stream, IL: Tyndale House, 2013), 172.

[33]C. S. Lewis, "First and Second Things," in *God in the Dock*, ed. Walter Hooper (Grand Rapids, MI: Eerdmans, 1970), 280.

jolted him out of this illusion. What if reality, transcendence, even God, were not passive but active? Modern art forms, shaped by modernity's characteristic illusions, express just such a boundary. But the awful reality of the Great War, Lewis believed, made clear that the scientist and materialist do not have the last word.[34] Lewis saw his work on myth and imagination as one way in which the paralyzing split between reason and imagination could be healed. Like Chesterton, Lewis found the realism of Shaw too simple and lacking depth, and during the war he began to read George MacDonald and was particularly captured by *Phantastes*. "It is as if I had been carried sleeping across the frontier, or as if I had died in the old country and could never remember how I came alive in the new."[35] The new country was *myth*, a true narrative that Lewis believed constituted an enthralling medium for conveying the sense of life as it is actually lived. In the 1930s he gradually began to develop his view of Christianity as a "true myth," to which doctrine was a secondary translation, a process he describes in *Surprised by Joy* (1955).

Reviewing the stories in Lewis's Narnia series that describe desire and longing as fundamental to the human journey to God, I have found myself asking: Why did Lewis not see the broken myths that proliferate in modern art as the "dim dreams" of the human stories he often writes about? Maybe contemporary images, too, might come to life. I believe there are two reasons for his inability to make this obvious connection. First, as he describes his hermeneutics of myth in the important essay "Transposition," all human desire is ultimately for a vision of God. Human experiences of longing transpose this higher desire onto lower ones, all of which provide a background for the theological virtue of hope. But here is the catch: these hungers— for sex, food, fame—express longings that nothing in this world can satisfy. What we long for lies outside this world, and these longings are "news from a country we have not yet visited"—a country on the other side of the wardrobe.[36] So the images of our lives are "shadows," not "figures," without final value; they are not the possible *locus theologicus* modern people take them to

---

[34]See Alister McGrath, *The Intellectual World of C. S. Lewis* (Oxford: Wiley-Blackwell, 2013), 40-46. For what follows on myth, see 61-62.

[35]Quoted in McGrath, *Intellectual World*, 57. For the whole discussion of myth, see 59-62.

[36]C. S. Lewis, "Transposition," in *Screwtape Proposes a Toast and Other Pieces* (London: Fontana, 1965), 98. I have developed this critique at greater length in William Dyrness, *Poetic Theology: God and the Poetics of Everyday Life* (Grand Rapids, MI: Eerdmans, 2011), 117-21.

be. Indeed, I believe a large part of the appetite for Lewis among evangelical Protestants lies in the way this dichotomy fits their popular theology of salvation as the assurance of heaven and an escape from the trials of this life.

The second reason Lewis had no interest in exploring the broken dreams evident in modern culture is that he spent little time listening to contemporary voices. While Lewis made no claim to be a theologian, as McGrath points out, for many modern believers he was the entryway into thinking theologically; in this he did something professional theologians were unable to do.[37] But the problem is that while he was deeply conversant with Augustine, Aquinas, and Richard Hooker, he never seriously engaged a theologian of the nineteenth or twentieth century. He did not explore Karl Barth or, more critically, Jacques Maritain, who, like Lewis, sought to bring medieval voices to contemporary attention. Here Lewis expresses the downside, or perhaps the reverse, of his rejection of chronological snobbery—our modern tendency to think only new books are worth reading. In contrast to Maritain, Lewis believed tradition could not be revised into a modern form; it could only be entered.[38] Lewis seeks to explore this ancient tradition in his imaginative writings, but he provides no guidance for those seeking to be faithful interpreters of modern culture.

Turning briefly to Orthodox views of modern culture, we find an interesting parallel to Lewis's judgment of modern art's captivity to long-term historical forces. Theologian Paul Evdokimov, for example, like other Orthodox writers, sees art already in the early Renaissance of the thirteenth century seeking an increasingly refined reflection of the natural world but gradually losing "the ability to directly grasp and portray the transcendent."[39] In a move that was confirmed in the high Renaissance, Evdokimov thinks, art was leaving its "heavenly biosphere" in the liturgy. The result is that modern art has been "liberated" from the holy mysteries to celebrate the autonomous subject. In his careful historical survey, Evdokimov notes that beginning in 1874, "we have paintings of what is circumstantial and occasional, as interpreted emotionally,"

---

[37]Lewis would say that theology is a matter for the church. For this paragraph, see McGrath, *Intellectual World*, 164-66.

[38]Lewis makes this clear in his essay "On the Reading of Old Books," in Hooper, *God in the Dock*, 200-207.

[39]Paul Evdokimov, *The Art of the Icon: A Theology of Beauty* (Redondo Beach, CA: Oakwood, 1990), 73.

a heroic but desperate attempt to find Tabor light in the world.[40] The modern artist is free with "a terrible liberty of representing the world in the image of his own devastated soul." Kazimir Malevich's supremacism offers a container with no dimensions; Jackson Pollock's speed-painting excludes all human consciousness. The one elicits no desire to pray; the other represents a refusal of the image of God. According to Evdokimov, the true symbol makes visible the invisible, allowing art to eschatologically anticipate the final synthesis. Modern art, though a refreshing departure from previous academicism and false taste, is at a dead end; it awaits a miracle to recover its priestly function.[41]

III

Here I return to the deep irony with which I ended the first section on the Catholic reception of modern art. What if, despite the frequent dismissal of modern culture and its art by religious thought leaders, the religious traditions they represent continue to influence the development of modern styles? One can argue that this is true in the actual history and development of modern styles. What is the evidence for the influence of religious traditions on the development of modern art forms themselves? Once one turns to the emergence of modern art with this question in mind, examples turn up everywhere, something that Jonathan Anderson and I sought to show in our recent book.[42]

One important consideration is the role of religion in contemporary Indigenous and minority expressions of art. It would be impossible to understand the history of Native American art in the United States, for example, without giving a large place to its religious traditions. Similarly, contemporary art in the Black church or in the immigrant Islamic communities cannot be understood without a firm grasp of the religious traditions of these groups.[43]

But what role has religion played in the development of the dominant traditions of Euro-American art over the last two centuries? Again, despite the

---

[40]Evdokimov, *Art of the Icon*, 75-76. In Orthodox theology, Tabor light is the light revealed on Mount Tabor at the transfiguration of Jesus.
[41]Evdokimov, *Art of the Icon*, 82, 84, 87, 94-95.
[42]Anderson and Dyrness, *Modern Art and the Life*.
[43]See Josef Sorett, *Spirit in the Dark: A Religious History of Racial Aesthetics* (New York: Oxford University Press, 2016); William Dyrness and Maria Fee, "Art as Practical Theology," in *Handbook of Art and Theology* (London: Bloomsbury, forthcoming); William Dyrness, "The Poetic Formation of Interfaith Identities: The Zapatista Case," in *Arts in Witness in Multifaith Contexts*, ed. Roberta King and William Dyrness (Downers Grove, IL: InterVarsity Press, 2019), 204-9.

condemnation of religious leaders and the studied ignorance of many histories of modern art, the marks of these traditions are everywhere if one looks closely. For example, early twentieth-century Russia was a cauldron of political upheaval as well as religious and artistic renewal. Beginning in the 1890s, two developments coincided: the revival of interest in Orthodox history and practice and the development of modern art in Russia. As in France, these movements—artistic and religious—were co-emergent.[44] Avant-garde artists were not only frequently raised in the Orthodox faith but also were deeply shaped by the visual culture of Russian Orthodoxy; indeed, many began their careers as seminarians and icon painters. Two were particularly significant for the rise of modern art: Natalia Goncharova (1881–1962) and Kazimir Malevich (1879–1935). Goncharova, probably the most important Russian avant-garde artist, attended church throughout her life and was deeply versed in Christian theology. Much of her imagery was adapted from Russian icons and featured apocalyptic imagery of the last times, such as *Archangel Michael* (see web 7.3). The avant-gardist group she launched in 1910 included many important modern artists, all of whom reflected deep religious influences, including Alexej von Jawlensky, Albert Gleizes, and Wassily Kandinsky.

Goncharova was also a mentor to the better-known Kazimir Malevich, founder of suprematicism, which featured nonobjective squares that were clearly framed and exhibited with Russian icons in mind (such as *Black Square*; see web 7.4). Recent scholarship has interpreted these stark images not only as expressions of a search for purity but also meditations on the absolute fullness and otherness of God—a visual example of the long Christian tradition of apophatic theology, which recognizes the limitations of human imagination. Typically, the authorities of the Orthodox Church refused to see the religious impulses behind these modern images, calling on the police to remove some of Goncharova's images as forms of blasphemy. Malevich's work was similarly denounced, just as Sergei Rachmaninov's *Vespers* (*All Night Vigil*, 1915), perhaps the most famous piece of modern Russian music, was initially rejected for canonical use in worship.

While Malevich was developing his nonobjective paintings in Russia, equally important avant-gardists, the Dadaists, were collaborating in ways that

---

[44]For what follows, see Anderson and Dyrness, *Modern Art and the Life*, 199–220.

bear a striking resemblance to the theological exploration of Malevich. Some Christian writers identify Dada as the epitome of modern art at its theological worst, such as Rookmaaker, who claims Dadaists "laugh away all that is of value in our world."[45] But Jonathan Anderson has shown that Hugo Ball, who stood at the fountainhead of Dada activity and experienced a reconversion to Catholicism, came to increasingly foreground mystical theology in his performance of Dada events, reflecting his deep study of early Christian Byzantine theology. In the extremely fraught world of the Great War, these avant-garde artists were not promoting a simple return to their inherited Christian traditions; they were clearly struggling with the "problems and possibilities of *referring*—whether visually or verbally—to the Holy."[46]

Just as modern artists in Russia could not have escaped the influence of the Orthodox faith, neither could artists at the birth of modernism in America escape the influence of their Puritan past. The continuity between the Calvinism of the Puritans and nineteenth-century writers and artists is profound. As Perry Miller pointed out half a century ago: "What is persistent from the covenant theology . . . to Edwards and to Emerson is the Puritan's effort to confront, face to face, the image of a blinding divinity in the physical universe, and to look upon that universe without intermediary of ritual."[47] This focus on the direct, unmediated experience of God fueled the Second Great Awakening of the early nineteenth century and had deep impact on the art of that century. It is clear, for example, that Thomas Cole (*Sunrise in the Catskills*; see web 7.5), Frederick Law Olmsted, and even Albert Pinkham Ryder felt the impact of these revivals and the immediacy of religious experience they highlighted. But a closer study of Cole and his only student, Frederic Edwin Church, shows that it was their sense of the active presence of God in history and creation, fueled by their shared Reformed faith, that led to the splendors of what we know as the Hudson River school of painting, and even to Olmstead's work on New York's Central Park. As Cole painted his famous *Course of Empire* series, he began to understand his own vocation in religious terms. As anonymous Gothic artists "worked to God," he believed his depiction of

---

[45]Rookmaaker, *Modern Art and the Death*, 129.
[46]Anderson and Dyrness, *Modern Art and the Life*, 241, emphasis original. This rich section of our book revisits work that Jonathan had done elsewhere.
[47]Perry Miller, *Errand into the Wilderness* (Cambridge, MA: Harvard University Press, 1956), 185. For this section, see Anderson and Dyrness, *Modern Art and the Life*, 246-53.

creation to be the artist's "lowly imitation of the creative power of the Almighty," which continued God's own creative processes.[48]

It is impossible for me to read Perry Miller's description of the "image of the blinding divinity in the physical universe" without thinking of the paintings of Vincent van Gogh. While van Gogh left the institutional forms of his father, a Reformed minister, he held onto a faith in something on high (*là-haut*), writing to his brother Theo in 1882 that "*the point is to grasp what does not pass in what passes. One of the things that will not pass* is the something on high and belief in God."[49] Though he failed at his earlier attempt to be a Christian missionary, he never lost the sense of God's presence inhering in the radiance of what he saw—whether the starry sky, a mulberry tree, or the weathered face of a peasant. The overriding preoccupation of van Gogh was not simply a belief in the infinite but belief in the blinding divinity of the world as an *inhabitable infinite*.[50]

The difference that religious perspectives make comes to clear expression in van Gogh's stormy relationship with Paul Gauguin. Debra Silverman argues that together these artists pointed the way to a new form of sacred art that carried uniquely modern sensitivities. Van Gogh for his part always retained what she calls a "visual Calvinism." Gauguin never lost the sacramental influence of the Catholic seminary where he studied as a young man. Though the latter formally rejected institutional Christianity, Silverman argues, this rejection "co-existed with a mentality indelibly stamped by the theological framework and religious values that framed him."[51] This framework was surely stimulated and enhanced by the religious values Gauguin saw in Tahiti and Martinique, and they came to special prominence in his brief time of working alongside van Gogh in Arles. While Gauguin, in *Vision of a Sermon* (see web 7.6), sought to shape images after the fashion of transcendent Catholic mysteries, van Gogh in *The Sower* (see web 7.7), which was painted the same year, portrays a spirituality within his twisting forms and lively palette.

---

[48]Louis Noble, *The Life and Works of Thomas Cole* (Cambridge, MA: Harvard University Press, 1964), 214, 251. See also Anderson and Dyrness, *Modern Art and the Life*, 248-49.

[49]Vincent van Gogh to Theo van Gogh, December 13-18, 1882, quoted in Anderson and Dyrness, *Modern Art and the Life*, 168, emphases original.

[50]Anderson and Dyrness, *Modern Art and the Life*, 169.

[51]Debra Silverman, *Van Gogh and Gauguin: The Search for Sacred Art* (New York: Farrar, Straus & Giroux, 2000), 101.

IV

It is appropriate to end this brief tour with these postimpressionists because it was the symbolism of that period that nurtured Georges Rouault during his studies at the L'École des Beaux-Arts in the 1890s. These avant-garde forms, so shocking to art critics and especially to religious leaders, nourished rather than impeded the religious vision that Rouault eventually developed. Even Rookmaaker recognized that Rouault embodied another way forward for modern art, even if he could not specify what that was.[52]

In sum, the religious impulses that I have described—and many others I have passed over—do not show up on the fringes of modern art history but at the very center of its creative impetus, and arguably they fueled its cutting edge. This is true even if nothing of this was visible to religious leaders as they surveyed with alarm the emergence of modern culture.

How do we respond to this disconnect? Among other things, we need to do more in our churches and seminaries to encourage people to engage with modern culture rather than retreat to some supposed idyllic past. This may result in not only a more relevant Christian witness but also a more resilient spirituality. If my reading of the Christian influence on modern art is right, the aesthetic shock that characterized many modern styles and the work of Georges Rouault may not be a barrier to religion but in fact may be a part of the gospel itself. Even amid the supposed secular culture we inhabit, modern art offers evidence that God has not left himself without a witness.

---

[52]Though sympathetic, Rookmaaker could not make out what to do with Rouault, whom he treats near the end of his survey. Why do we take Picasso as the man of our time, Rookmaaker asks? Rouault is proof that another direction could have been taken in modern art, though he is not sure what that might be. Though Rouault prophesied against the evil times in which he lived, Rookmaaker notes, his figures are still symbols in a negative sense, coming only later to a more compassionate view. See Rookmaaker, *Modern Art and the Death*, 156-57.

Alphabet Soup

—See Color Plate 9—

Ryan Lauterio

Out of nothing, the Lord God spoke creation into existence, a creative act that moved reality from formlessness and void into loving habitability, a reality with humanity and all living things placed squarely in a rich aesthetic world of abundance and makerly possibility. Available to us was a worshipful life of deep purpose and satisfaction gifted by the triune God. Unfortunately, sin and death entered the world, breaking humanity from beholding God's face and putting us into the void of death and chaos that comes from a sinful life outside God's holy and loving presence.

In the background of my artwork exists the tension of being rescued from the void and saved from sin and death by grace through faith in Jesus Christ. As followers of Jesus and as painters, Rouault and I have both experienced the tension of our respective contemporaries rejecting the idea that Christianity has anything valuable to say about the world (let alone art). Rouault's work and my recent body of paintings both take an honest look at where humanity is and perhaps where it is heading. *Alphabet Soup* does this by rendering a tense field where image, gesture, figure, and form struggle in a groaning, dynamic exchange, separated in a liminal state, as figures teeter between cohering or imploding.

In Rouault's work, figures seem to groan, suffering under the weightiness of lack. Figures rendered in rough outlines bear evidence through the human touch of the artist's compassionate sensibilities. The characteristic black outlines that run across the surface of Rouault's prints and paintings are more than mere lines. They seem to present a spatial effect that could be described as "void-contours." These void-contours often isolate the figure and form from its surroundings, thus bringing to bear an estrangement that pervades the inscape of his works with the paradoxical tension of death lurking amid life. We must have eyes to see well what exists with nuance in Rouault's use of color as visible light and form, much like Hans Hofmann's theory of color as light.[1] Rouault's stark primary colors seem to optically emerge toward the viewer, filling and narrowing the void contours to signal the possibility of humanity's redemption.

In *Alphabet Soup*, the black is the same void, hungry for color and light to emerge and create separation that enjoins and clarifies until things are placed back into order. Silhouetted children, voided yet habitable in terms of image, stand waiting, suspended in a moment of tension, looking toward a figurative monolith that, in terms of effects and gestural thrust, implodes while assembling itself in a clumsy, garish way. The painting is visually held together by the geometric orange and green bands that serve as a kind of outside-time framework and structure for the inscape of the grayscale interior. Rouault's use of primary color within his paintings provided a vivid structure and frank depiction of his theological convictions. In my work, these integrated painted frames carry theological implications while formally expressing a similar idea of color and attitude to Rouault's, as the effects of the color and form institute spatial stability. These stabilizing color effects provide grounding to the internal struggle of the central figure, which is consumed and suffering under a self-aggrandized, futile battle to actualize outside its ontological reality, unaware of the grace color provides by grounding its existential wrestling.

Alphabet Soup converses with Rouault's work in that he depicts humanity with an honesty that hides nothing. A generative interplay between my work and that of Rouault for future enrichment around important theological realities has productive potential, especially when considering that the rich and complex history of our understanding of human beings made in God's image is perhaps under the most significant

---

[1] "Whether you use it in a decorative sense, or in the sense of a grand symphonic poem, the important thing always to be remembered is that the chief function of color is to create light." Hans Hoffman, *Color Creates Light: Studies with Hans Hoffman* (Salt Spring Island, BC: Trillistar InterArts, 2011), 275.

amount of tension, debate, and stress we have seen in many lifetimes. My work aims to dialogue with the heart of Rouault's work while metaphorically and effectually depicting the tension between theological views of humanity and contemporary secular views of humanity.

Finally, I cannot help but think about Jesus coming again as one clothed in rainbows of living color: the Jesus in whom all things hold together, live, and have their being; the one who died to make all things new and uphold all things by the power of his word; the one who came to break down the dividing wall of hostility and went into the void to die so that we might know life eternal and have it forever as heaven and earth overlap. Indeed, all of what King Jesus has done is a consummation and assurance for us who believe. We will live in this new heavenly earth with him, as he, the light of the world, clothes us in living color. A careful look at the breadth of Rouault's work will point to this hope, time and time again, without ever diminishing the suffering we endure as we wait for the fullness of humanity redeemed with Christ our Lord.

8

"The Stark Elation of Seeing the Thing as It Is"

Georges Rouault's Miserere *at One Hundred (1922–2022)*

Stephen Schloesser

> *Our entire task in this life consists in healing the eyes of the heart so that they may be able to see God.*
>
> SAINT AUGUSTINE, "SERMON 38 ON THE NEW TESTAMENT"

Numerous essays and other recent publications marked the centenary of 1922, long considered the mythical "Year I" (echoing the 1793 French Revolutionary calendar) of the post–World War I epoch of modernism.[1] Or at least this is how Ezra Pound famously dubbed it in light of how 1922 was bookended by two literary meteors: on February 2, the publication of James Joyce's *Ulysses* by Shakespeare and Company in Paris (to evade obscenity laws); and later that fall the publication of T. S. Eliot's *The Waste Land* in October (UK), November (US), and December (in book form, following its previous publication in magazine form).[2] The year 1922 is also when the first English

---

[1] Kevin Jackson, *Constellation of Genius: 1922: Modernism Year One* (New York: Farrar, Straus & Giroux, 2013).

[2] James Joyce and Catherine Flynn, *The Cambridge Centenary Ulysses: The 1922 Text with Essays and Notes* (New York: Cambridge University Press, 2022); T. S. Eliot, Valerie Eliot, and Ezra Pound, *The Waste Land: A Facsimile and Transcript of the Original Drafts Including the Annotations of Ezra Pound*, rev. ed. (New York: Liveright, 2022); Jed Rasula, *What the Thunder Said: How* The Waste Land *Made Poetry Modern* (Princeton, NJ: Princeton University Press, 2022); Matthew Hollis, *The Waste Land: A Biography of a Poem* (New York: Norton, 2022).

translation installment appeared of Marcel Proust's sprawling *À la recherche du temps perdu* (*In Search of Lost Time*). This first of several volumes was published before Proust died on November 18, almost exactly four years since the armistice of November 11, 1918, concluded the Great War.[3] The war's carnage had swept away the old world and made way for the birth of the modern.[4] Willa Cather later judged in retrospect, "The world broke in two in 1922 or thereabouts."[5]

Although emerging from a cultural context and wartime experience significantly different from that of the British and Americans, France also saw a new era signaled in 1922—an ambiguously bivalent era represented by both neoclassicism and surrealism.[6] Writing in 1923, one critic observed, "The artist today no longer disdains the antique. He simply knows how to see it in a modern way, to make allusions, discreet quotes, highly modified borrowings that take the form of a homage. Thus, instead of going against tradition, our modern art easily ties in with it, adjusts it to itself."[7] Few works exemplified

---

[3]Patti Miller, "Reading Proust Aloud: 'How Can It Be That Deeply Flawed and Terrible Humans Have the Capacity to Create?,'" *The Guardian*, November 12, 2022, www.theguardian.com /books/2022/nov/12/reading-proust-aloud-how-can-it-be-that-deeply-flawed-and-terrible -humans-have-the-capacity-to-create. For the Bibliothèque Nationale de France commemoration, see "France's National Library Celebrates Proust 100 Years After His Death," RFI, November 18, 2022, www.rfi.fr/en/culture/20221118-french-national-library-celebrates-proust-100-years-after -his-death; "Marcel Proust: La fabrique de l'oeuvre," October 11, 2022–January 22, 2023, www.bnf .fr/fr/agenda/marcel-proust.

[4]Modris Eksteins, *Rites of Spring: The Great War and the Birth of the Modern Age* (Boston: Houghton Mifflin, 1989).

[5]Bill Goldstein, *The World Broke in Two: Virginia Woolf, T. S. Eliot, D. H. Lawrence, E. M. Forster, and the Year That Changed Literature* (New York: Picador, 2018); see also Michael North, *Reading 1922: A Return to the Scene of the Modern* (New York: Oxford University Press, 1999).

[6]Stephen Schloesser, *Jazz Age Catholicism: Mystic Modernism in Postwar Paris, 1919–1933* (Toronto: University of Toronto Press, 2005), 11-14.

[7]*L'Atelier Primavera et la décoration moderne, 1913–1923* (Paris: Magasins du Printemps, 1923) 20; quoted in Charlotte Benton, Tim Benton, and Ghislaine Wood, eds., *Art Deco 1910–1939* (Boston: Bulfinch, 2003), 91. Compare Brandon Taylor, "The 1920s: Looking Forward, Looking Back," in *Make It Modern: A History of Art in the 20th Century* (New Haven, CT: Yale University Press, 2022), 78-143. "The decade that followed the end of the First World War can be broadly characterized as one of recovery: not merely recovery from the hiatus of war, but recovery of past standards of stability and security, even of national redefinition against the background of rapid and destabilizing change" (79). Michael North observes ironically that the "modern itself is an unstable category when the new, in literature and in fashion, comes into being in such close association with the ancient" (quoted in Schloesser, *Jazz Age Catholicism*, 12). See also Daniel J. Sherman, *The Construction of Memory in Interwar France* (Chicago: University of Chicago Press, 1999); Romy Golan, *Modernity and Nostalgia: Art and Politics in France Between the Wars* (New Haven, CT: Yale University Press, 1995); and Kenneth E. Silver, *Esprit de Corps: The Art of the Parisian Avant-garde and the First World War, 1914–1925* (Princeton, NJ: Princeton University Press, 1989).

this paradoxical postwar context as much as Jean Cocteau's 1922 production
of the ancient Greek Sophocles's *Antigone* at the Théâtre de l'Atelier in the
Montmartre district of Paris.[8] Cocteau's version of the neoclassical, a primitivist modernism (or modernist primitivism), starring Antonin Artaud as the
blind seer Tiresias, featured Cocteau's own translation accompanied by Pablo
Picasso's scenery, Coco Chanel's costumes, and Arthur Honegger's music.

That same year, Jacques Maritain, Georges Rouault's close friend and
patron, published his own primitivist modernist manifesto titled simply *Antimoderne* (*Antimodern*).[9] Maritain's open letter to Cocteau interpreted the
Antigone phenomenon in terms of external semblance and hidden reality:
"You have an admirably jealous longing for freedom. How well I understand
your love for Antigone! Yet she herself tells us, and that is why she is dear to
you, that in breaking human law, she was following a better commandment—
the unwritten and unchangeable laws."[10] Art historian Vincent Scully suc-
cinctly summarizes the cultural work performed by classicism and its varieties:
"Classicism is Memory and Sorrow."[11]

Of the numerous centenary commemorations published in 2022–2023, one
especially stands out. James Parker's "T. S. Eliot Saw All This Coming" appeared in the *Atlantic* with the subheading, "One hundred years after the publication of *The Waste Land*, its vision has never been more terrifying." Parker
concludes with an attempt to explain the poem's phenomenal impact: "Why?
Because it couldn't be denied. Because it was brain-thunder. Because it was
magic, and it ripped the shaman apart. Because it itemizes our illnesses like
no poem before or since, offering nothing, nothing at all, but *the stark elation
of seeing the thing as it is*."[12]

Parker's line seems a fitting (albeit fittingly paradoxical) epigraph for
Georges Rouault's monumental *Miserere* series, begun in earnest in 1922.[13] For

---

[8]For Jean Cocteau's neoclassicist realism, see Schloesser, *Jazz Age Catholicism*, 142-48.
[9]Schloesser, *Jazz Age Catholicism*, 162-67, 170-72.
[10]Schloesser, *Jazz Age Catholicism*, 186.
[11]Vincent Scully, quoted in Schloesser, *Jazz Age Catholicism*, 141.
[12]James Parker, "T. S. Eliot Saw All This Coming," *Atlantic* (January/February 2023), emphasis added,
    www.theatlantic.com/magazine/archive/2023/01/ts-eliot-the-waste-land-poem-anniversary
    /672231/.
[13]See Stephen Schloesser, "1921–1929: Jazz Age Graphic Shock," in *Mystic Masque: Semblance and
    Reality in Georges Rouault, 1871–1958*, ed. Stephen Schloesser (Boston: McMullen Museum of Art,
    2008), 134. For Rouault overview, see Schloesser, "Georges Rouault: Masked Redemption," in *Jazz
    Age Catholicism*, 213-44.

Rouault, too, the fundamental task is "seeing the thing as it is." All is not as it seems, however, and the gap between surface appearance and deeper reality underlies numerous dramatic situations portrayed in Rouault's work: the worlds of prostitutes, judicial figures (lawyers, judges, and the accused), society's wealthy and powerful, wandering circus figures, and Christ himself, often on the road. In the *bal masqué* (masked ball) that is Rouault's human comedy, the epistemological act of judging appearances plays a commanding role. Rouault's tragicomic world is marked by misjudgments, misapprehensions, and epistemological uncertainty. Judicial figures must necessarily make their judgments based on the limitations of sense data, the selective memories of witnesses, and the frequently sophistic arguments of lawyers. As a consequence, the innocence of criminals is too often misjudged.[14] Similarly, since clowns and prostitutes intentionally paint their faces and don colorful costumes to entertain others, the viewer misjudges these lives based on external appearances. Rouault explicitly uses these figures who paint their faces as types for humans' dissimulating activity when he asks in plate 8 of the *Miserere*: *Who among us does not wear a mask?* The *Miserere* is a monumental work resisting any simple overview. As a representative sampling, then, what follows are five excerpted moments illustrating Rouault's mystic masque.[15]

Tears in Things

The most striking example of the 1920s neoclassical vogue in the *Miserere* is *There are tears in things . . . (Sunt lacrymae rerum . . . ;* M27; see fig. P.1), Rouault's depiction of the blind poet Orpheus and his lyre. Rouault's original verses written for this image allude more directly to Orpheus's grief as he loses Eurydice, a punishment for having broken the command not to turn around and look at her as she was emerging from the underworld:

> Eurydice! Eurydice!
> Orpheus cries out mournfully

---

[14]Compare the roles played by judges in the cinematic work of Krzysztof Kieślowski (1941–1996). See especially the fifth episode ("Thou Shalt Not Kill") of *Dekalog* (1988); *A Short Film About Killing* (1988); and *Rouge* (Red) in the Three Colors trilogy (1994).

[15]The following six commentaries are an abridgement of Stephen Schloesser, "Notes on the Miserere Plates Exhibited in *Mystic Masque*," in Schloesser, *Mystic Masque*, 157–80. The unabridged essay, complete with endnotes and original French titles, is available online, https://archive.org/details /mysticmasquesembooschl.

watching vanish
the fugitive form
the beloved form.

Perhaps in order to universalize the sentiment and give it the neoclassical timelessness implied by Latin, Rouault replaced this text with the brief three-word quotation from Virgil's *Aeneid*: "Sunt lacrymae rerum." Bernard Doering sets the context for the quoted lines:

> When Aeneas arrives at Carthage and, in a temple there, sees a frieze depicting the fall of Troy and the deaths of the Trojan heroes, of his family and his friends, his eyes filled with tears (*lacrimans*), he exclaims with profound sadness: *Sunt lacrymae rerum et mentem mortalia tangent* (There are tears at the very heart of things, and the mortal nature of those things troubles the human mind).[16]

Virgil's heart-rending cry points beyond fleeting surface appearances to the deeper, hidden reality of things. Agony and anxiety are not accidental traits of being human; they are essential to our consciousness of being thrown into time and knowing that a day will come when we will cease to exist.[17]

The linkage of Christ and Orpheus goes back to early Christianity and was recovered by nineteenth-century interests in esoteric religions and occult philosophies, "a desire to create broad, all-encompassing systems of humanity's development—past, present, future."[18] Gustave Moreau, Rouault's beloved mentor, was a key figure in this syncretic intellectual environment in which the multivalent figure of Orpheus played a central role as "poet, musician, initiate, magician, heroic intruder in Hades, lamenting lover, victim of Dionysian fury, but especially harbinger of civilization, archetypal artist, leader of cults, and priest."[19] Examples of Moreau's depictions of Orpheus include *Orpheus at the Tomb of Eurydice* (see web 8.1; painted in 1891, the year before Rouault

---

[16]Bernard Doering, "Lacrimae Rerum—Tears at the Heart of Things: Jacques Maritain and Georges Rouault," in *Truth Matters: Essays in Honor of Jacques Maritain*, ed. John G. Trapani (Washington, DC: Catholic University of America Press, 2004), 206-7.

[17]See discussion of Blaise Pascal and Martin Heidegger on anxiety in Schloesser, "1921–1929," 139, 150-51; compare Schloesser, "1871–1901: Realism, Symbolism, Mystic Modernism," in Schloesser, *Mystic Masque*, 37.

[18]Dorothy M. Kosinski, "Gustave Moreau's 'La Vie de l'humanité': Orpheus in the Context of Religious Syncretism, Universal Histories, and Occultism," *Art Journal* 46, no. 1 (Spring 1987): 13; quote altered for gender inclusivity.

[19]Kosinski, "Gustave Moreau's 'La Vie de l'humanité,'" 13.

entered Moreau's atelier) and *Orpheus* (1865), also known as *The Thracian Girl Carrying the Head of Orpheus.*

Almost twenty-five years before beginning the *Miserere*, Rouault had painted and exhibited his own *Orpheus* at the 1899 Salon des artistes français. Executed in the academic salon style, it can perhaps be seen as a vehicle of mourning and an ode to Moreau, who had died a year earlier (April 1898). Rouault's representation of Orpheus in the *Miserere* (see fig. P.1), as well as its pre-1926 studies and post-1926 variants, is a very different image. With his lyre strapped over his left shoulder, Orpheus kneels on one bended knee and balances himself on his right. The figure and posture of Orpheus's head is directly echoed in two other *Miserere* plates: *Are we not all forced laborers?* (M6; see fig. 2.1) and *The blind have sometimes consoled the sighted* (M55; see web 8.2); and it is indirectly echoed in two others: *Alone, in this life of pitfalls and mischief* (M5) and *Virgin of the seven swords* (M53), an image of Mary (the mother of Christ) alluding to a late medieval and early modern devotion to Our Lady of the Seven Sorrows (or Seven Swords). The layers of meaning amplify one another: enchainment or enslavement, solitude and loneliness, blindness (physical blindness enabling the deeper insight of the poet-singer Homer and the seer Tiresias), and bereavement (both Orpheus and Christ's mother see their beloved taken away from them).

The style of *Sunt lacrymae rerum* itself is thoroughly neoclassical in the 1920s mode, as exemplified by the purism of Le Corbusier, the neoclassicism of Cocteau, Picasso, and Igor Stravinsky, and the industrial-mechanical tubism of Fernand Léger.[20] Like Picasso's *Three Women at the Spring* (see web 8.3), painted at Fontainebleau in the summer of 1921, Orpheus's clothing and fingers evoke fluted classical columns, as does the top of his lyre; his musculature is pronounced in the classical style (note his right calf); and the figure taken as a whole consists of well-defined volume and relief made possible by the play of luminosity and shadow.

Although Orpheus sometimes appears as a sighted figure in literary variants, his blindness is essential to Rouault's interpretation. His lack of external sight suggests a more profound internal vision, allowing him to sing his plaintive revelation, "There are tears in things." If, as observed above, classicism is

---

[20]The childhood name of Le Corbusier was Charles-Édouard Jeanneret.

indeed "memory and sorrow," Rouault's representation of Orpheus is ideally suited to his universal lament over the human condition. This condition is portrayed in countless variations throughout the *Miserere*.

TRIPTYCH: REVILED JESUS TAKES REFUGE IN THE BAREFOOT WANDERER

If this trio were physically constructed as a triptych, the outer two plates would constitute the wings: *Jesus reviled . . .* (M2; see fig. 8.1) and *takes refuge in your heart, barefoot wanderer of misfortune* (M4; see fig. 8.3). The middle panel would bridge the two: *forever scourged . . .* (M3; see fig. 8.2). The ellipses used in the titles are Rouault's own and meant to indicate linkages between the poetic phrases and the plates. This small poem reads:

> Jesus reviled . . .
> forever scourged . . .
> takes refuge in your heart,
> barefoot wanderer of misfortune.

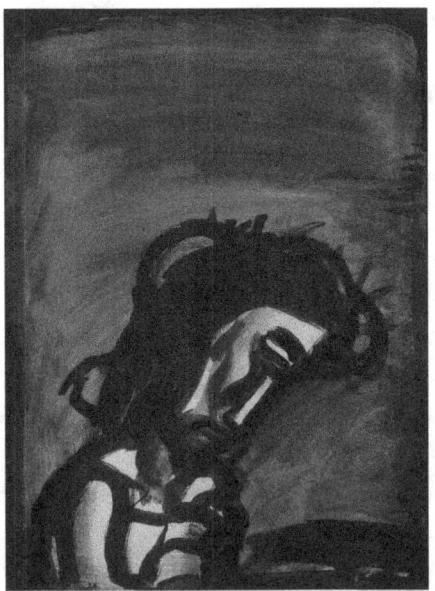

Figure 8.1. Georges Rouault, *Jésus honni . . . (Jesus reviled . . .)*, *Miserere* plate 2, 1921–1922. Etching on paper, 21 5/8 × 15 3/4

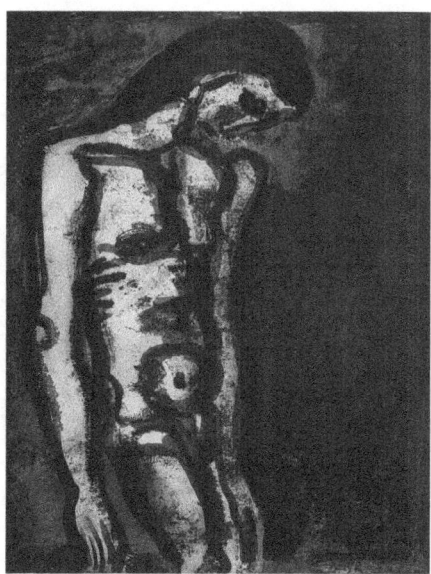

Figure 8.2. Georges Rouault, *toujours flagellé . . . (forever scourged . . .*), *Miserere* plate 3, 1922. Heliogravure, aquatint, and roulette printed in black on paper, 19 1/8 × 14 1/4

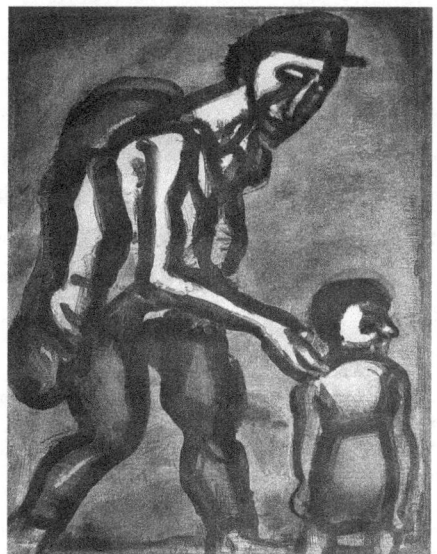

Figure 8.3. Georges Rouault, *se réfugie en ton coeur, va-nu-pieds de malheur. (takes refuge in your heart, vagabond of misfortune.*), *Miserere* plate 4, 1922. Heliogravure, aquatint, and roulette on cream laid paper, 18 15/16 × 14 11/16

The connections between the figures clarify Rouault's incarnational-sacramental vision. In the first plate of the triptych, *Jesus reviled* . . . , we see only the bowed head, a profile view of what will later be titled *Behold the Sorrow* (*Ecce Dolor*, from *Passion*; see web 8.4), a medieval figure (the "man of sorrows"). This bowed head emerges directly from that in the bottom half of the preceding plate that opens the folio, *Miserere mei, Deus* (M1, *Have mercy on me, God*). In the second plate of the triptych, *forever scourged* . . . , the viewer pulls back and sees three-quarters of Christ's full body. If Rouault's interest were purely historical, the viewer would now expect the third plate in the triptych to view Christ from yet another fuller angle.

Like his mentors Moreau and Léon Bloy, however, Rouault was a symbolist at heart. The third plate surprises the viewer as the historical Jesus of the previous two becomes identified here and now with the wayfarer: the *va-nu-pieds*—translated literally as *going barefoot* (i.e., going with nude feet)—and being equivalent to a beggar, vagabond, tramp, or "bum" (*clochard*). The image of the homeless wanderer is a favorite of Rouault's and owes its lineage to Jacques Callot's beggars, *Bohemians*, and *Gypsies*; to Honoré Daumier's fugitives, emigrants, and traveling saltimbanques; and to Édouard Manet's gypsies.[21]

The triptych form allows Rouault to engage his passion for surprising (and sometimes shocking) inversions. As the viewer moves through the *Miserere* series, going from one image to another, two successive images of the historical Jesus lead the viewer to expect an exalted subject in the third. At precisely this moment, however, Rouault unexpectedly inserts society's most marginal type—the homeless person—and makes the wanderer the present-day incarnation of the historical Jesus. In this upending inversion, the most

---

[21]The image of the wanderer has deep resonances in Christian theology and philosophy. For antiquity, see Peter Brown's discussion of "resident aliens" in *Augustine of Hippo: A Biography*, new ed. (Berkeley: University of California Press, 2000), 323; see also M. A. Claussen, "'Peregrinatio' and 'Peregrini' in Augustine's 'City of God,'" *Traditio* 46 (1991): 33-75; Schloesser, "1921–1929," 140-41. For modernity, see Gabriel Marcel, *Homo Viator* (New York: Harper & Row, 1962); and Josef Pieper, *On Hope* (San Francisco: Ignatius, 1986), translation of *Über die Hoffnung* (1935). For postmodernity, see Charles Lock, "Michel de Certeau: Walking the via Negativa," *Paragraph* 22, no. 2 (1999): 184-98. For contemporary relevance, see vănThanh Nguyễn, *What Does the Bible Say About Strangers, Migrants, and Refugees?* (New York: New City, 2021); Peter C. Phan, ed., *Christian Theology in the Age of Migration: Implications for World Christianity* (Lanham, MD: Lexington Books, 2020); Richard Kearney and Kascha Semonovitch, eds., *Phenomenologies of the Stranger: Between Hostility and Hospitality* (New York: Fordham University Press, 2011).

powerful now "takes refuge in" (*se réfugie*) the heart of the most vulnerable. In the mystic masque, appearances surprise.

DIPTYCH/TRIPTYCH: MASKS

Another triptych constitutes the heart of judging rightly between semblance and reality. The question-and-response form linking two plates—*Are we not slaves? . . .* (M6; see fig. 2.1) and *believing ourselves to be kings* (M7; see fig. 2.2)—suggests they should be seen as a diptych. But when the title for the third following plate is added—*Who does not wear a mask?* (M8; see fig. 2.3)—the three lines are seen to be a short poem that rhymes in French (i.e., *forçats* rhyming with *pas*; both near-rhyming with *rois*). This transforms the diptych into a triptych:

> *Ne sommes-nous pas forçats?*
> *nous croyant rois.*
> *Qui ne se grime pas?*
> Are we not slaves?
> believing ourselves to be kings.
> Who does not wear a mask?

Although the term *forçat* can simply refer to a convict or prisoner, its etymological roots evoke a forced laborer of some kind—including convict laborers, as in ship galley slaves—and it derives from the French verb *forcer* ("to force," as in English). Rouault would have encountered both the word and image in his readings of Voltaire's *Candide* as a child, Fyodor Dostoevsky beginning in 1911, and Alfred Jarry's *Ubu Roi* (King Ubu), on which he was working at the time for his patron, Ambroise Vollard.[22]

In the initial diptych, *Are we not slaves? . . . believing ourselves to be kings*, Rouault transforms Jarry's farce into a universal image of the tragicomic human condition. Like the grinning King Ubu watching over his back, we dress ourselves in royal robes and headgear. But looking over his shoulder, King Ubu sees himself mirrored and nude—an emperor without clothes—a convict, galley slave, forced laborer. It is, as Blaise Pascal observed, a problem of imagination conflicting with knowledge.[23]

---

[22]For Rouault and Ubu, see Stephen Schloesser, "1902–1920: The Hard Metier of Unmasking," in Schloesser, *Mystic Masque*, 97-98.
[23]See Schloesser, "1902–1920," 89.

The diptych expands into a triptych with the tragic clown in the third plate—
Who does not wear a mask? (*Qui ne se grime pas?*)—one of Rouault's most powerful images, both here and in its variant painted sometime after 1930. The verb
se grimer means "to paint one's face" (with greasepaint) in order to perform for
the audience. By extension, it also means to disguise or mask oneself. The
clown's rhetorical question broadens King Ubu's mask into a more universal
condition: "Who does not apply face paint? Wear a mask? Disguise oneself?"
The question can be traced back to Rouault's 1905 encounter with an old vagabond clown, an encounter echoing the experience of *dédoublement* narrated
in Charles Baudelaire's prose-poem "The Old Acrobat."[24] "I saw quite clearly
that the 'Clown' was me, was us, nearly all of us," Rouault had written nearly
two decades earlier. "This *rich* and *glittering* costume, it is given to us by life
itself, we are all *more or less clowns*, we all wear a glittering costume."

Rouault's types are distinguished by this invisible epistemological division:
a difference in knowledge and judgment. While Rouault's antagonists act out
their lives in self-deception, his protagonists are self-aware of the disjunction
between semblance and reality. Mind the gap.

Triptych/Tetraptych: Judgments and Justice

Another triptych transports us from one performative setting to another: from
the traveling circus tent to the courtroom. Once again, Rouault's ellipses in
the plates' titles (which rhyme in French) indicate that they are to be connected as a group.

> The condemned is led away . . .
> while his lawyer, in hollow phrases, proclaims his complete innocence . . .
> beneath a Jesus on the cross forgotten there.

In the first plate, *The condemned is led away . . .* (M18; see web 8.5), the figure
of a condemned man calls to mind the earlier plate considered above, *forever
scourged . . .* (M3; see fig. 8.2). Even as this condemned man resonates with
Christ "forever scourged" and with the "barefoot wanderer" in whose heart he
takes refuge, he now adds his own layer of new meaning. The second plate—
while his lawyer, in hollow phrases, proclaims his complete innocence (M19, *son
avocat, en phrases creuses, clame sa total inconscience . . .*; see web 8.6)—is drawn

---

[24]See Schloesser, "1902–1920," 82-83, emphasis original.

directly from the pages of caricature artist Honoré Daumier. Daumier and Rouault mock the same "unconsciousness" (*inconscience*), the feigned innocence or lack of any responsibility for the guilty verdict delivered by the judges.

The triptych's third plate—*beneath a crucifix forgotten there* (M20; see web 8.7)—carries multiple meanings. The first and most literal meaning is historical: in 1905, one of the provisions of the Act of Separation of Church and State was the removal of crucifixes from courtrooms. (Daumier's courtrooms frequently have the large crucifix looming over the judges' heads, even when they are falling asleep beneath them out of disinterest.) On this literal level the simple meaning is: there is no crucifix on the wall where there used to be one.

On a deeper level, Rouault plays on the lawyer's unconsciousness. While he claims not to be conscious of any complicity he might have had in the judgment handed down, he is also not conscious of the higher authority or principle that is judging the proceedings, whether the players in this masque are aware of it or not. This was the meaning that Léon Bloy, Rouault's onetime mentor, had attributed to the judicial proceedings in the Dreyfus Affair (1894–1906).[25] A seeming contradiction in his day, a Catholic who was also pro-Dreyfus, Bloy viewed the world as a historical, symbolist pageant.[26] The particular dramas we see played out on history's limited stages point beyond themselves to a cosmic drama that will ultimately be unveiled and revealed only at the apocalypse.[27]

The title of Bloy's 1900 essay "Je m'accuse" (I accuse myself) is a wordplay on Émile Zola's "J'accuse!" (1898), the open letter that reignited the Dreyfus Affair. On history's visible stage, Bloy argued, Colonel Dreyfus had been unjustly convicted for "the presumption of a known crime, for which he appears

---

[25]The Dreyfus Affair was a political scandal that caused division within the French Third Republic from the trial of Captain Alfred Dreyfus in 1894 until his rehabilitation in 1906. See Maurice Samuels, *Richard Dreyfus: The Man at the Center of the Affair* (New Haven, CT: Yale University Press, 2024); Piers Paul Read, *The Dreyfus Affair: The Scandal That Tore France in Two* (New York: Bloomsbury, 2012); Ruth Harris, *Dreyfus: Politics, Emotion, and the Scandal of the Century* (New York: Metropolitan Books, 2010); Michael Burns, Michael, *France and the Dreyfus Affair: A Documentary History* (Boston: Bedford/St. Martins, 1999).

[26]See Stephen Schloesser, "History as Revelation: Léon Bloy, Flannery O'Connor, and Symbolist Exegesis of the Commonplace," in *Revelation and Convergence: Flannery O'Connor and the Catholic Intellectual Tradition*, ed. Mark Bosco and Brent Little (Washington, DC: Catholic University of America Press, 2017), 10-50. See also Schloesser, *Jazz Age Catholicism*, 69.

[27]*Apocalypse* derives from the Greek *apokalyptein*, meaning "to uncover" or "to reveal"; from *apo-* ("un-") + *kalyptein* ("to cover").

to be absolutely innocent and not responsible"—that is, treason. This was the visible surface semblance of the national drama. Bloy, however, saw Dreyfus (who, like his invisible counterpart, Christ, was Jewish) being "punished for an *unknown* crime"—that is, an invisible or unrecognized deeper crime: human sin. Thus the Dreyfus Affair, in Bloy's idiosyncratic symbolist reading, was only "an illusion"—a mystic masque—"*the human and hideous appearance of a DIVINE COURT CASE for which the moment has not yet come to be revealed in the light.*" Since Bloy (like Joris-Karl Huysmans, onetime friend of both Bloy and Rouault) firmly believed in the doctrine of vicarious redemption, he saw Dreyfus as suffering on behalf of Bloy's own sins. Hence, "Je m'accuse."[28]

On yet a third level, Rouault has curiously altered the typical French phrase for "crucifix"—that is, "Christ en croix" (Christ on the cross)—by substituting the more devotional "Jesus on the cross." The slight word change alters the meaning significantly. Rather than meaning "beneath a forgotten crucifix," it conveys instead a forgotten Jesus—the living personal sense implied in the *Miserere* plate whose legend is taken from Pascal: "*Jesus will be in agony, until the end of the world*" (M35; see web 3.14). Both Pascal and Rouault take this literally: Jesus will always be in agony—here and now, in particular historical circumstances—like this condemned man in front of his lawyer. The whole world is, in Bloy's words, "*a DIVINE COURT CASE*" awaiting its true revelation.

As if to make this almost redundantly clear, the reader turns to the next plate and encounters yet another twist. Although the lack of ellipses seemed to indicate that the triptych was the end of this episode, a surprise comes with "*He was oppressed and afflicted, yet he opened not his mouth*" (M21; see fig. 3.3). The legend is a direct quotation from Isaiah 53:7, and the bodily configuration is a nearly exact reiteration of the "condemned man." It also clearly refers back to *forever scourged . . .* (M3; see fig. 8.2).

In terms of the connections between poetic phrases, this grouping (M18-19-20) is a triptych. But the nearly exact bodily arrangements of the condemned man and Christ as the suffering servant (M21) expand the episode into a four-paneled polyptych. Like early modern polyptychs (for example, Matthias Grünewald's *Isenheim Altarpiece,* used by Huysmans as the foundation of his decadent aesthetic), Rouault's *Miserere* plates—especially in the

---

[28]Schloesser, *Jazz Age Catholicism,* 43-44.

original deluxe folio edition with freestanding removable broadsheets—can function as altarpiece wings.[29] When a wing is shut, a diptych or triptych can mean one thing; when a wing opens, another layer of meaning is added: a diptych becomes a triptych, a triptych becomes a tetraptych, and semantic reverberations multiply.

RECOGNITION ON THE ROAD

One metaphorical variation on the lack of sight is the inability to recognize what is standing right in front of us. The plate *Lord, it is You, I recognize You* (M32; see web 2.2) considers this theme as Rouault's poetic fragment sets the scene.

> Lord,
> It is you, I recognize you
> Even if far from Emmaus
> I always find you again [*retrouve*].[30]

Rouault's fragment alludes to the scriptural account of the road to Emmaus (Lk 24:13-35), and his choice for depicting this moment of the opening of the eyes invites reflection. He was certainly aware of the scriptural account in which the act of recognition comes not on the road but rather at the supper table's breaking of bread. Rouault's own depiction of it nearly twenty-five years earlier, *Christ and the Disciples at Emmaus* (1899), exhibited at that February's Salon des artistes français (along with his *Orpheus*), was modeled after Rembrandt's *The Supper at Emmaus* (1648). Not only would Rouault have seen Rembrandt's painting at the Louvre, but his own photographic copy is preserved in the Rouault archives. In short, his decision to relocate this moment away from its traditional supper setting was intentional.

Why? It seems that Rouault is deliberately conflating two recognition scenes: the one at Emmaus and the one in which the doubting apostle Thomas refuses to believe unless he puts his "finger where the nails were" in Christ's

---

[29]For Huysmans's revolutionary use of Matthias Grünewald's *Isenheim Altarpiece* (ca. 1512–1516) now conserved at the Unterlinden Museum at Colmar, Alsace (France), see Schloesser, *Jazz Age Catholicism*, 40-43.

[30]"Seigneur / C'est vous, je vous reconnais / Même loin d'Emmaüs / Toujours je vous retrouve." The resonance of the verb *retrouver* is difficult to reproduce in English. Literally, it translates as "re-find" (*re-trouver*); compare *reconnais* (literally, "to re-know" or "know again") with the English *recognize*.

hands and his "hand into his side." A week later, Christ comes and stands among them, saying to Thomas: "Reach out your hand and put it into my side." Thomas does so and recognizes him with the exclamation, "My Lord and my God!" Christ concludes, "Blessed are those who have not seen and yet have believed" (Jn 20:25-29).

Rouault has telescoped these two events to make his point about appearances and reality. The words of recognition (*je vous reconnais*) come from the Emmaus narrative, while the address "My Lord" (*Seigneur*) comes from the Thomas story—and indeed, the figure to the right is extending his hand to place it in the side of Christ, in the wound left by the soldier's piercing of Jesus' side with a lance (Jn 19:34). It is also understandable that for Rouault this revelatory moment takes place *on the road*—the road, as seen above, is privileged space for Rouault. (Compare the *Christ and Disciples* in the *Passion* series [see web 8.8]—presumably this is also the road to Emmaus.) Moreover, this moment of revelation and recognition then fits with the key image that binds together both halves of the *Miserere*, namely, the moment of compassion and revelation on the way of the cross that is Veronica's veil: *and Veronica with the soft linen still walks along the road . . .* (M33; see fig. 4.1).[31]

Finally, the figure of Christ in *Lord, it is You* is the mirror image of *"He was oppressed and afflicted, yet he opened not his mouth"* (M21; see fig. 3.3), a doubling that matches the doubting Thomas story. It is only by putting his hand in the *wounds* of Christ that Thomas will believe in the *healing* power of Christ.[32] The accumulation of visually echoing images continues adding complexity to the layers of meaning: *forever scourged . . .* (M3; see fig. 8.2); *The condemned is led away* (M18; see web 8.5); *"He was oppressed and afflicted"* (M21); *Lord, it is You, I recognize You* (M32; see web 2.2). Rouault's vision of the world—symbolist, sacramental, and incarnational—is captured in both the image and the words, "Even far from Emmaus / I always re-find [*retrouve*] you." Rouault links the wounds and the revelation-recognition: healing comes

---

[31]For a theological exploration of Rouault's decision to conclude both halves of the *Miserere* with Veronica's veil—her act of compassion en route—see James F. Keenan, SJ, "Et Veronique au tendre lin passe encore sur le chemin," in Schloesser, *Mystic Masque*, 437-48. See also Tomáš Halík, "Veronica and the Imprint of the Face," in *Touch the Wounds: On Suffering Trust, and Transformation*, trans. Gerald Turner (Notre Dame, IN: University of Notre Dame Press, 2023), 105-13.

[32]Compare Halík's reflections on Thomas in the chapter "The Gate of the Wounded," in *Touch the Wounds*, 1-10.

(paradoxically) by means of the wounds. Hence the final plate of the *Miserere*: *"It is by his wounds that we are healed"* (M58; see web 8.9).

SEEING THINGS AS THEY ARE

If James Parker's assessment is correct, T. S. Eliot's *The Waste Land* indelibly marked the postwar world in 1922 because it offered "the stark elation of seeing the thing as it is." Rouault offered a similarly stark assessment: *Sunt lacrymae rerum*. There are tears in things. A century later, we are still learning to see things as they are.[33] Natalie Carnes's theological engagement with Gregory of Nyssa aims at recovering beauty as a category adequate to the twenty-first century. Carnes first sets out the problem: "Beauty has been implicated in misogyny, racism, war, and genocide. Even more: It is part of the entertainment that distracts us from these weighty concerns. Let's not be sentimental about beauty. It has a past that calls for sackcloth and ashes."[34] She then sketches a path forward in response:

> Yet beauty's home, I argue, is not the sanitized spaces of bourgeois living. While modernity's articulation of beauty, like strands of philosophy, has often deflected the difficulties of reality like horror and ugliness, Gregory's beauty, like his theological language, is formed in the difficulties of reality. It is a beauty that, while not reducible to ugliness or horror, cannot be found apart from them. . . . Perceiving the beauty of Christ requires right attention to the ugliness of affliction.[35]

---

[33]For example, see Brian McLaren's three seasons of podcasts, *Learning How to See*, hosted by the Center for Action and Contemplation: https://cac.org/podcast/learning-how-to-see/. See also Annie Dillard's now-classic reflections on seeing in *Pilgrim at Tinker Creek* (New York: Harper & Row, 1974).

[34]Natalie Carnes, *Beauty: A Theological Engagement with Gregory of Nyssa* (Eugene, OR: Cascade Books, 2014), xii.

[35]Carnes, *Beauty*, xiv, 152. Carnes explores these issues with a systematic approach in *Image and Presence: A Christological Reflection on Iconoclasm and Iconophilia* (Stanford, CA: Stanford University Press, 2018). "Images need negation to be images," writes Carnes. "The negation at the heart of imagining is not an eradication nor an erasure. Neither is it a degradation of the image. It is a breaking open that leads to greater revelation. It is a way of saying images mediate presence-in-absence and likeness-in-unlikeness. When absence and unlikeness are elided, the image becomes an idol. This is a failure of negation, and without the negation, the image ceases to be an image." (7). See also Hans Urs von Balthasar: "This law extends to the inclusion in Christian beauty of even the Cross and everything else which a worldly aesthetics (even of a realistic kind) discards as no longer bearable. . . . Our task, rather, consists in coming . . . to see his 'formlessness' as a mode of his glory because a mode of his 'love to the end,' to discover in his de-Formation (*Ungestalt*) the mystery of trans-Formation (*Übergestalt*)." Von Balthasar, *The Glory of the Lord: A*

The monumental *Miserere* series, begun in earnest in 1922, is a road trip, a journey toward perceiving beauty rightly, interwoven throughout by the play of surface semblance and deeper reality. There are tears at the very heart of things all along the road. Jesus—who has nowhere to lay his head (Lk 9:58; Mt 8:20)—takes refuge (paradoxically) in the wandering homeless and migrants as well as the incarcerated and forced laborers. Those thinking themselves to be kings are deluded, while self-masking clowns see truly. Moments of re-cognition on the road come and go. Veronica's act of compassion—en route—rebounds in a revelation, a true icon unveiled on her veil: *and Veronica with the soft linen still walks along the road . . .* (M33; see fig. 4.1). This is Rouault's mystic masque: semblance and reality.

Theological Aesthetics, trans. Erasmo Leiva-Merikakis, ed. Joseph Fessio and John Riches, vol. 1, *Seeing the Form* (San Francisco: Ignatius, 1983), 124, 160.

Crown

—See Color Plate 10—

Melanie Spinks

Jesus says, "What people value highly is detestable in God's sight" (Lk 16:15). That is not exactly the way to win friends and influence people, especially given Jesus' audience. This was a people who wanted a king and were looking for one to come. It is interesting what Jesus had to say about the current royal house and its entourage. Regarding John the Baptist, he asks, "What did you go out to see? A man dressed in fine clothes? No, those who wear fine clothes are in kings' palaces" (Mt 11:8). Jesus is the King of kings, seated at the Father's right hand. But he did not come in the royal brand that everyone expected.

With *The Old King* (see web 5.2), Georges Rouault painted a portrait of a king that is anything but a spoiled youth withdrawn from the world, hiding in pampered luxury, decked in fine clothing, sheltered from responsibility, and overly sensitive to the realities and hardships of life. Notice his countenance, rendered with hard lines, delineating a heavy brow and firm jaw; behold the aged, weathered complexion suggested in that texture of grit. Here is a king who is acquainted with grief and suffering. This king rules soundly and soberly with fixed attention and deep contemplation. He wears a jeweled crown of gold as he stewards the weighty responsibilities on his shoulders.

Rouault gives us another depiction of a king. "Here is the man!" (Jn 19:5). This King Jesus also wears a crown: a humble one of twisted thorns (see web I8.1). As it is written, they "twisted together a crown of thorns and set it on his head. They put a staff in his right hand. Then they knelt in front of him and mocked him. 'Hail, king of the Jews!' they said" (Mt 27:29). Jesus also with lowered gaze bears the weight of the world, only in a much more profound way. He too is not soft. He is no victim. Rendered with hard, visceral strokes and gritty impasto, the King of kings soundly and soberly wears a crown in the moment of his grief and suffering as he willingly bears the weight of sin and death laid on his shoulders.

Two kings, two crowns. Messiah ben Joseph, the suffering servant, comes before Messiah ben David, the exalted king.

The composition of two crowns is an important theme in church history. I had drawn the crowns on paper about a decade ago. Contemplating Rouault over this year (particularly as a sculptor, which is my expertise), I was inspired by the visceral feel of texture and line that seem almost carved into the canvas, demarcating shape and gesture with complex surface and depth. I framed the two crowns in the woody medium, nodding to Rouault's strong physicality. Wood in the temple is the material of humanity. The parallels of days three and six in the creation narrative reveal that humanity's destiny is mysteriously bound up in the life of the trees. Throughout the stories that follow, a tree is present at the crux of major human decisions. In my work the wood is tattered and worn, much like our King. Remember that Jesus said, "A servant is not greater than his master" (Jn 15:20). Gold, the metal of divinity, haloes the scene in tondo form, a symbol of a reality that is already and not yet complete. In the temple, gold is wrapped over the wooden objects, symbolizing the humanity and divinity that would mysteriously come together in Christ's incarnation. Silver (notice the cruciform light burst emanating from the center) is the metal of redemption. As the foundation of the temple, this precious metal symbolizes Christ's perfect, pure, and complete redemptive work on our behalf.

This work testifies to our Lord and King, who has taken both crowns on his brow. Because "a servant is not greater than his master," we know that the way up is by following the way down; suffering and dying to self comes before resurrection and rewards. Jesus was "crowned with glory and honor because he suffered death, so that by the grace of God he might taste death for everyone" (Heb 2:9).

So if you are under trial, take heart. John writes that we all enter the kingdom as victors, which means that there are battles to be fought. Our victories in him are rewarded with a crown as well, given by God so that we can give it back to God. "Blessed is the one who perseveres under trial because, having stood the test, that person will receive the crown of life that the Lord has promised to those who love him" (Jas 1:12).

9

Resonating with Rouault

Wesley Vander Lugt

I have discovered that my conversations with people about modern and contemporary visual art—or any art, for that matter—often revolve around the theme of resonance. On the one hand, there are the conversations sparked when a work of art resonates deeply, and we wrestle together to find appropriate language to explain that moving, decentering experience, one that opens the door to encountering God. On the other hand, there are the conversations that arise when a work of art does *not* resonate, raising difficult questions of taste, preference, and the possibility of resonating with art that one does not understand or enjoy.

The essays in this volume demonstrate that the art of Georges Rouault continues to resonate with contemporary viewers today, but that has not always been the case, as several of the contributions show. What is it that makes singular works of art by Rouault—or his whole oeuvre—resonate with some people at some times and not others? What is happening when we claim to resonate with art, and what are the results of such resonance? Can someone cultivate resonance with an artwork, or does it just happen, emerging and fluctuating based on personality, situation, education, and other factors? In this concluding chapter, I address these questions by providing a brief overview of resonance theory in the disciplines of acoustics and sociology, transpose these insights into the arenas of art and spirituality, and then propose how to create conditions for experiencing deeper resonance with the art of Rouault.

INTRODUCING RESONANCE

A maxim commonly attributed to Albert Einstein states that "everything in life is vibration." This is most evident in the field of acoustics, where the vibration and frequencies of one body amplify the frequencies of another. If you strike a tuning fork, for example, and place it in proximity with another tuning fork, they will resonate with each other at the same frequency. The word *resonance* is in fact from the Latin word *resonare*, meaning "to resound." When different bodies resonate with each other, such as the strings on a piano, it is not that the sound of one merely echoes off the other. Rather, the frequencies of one string activate or excite the resonant frequencies of the others: there is an initial sound and a *re-sound*. Resonance is thus a matter of amplifying the unique voice and vibrations of each body.

Acoustic resonance has an analog in social life, as people with different experiences and personalities can resonate when they are in proximity, share a common experience, engage in dialogue, or find other ways of resounding with each other. Broadly speaking, therefore, resonance is what German sociologist Hartmut Rosa calls "a form of relation." Resonance does not occur automatically between all bodies, which means that resonance is not a material or substantial concept but is rather a relational one.[1] Rosa explains how resonance emerges when there is relational responsiveness between two subjects with their own unique energy and agency. You might experience resonance when you meet up with an old friend and enjoy the improvisational back and forth of conversation or when you collaborate meaningfully with a coworker on a project. You can also resonate with other living creatures and even inanimate things such as artwork when you encounter what Rosa calls "an energetically charged form of contact."[2] Resonance is possible even across the greatest possible distance—between human creatures and their Creator God—through dynamics of revelation, encounter, incarnation, grace, and trust.

A resonant relationship may or may not make someone feel happy, since resonance can produce a range of emotions, even so-called negative emotions such as grief or confusion. Resonance does not entail a specific emotional state but is a matter of genuine encounter, responsiveness, and a willingness to be moved, affected, and transformed. Consequently, the opposite of resonance is not *dissonance*—a musical term referring to tones in tension or

---

[1]Hartmut Rosa, *Resonance: A Sociology of Our Relationship with the World*, trans. James C. Wagner (Medford, MA: Polity, 2019), 285, 166.
[2]Rosa, *Resonance*, 137.

disharmony with each other—but rather *alienation*, a mode of relating characterized by indifference, disconnection, and muteness. If, as Rosa maintains, alienation is the prevailing mode of relating in our contemporary world, then "at the root of resonance lies the shout of the unreconciled and the pain of the alienated. At its center is not the denial or repression of that which resists us, but the momentary, only vaguely perceptible certainty of a transcending 'nevertheless.'"[3] In other words, resonance becomes possible when we recognize, like Rouault did, that "there are tears at the heart of things" that call for mercy and reconciliation.

RESONATING WITH ART

In keeping with Rosa's groundbreaking work on resonance, theater and opera director Anne Bogart explains how resonance is not the same as harmony or consonance. Instead, it is a vibrant, creative form of interaction that can shape assumptions, identity, and forms of action in the world. Bogart addresses how resonance can emerge in both artistic creation and reception and how "the reverberations engendered in the moment of an artistic encounter can have a profound effect on the body, on neural pathways, and consequently upon one's actions in the world, and subsequently, in the world at large."[4] Bogart and Rosa agree that resonating with a work of art is not merely about enjoyment but rather is a mutually transformative encounter.[5] Again, the opposite of resonance is not dissonance, but dullness, boredom, and a lack of vibrant exchange.

According to Rosa, resonating with an artwork requires a "strong evaluation," a concept he adopts from philosopher Charles Taylor. A strong evaluation is a determination of value independent of personal desires, preferences, or inclinations. A strong evaluation of Rouault's art would include the determination that his work is valuable and important whatever one's artistic preferences might be. Having a strong evaluation of Rouault's art makes a resonant relationship possible whether or not I am existentially drawn to it or react to it as pleasing. Rosa observes that when we acknowledge a work's inherent value, the work can then demand something from us, including "certain

---

[3]Rosa, *Resonance*, 187-88.
[4]Anne Bogart, *The Art of Resonance* (New York: Menthuen Drama, 2021), 11, 8.
[5]Rosa notes, "What we experience as beauty is the expression of the possibility of a resonant relationship with the world" (*Resonance*, 285).

receptive or productive attitudes and actions." In a world that is "predominantly silent and often repulsive," learning to resonate with art like Rouault's can help us learn resonance within other relationships, to "rehearse various ways of relating to the world" that is broken and bleeding.[6] This is especially true of Rouault's art, which invites us to consider the possibility of resonance with those often relegated to the margins of society and therefore resonance with Jesus, who himself suffered as an outcast.

CULTIVATING RESONANCE WITH ROUAULT'S ART

What happens, however, if when encountering Rouault's art one does not immediately experience the kind of resonance described above? What if his *Miserere* series does not produce "an energetically charged form of contact" and leaves the viewer feeling empty? What if the *Passion* series seems mute, devoid of any demand on one's evaluations, emotions, or beliefs? What if, to put it crudely, someone just does not like Rouault's art and prefers different styles or themes? Is it possible to cultivate resonance with art when it does not naturally or immediately occur?

Ultimately, resonance is not something that we can conjure and control, but we can create certain conditions that enable greater availability for resonance.[7] Anne Bogart speaks of the power of triads in the creative process, and when it comes to creating the right conditions for resonating with the art of Rouault, I would suggest the triad of availability, perception, and response, which loosely corresponds to Bogart's triad of "ready, set, go."[8]

Creating the right conditions for resonance with Rouault's art begins with a commitment to be fully present and available to whatever the artwork has to offer. To be available is to put aside what one might want or expect the artwork to offer, ready to encounter it on its own terms. This receptive disposition is essential for creating space for transformative resonance. Theater artists often speak of this fundamental disposition of availability as the precondition for true creativity. Jacques Lecoq, for example, explains how availability (*disponibilité* in French) is the essential state of "discovery, of openness,

---

[6]Rosa, *Resonance*, 133-34, 185, 286.
[7]For more on the relationship between resonance and uncontrollability, see Hartmut Rosa, *The Uncontrollability of the World*, trans. James C. Wagner (Medford, MA: Polity, 2020).
[8]Bogart, *Art of Resonance*, 70-72.

of freedom to receive" that allows the magic of aesthetic exchange to happen.[9] The same is true with other forms of artistry, whether in the process of artistic creation or in reception. Without availability and a readiness to receive all that the artwork has to offer, the artistic event and exchange will often remain mute and alienating.

Slow art is a growing movement that exists to help people experience resonance with art by receiving visual art as it is meant to be received. In technological and media-saturated societies, we are accustomed to consuming visual art in the same way we consume other images: quickly, inattentively, and impatiently. One of the reasons people often feel exhausted after walking through an art museum is that the average amount of time spent before a painting—which holds a freight of meaning and potential for resonance—is fifteen seconds, and often it is much less than that. Within the scope of our fast-paced, internet-shaped lives, fifteen seconds might seem like a long time, but it is not nearly enough time to be fully present and available for resonance and transformation.[10]

The website for Slow Art Day describes the practice of presence and availability as "passionately retro," recognizing our need to return to a simple act that has a powerful ability to produce joy and resonance: slowing down and gazing. As such, "What sounds like a possibly boring act (if watching paint dry is boring, then watching dry paint must be even more so), is quite the opposite."[11] Being with a work of visual art for more than fifteen seconds is anything but boring, but sometimes you must push through what may seem boring or unproductive to create conditions for resonance.

For example, learning how to resonate with Rouault's *Who does not wear a mask?* (M8, see fig. 2.3), begins with slowing down and committing to be fully present and available, open to a reciprocal encounter in which the work has its own agency and voice. This commitment to be available is driven by a strong evaluation that the work is valuable and contains a compelling offer, an

---

[9]Jacques Lecoq, *The Moving Body: Teaching Creative Theatre*, trans. David Bradby (New York: Methuen Drama, 2009), 36.

[10]Rosa comments, "When guided, timed streams of spectators are provided twenty seconds on average to encounter Mona Lisa's smile, or when viewers are even led past exhibits on conveyor belts (as they are past the Crown Jewels in the Tower of London), then there simply is no time for any sort of adaptive transformation" (*Resonance*, 295).

[11]See "About," Slow Art Day, accessed March 21, 2024, www.slowartday.com/about/.

evaluation driven by acknowledging the artist's skill, the artwork's location in relation to artistic traditions, the reception in both historical and contemporary art worlds, and the inherent value of the art as an act of "sub-creation," to use J. R. R. Tolkien's word for our capacity to image God through creativity and the making of secondary worlds. Part of my hope for this volume is that it will bolster a strong evaluation of Rouault's art—a belief that his work *deserves* our attention—and that it will motivate those who read this book to cultivate availability for deeper resonance with Rouault.

After the surprisingly hard work of slowing down and remaining available for resonance, the next step in creating the right conditions for resonance is to move beyond looking to attentive perception. Anyone can look at Rouault's *Who does not wear a mask?* and say they have seen it, but have they *perceived* it? Recently I was talking to friends who had just returned from Paris, and they shared with me how they "did" the Louvre, the Pompidou, and the Musée d'Orsay, but they did not have time to "do" any others, as if art museums are places to conquer and check off a list of places consumed. (This may be a distinctly American disease, but I am afraid it has global reach.) The prevalence of this conquest mindset is why the founders of Slow Art Day encourage participants to choose five works of art to be with and perceive throughout the morning and then discuss with others over lunch. The goal is not to browse through the whole modern art wing and see as much as you can but to genuinely perceive five works, to appreciate their meaning, contribution, offer, invitation, and demand on you as a viewer.

Marguerite Duras once said, "The art of seeing has to be learned."[12] That, I believe, is another benefit of a volume like this one that brings together various experiences, expertise, and contemporary responses to deepen our perception of Rouault's art and to open new ways of seeing. The various perspectives of biography, technique, art history, cultural analysis, theology, philosophy, and contemporary reception in therapy, ministry, and community organizing all move us beyond mere *looking* at Rouault's art to *perceiving* his art on various levels of meaning. For example, Schloesser's proposal that *Who does not wear a mask?* is the last image of a triptych within the *Miserere* was, at least for me, a revelation of new perception regarding Rouault's intended narrative, that

---

[12]Quoted in Bogart, *Art of Resonance*, 55.

whether we are laboring under force (M6, *Are we not all slaves?* . . . ; see fig. 2.1) or laboring under farce (M7, *believing ourselves to be kings*; see fig. 2.2), we are all clowns, switching between various masks along our life journey.[13] This corroborates with Rouault's encounter with a clown who was traveling with a nomad caravan and Rouault's realization that "the 'clown' was me, was us, nearly all of us. . . . We are all more or less clowns, we all wear a glittering costume."[14] Instead of leaving us in a place of despair, however, we then encounter plate 9 of the *Miserere* and Rouault's way of hinting at hope: *Sometimes it happens that the road is beautiful* (see web 9.1), the road where we meet the Christ who himself took on a mask, experienced our shame, was rejected, despised, and died in order that we might be redeemed and remade. As perception grows, so does the possibility for resonance.

Perceiving a work of art begins with personal encounter and grows through interpersonal dialogue and discovering multiple layers of meaning. The initial encounter with the work does not necessarily need to be pleasant or revealing to hold promise for resonance. In fact, an initial experience of distaste (I don't *like* that), confusion (I don't *get* that), or even revulsion (I don't see how *anyone* could like that), rather than shutting down the possibility for resonance, can be accepted as an opportunity to remain present, ask more questions, stay with the trouble, and submit to the decentering process of mutual discovery. Resonance begins to emerge not only when we perceive and interpret the artwork but also when the artwork begins to interpret us.

A final step toward cultivating the right conditions for resonance with Rouault is adaptive response, which is more robust than mere reaction. An initial reaction to *Who does not wear a mask?* may generate something meaningful, but as Bogart explains, "Response blends both logic and emotion and generates choice."[15] The first choice, of course, is whether to look and be done with the artwork, the experience quickly becoming a fading memory, or to keep returning to the artwork and to add it to what David Dark calls an "attention collection," the works of art and culture that grab and keep your attention in some kind of formative way.[16]

---

[13]See Stephen Schloesser's chapter in this book, under the subhead "Diptych/Triptych: Masks."

[14]Quoted in Franco Mormando, "Of Clowns and Christian Conscience," *America* 199, no. 17 (2008): 18.

[15]Bogart, *Art of Resonance*, 148.

[16]David Dark, *Life's Too Short to Pretend You're Not Religious* (Downers Grove, IL: InterVarsity Press, 2017), 44-58.

The kind of response engendered by a resonant connection with a work of art is not merely an intellectual or emotional responses, although it can include those, but a response of what Rosa calls "adaptive transformation" as we rehearse different ways of relating to the world and to others. Responding to Rouault's artwork is more than a matter of disinterested contemplation, because his art invites us to adopt a different way of seeing and being in the world.[17] Rosa posits:

> What drives modern subjects to visit museums and movie theaters, concert halls and opera houses, and to read novels, poems, and plays as if their lives depended on it is the fact that these activities allow them, at least at a pathic level, to test out and rehearse in a playful, exploratory way widely different modes of relating to the world—solitude and abandonment, melancholy, attachment, exuberance, anger and rage, hate, and love—and thereby moderate and modify their own relationships to the world.[18]

What kind of adaptive response and transformation might emerge when you meet the gaze of Rouault's clown and experience resonance there? Might this engender a response of meeting the gaze of real neighbors whose masks you deem marginal or unpleasant to encounter? How might cultivating resonance with the etched face and eyes of this clown prepare us to find resonance with the Christ who, as Gerard Manley Hopkins poetically expresses, "plays in ten thousand places" through the bodies and lives of God's image bearers?[19]

Furthermore, how might we respond with respect to our own identity and self-discovery as clowns who, to use the language of the apostle Paul, are invited to put on Christ (Rom 13:14; Gal 3:27; Col 3:12)? What does it look like to take off the mask of the old self and put on this new self not as hypocrites but as those longing to be true to who we are already are by an act of grace (Eph 4:24; Col 3:10)? If we all wear a mask, why not wear the best one, the one that helps us see the beautiful road of faith, hope, and love?

These are the kinds of questions that emerge when we move from sustained availability and attentive perception to adaptive response regarding Rouault's

---

[17]For a critique of the supposed "great tradition" of disinterested contemplation as a response to visual art, see Nicholas Wolterstorff, *Art Rethought: The Social Practices of Art* (Oxford: Oxford University Press, 2015).

[18]Rosa, *Resonance*, 285-86.

[19]Gerard Manley Hopkins, "As Kingfishers Catch Fire," in *Poems and Prose* (New York: Penguin, 1953), 51.

Who does not wear a mask? Taken together, these postures and actions of availability, perception, and response can create the conditions for deep and ongoing resonance with the art of Rouault. This resonance is an ongoing and uncontrollable gift that offers fresh encounter, surprising revelation, and adaptive transformation for imagining and embodying resonant relationships in everyday life and with the God who is present in the most unlikely places.

Artistic Conclusion

Leslie Anne Bustard

Rouault's angel is "angelic"—halfway between heaven and earth.
MAKOTO FUJIMURA, *ROUAULT-FUJIMURA: SOLILOQUIES*

"After Rouault's *Appearance on the Road to Emmaus*"[1]

Things into which angels long to look . . .
Cleopas, learning that Jesus was no longer in the tomb,
walked with a friend to Emmaus from Jerusalem
and then listened to a stranger speak
surprising words concerning Christ.
That day was bright and sharp—
bursting into spring-life with its blues, and greens, and reds.
Each single blade of grass, each flower,
each step on the path
proclaimed a new promise to those burning hearts.
At a table spread with bread and wine,
his eyes would be opened,
and a stranger would be revealed.

"After Rouault's *Christ and the Woman Saint*"[2]

I could be that woman kneeling before Christ.
As he leans in, his eyes look for mine.
I bend my head, unsure of his gaze.
His hand offers me a quiet invitation.
Yes, this could be me. It could be Rachel weeping
or Mary sitting at Christ's feet.
Or it could be my daughter, my mother, or
my neighbor. Here is Jesus saying, "Come
to me for rest, all you who are weary."
Sister, for you, too, he offers his hand.

---

[1] Rouault's title for this painting is *Le Christ et les disciples* (*Christ and Disciples*). See web 8.8.
[2] See web AC.1.

Bibliography

"About." Slow Art Day, accessed March 21, 2024. www.slowartday.com/about/.

Alfeyev, Hilarion. *The Spiritual World of Isaac the Syrian*. Collegeville, MN: Cistercian Publications, 2000.

Anderson, Jonathan, and William A. Dyrness. *Modern Art and the Life of a Culture: The Religious Impulses of Modernism*. Downers Grove, IL: InterVarsity Press, 2016.

Art Equity Reimagined. https://artsreimagined.org.

"Artists Make New York's Guggenheim Site of Protest Against Killing of Mahsa Amini." Art Forum, October 24, 2022. www.artforum.com/news/artists-make-new-york-s-guggenheim-site-of-protest-against-killing-of-mahsa-amini-89476.

Balthasar, Hans Urs von. *The Glory of the Lord: A Theological Aesthetics*. Vol. 1, *Seeing the Form*. Translated by Erasmo Leiva-Merikakis. Edited by Joseph Fessio and John Riches. San Francisco: Ignatius, 1983.

Barr, Alfred. *What Is Modern Painting?* New York: Museum of Modern Art, 1943.

Béguin, Albert. *Léon Bloy: A Study in Impatience*. New York: Sheed & Ward, 1947.

Benton, Charlotte, Tim Benton, and Ghislaine Wood, eds. *Art Deco 1910–1939*. Boston: Bulfinch, 2003.

Berry, Wendell. *Sex, Economy, Freedom, and Community*. New York: Pantheon, 1993.

Bibliothèque Nationale de France. "France's National Library Celebrates Proust 100 Years After His Death." RFI, November 18, 2022. www.rfi.fr/en/culture/20221118-french-national-library-celebrates-proust-100-years-after-his-death.

———. "Marcel Proust: La fabrique de l'oeuvre." October 11, 2022–January 22, 2023. www.bnf.fr/fr/agenda/marcel-proust.

Bloy, Léon. *The Desperate Man*. Paris: Alphonse Soirat, 1887.

———. *La Femme pouvre*. Translated by I. J. Collins. South Bend, IN: St. Augustine's, 2015.

———. *Oeuvres de Léon Bloy*. 15 vols. Edited by Joseph Bollery and Jacques Petit. Paris: Bernouard, 1964–1975.

———. *The Poor Woman*. Paris: Mercure de France, 1897.

Bogart, Anne. *The Art of Resonance*. New York: Menthuen Drama, 2021.

Bollery, Joseph, and Jacques Petit, eds. *Oeuvres de Léon Bloy.* 15 vols. Paris: Bernouard, 1964–1975.

Brady, Mary. *Thought and Style in the Works of Léon Bloy.* Washington, DC: Catholic University of America Press, 1946.

Breathe Project. https://breatheproject.org/.

Brown, Peter. *Augustine of Hippo: A Biography.* New ed. Berkeley: University of California Press, 2000.

Brueggemann, Walter. *The Prophetic Imagination.* 40th anniversary ed. Minneapolis: Fortress, 2018.

Burns, Michael. *France and the Dreyfus Affair: A Documentary History.* Boston: Bedford/St. Martins, 1999.

Campbell, Mary Schmidt. *An American Odyssey: The Life and Work of Romare Bearden.* New York: Oxford University Press, 2018.

Carnes, Natalie. *Beauty: A Theological Engagement with Gregory of Nyssa.* Eugene, OR: Cascade Books, 2014.

——— . *Image and Presence: A Christological Reflection on Iconoclasm and Iconophilia.* Stanford, CA: Stanford University Press, 2018.

Charensol, Georges. *Georges Rouault, l'homme et l'oeuvre.* Paris: Quatre Chemins, 1926.

Chesterton, G. K. *Alarms and Discursions.* New York: Dodd, Mead, 1911.

——— . *All Things Considered.* New York: John Lane, 1910.

——— . *Varied Types.* New York: Dodd, Mead, 1903.

——— . *What's Wrong with the World.* New York: Dodd, Mead, 1910.

Claussen, M. A. "'Peregrinatio' and 'Peregrini' in Augustine's 'City of God.'" *Traditio* 46 (1991): 33-75.

Clément, Olivier. *The Roots of Christian Mysticism: Texts from the Patristic Era with Commentary.* Hyde Park, NY: New City, 2013.

Corrin, Jay P. *G. K. Chesterton and Hilaire Belloc: The Battle Against Christendom.* Athens: Ohio University Press, 1981.

Courthion, Pierre. *Rouault.* London: Thames & Hudson, 1962.

Couturier, M. A. "Rouault et le publique ecclésiastique." *L'Art Sacré* (September 1938): 245-47.

Dahme, Stephen. "'Pilgrim of Art': Artistic Autonomy and Christian Commitment in Rouault's Late Work." In *Mystic Masque: Semblance and Reality in George Rouault, 1971–1958,* edited by Stephen Schloesser, 379-87. Boston: McMullen Museum of Art, 2008.

Dark, David. *Life's Too Short to Pretend You're Not Religious.* Downers Grove, IL: InterVarsity Press, 2017.

Deane-Drummond, Celia. *The Ethics of Nature.* Oxford: Wiley-Blackwell, 2004.

Desmond, William. *God and the Between*. Oxford: Wiley-Blackwell, 2008.

Dillard, Annie. *Pilgrim at Tinker Creek*. New York: Harper & Row, 1974.

Doering, Bernard. "Lacrimae Rerum—Tears at the Heart of Things: Jacques Maritain and Georges Rouault." In *Truth Matters: Essays in Honor of Jacques Maritain*, ed. John G. Trapani, 205-23. Washington, DC: Catholic University of America Press, 2004.

Dubois, Elfieda. *Portrait of Léon Bloy*. London: Sheed & Ward, 1951.

Dyrness, William. "The Poetic Formation of Interfaith Identities: The Zapatista Case." In *Arts in Witness in Multifaith Contexts*, edited by Roberta King and William Dyrness, 204-19. Downers Grove, IL: InterVarsity Press, 2019.

——— . *Poetic Theology: God and the Poetics of Everyday Life*. Grand Rapids, MI: Eerdmans, 2011.

——— . *Rouault: A Vision of Suffering and Salvation*. Grand Rapids, MI: Eerdmans, 1971.

——— . "Rouault and Maritain and the Shaping of a Catholic Modernity." Paper presented at The Artist as Truth Teller symposium on Georges Rouault, Institute Catholique de Paris, June 17, 2022.

——— . "Seeing Through the Darkness: Georges Rouault's Vision of Christ." *Image 67* (Winter 2020). https://imagejournal.org/article/seeing-through-the-darkness/.

Dyrness, William, and Maria Fee. "Art as Practical Theology." In *Handbook of Art and Theology*. London: Bloomsbury, forthcoming.

Edwards, Denis. *The Natural World and God: Theological Explorations*. Adelaide, Australia: ATF, 2017.

Eksteins, Modris. *Rites of Spring: The Great War and the Birth of the Modern Age*. Boston: Houghton Mifflin, 1989.

Eliot, T. S. *Collected Poems (1902–1962)*. New York: Ecco, 1991.

Eliot, T. S., Valerie Eliot, and Ezra Pound. *The Waste Land: A Facsimile and Transcript of the Original Drafts Including the Annotations of Ezra Pound*. Rev. ed. New York: Liveright, 2022.

Evdokimov, Paul. *The Art of the Icon: A Theology of Beauty*. Redondo Beach, CA: Oakwood, 1990.

"Exploring COVID-19 Impacts Through Visual Art." New Sun Rising, accessed March 22, 2024. www.newsunrising.org/virtual-gallery-exploring-covid-19-impacts/.

Fine, Ruth, ed. *The Art of Romare Bearden*. Washington, DC: National Gallery of Art, 2003.

Flora, Holly, and Soo Yun Kang. *Georges Rouault's* Miserere et Guerre: *This Anguished World of Shadows*. Exhibition catalog. New York: Museum of Biblical Art, 2006.

Fondation Georges Rouault. https://rouault.org/en/.

Francis (pope). *Laudato Si': On Care for Our Common Home*. Vatican City: Libreria Editrice Vaticana, 2015.

Fujimura, Makoto. *Refractions: A Journey of Faith, Art, Culture*. Colorado Springs: Nav-Press, 2009.

Genesis Collective. www.gcollective.org.

George, Waldemar, and Geneviève Nouaille-Rouault. *L'Univers de Rouault*. Paris: Screpel, 1971.

"Georges Rouault, Le clown blessé [1932]." Centre Pompidou, accessed March 18, 2024. www.centrepompidou.fr/en/ressources/oeuvre/cKazzn.

Getlin, Frank, and Dorothy Getlin. *Georges Rouault's* Miserere. Milwaukee: Bruce, 1964.

Golan, Romy. *Modernity and Nostalgia: Art and Politics in France Between the Wars*. New Haven, CT: Yale University Press, 1995.

Goldstein, Bill. *The World Broke in Two: Virginia Woolf, T. S. Eliot, D. H. Lawrence, E. M. Forster, and the Year That Changed Literature*. New York: Picador, 2018.

Greene, Carroll. *Romare Bearden: The Prevalence of Ritual*. New York: Museum of Modern Art, 1971.

Groody, Daniel, and Gustavo Gutiérrez. *The Preferential Option for the Poor Beyond Theology*. Notre Dame, IN: University of Notre Dame Press, 2014.

"Guide to the Beaver Valley Labor History Society Collection, 1909–1981." USL Digital Collections, University of Pittsburgh, October 28, 2022. https://digital.library .pitt.edu/islandora/object/pitt%3AUS-PPiU-ais198108/viewer.

Gunton, Colin. *The One, the Three and the Many*. Cambridge: Cambridge University Press, 1993.

Halík, Tomáš. *Touch the Wounds: On Suffering Trust, and Transformation*. Translated by Gerald Turner. Notre Dame, IN: University of Notre Dame Press, 2023.

Harris, Ruth. *Dreyfus: Politics, Emotion, and the Scandal of the Century*. New York: Metropolitan Books, 2010.

Hart, David Bentley. *The Hidden and the Manifest: Essays in Theology and Metaphysics*. Grand Rapids, MI: Eerdmans, 2017.

——— . *Theological Territories: A David Bentley Hart Digest*. Notre Dame, IN: University of Notre Dame Press, 2020.

Hertneky, Paul. *Rust Belt Boy: Stories of an American Childhood*. Peterborough, NH: Bauhan, 2016.

Hibbs, Thomas. *A Theology of Creation: Ecology, Art, and Laudato Si'*. Notre Dame, IN: University of Notre Dame Press, 2023.

Hibbs, Thomas, and Makoto Fujimura. *Rouault-Fujimura: Soliloquies*. Baltimore: Square Halo Books, 2009.

Hoffman, Hans. *Color Creates Light: Studies with Hans Hoffman*. Salt Spring Island, BC: Trillistar InterArts, 2011.

Hollis, Matthew. *The Waste Land: A Biography of a Poem*. New York: Norton, 2022.

Hopkins, Gerard Manley. *Poems and Prose*. New York: Penguin, 1953.

Hunter, James Davison. *To Change the World: The Irony, Tragedy, and Possibility of Christianity in the Late Modern World*. New York: Oxford University Press, 2010.

Inside Out Project. www.insideoutproject.net/.

Jackson, Kevin. *Constellation of Genius: 1922: Modernism Year One*. New York: Farrar, Straus & Giroux, 2013.

Jenkins, Willis. *Ecologies of Grace: Environmental Ethics and Christian Theology*. Oxford: Oxford University Press, 2008.

Jewell, Edward Alden. "Religious Art Seen in Modern Display: 24 Painters Show Works in an Exhibition to Aid Grosvenor Neighborhood House Avery's Bare Style." *New York Times*, January 9, 1946.

Johnson, Elizabeth. *Ask the Beasts: Darwin and the God of Love*. London: Bloomsbury, 2014.

Joyce, James, and Catherine Flynn. *The Cambridge Centenary Ulysses: The 1922 Text with Essays and Notes*. New York: Cambridge University Press, 2022.

Kang, Soo Yun. *Rouault in Perspective: Contextual and Theoretical Study of His Art*. Lanham, MD: International Scholars, 2000.

Karmel, Pepe. "The Negro Artist's Dilemma: Bearden, Picasso, and Pop Art." In *Romare Bearden, American Modernist*, edited by Ruth Fine and Jaqueline Francis, 249-68. Washington, DC: National Gallery of Art, 2011.

Kearney, Richard, and Kascha Semonovitch, eds. *Phenomenologies of the Stranger: Between Hostility and Hospitality*. New York: Fordham University Press, 2011.

Keenan, James F. "Et Veronique au tendre lin passe encore sur le chemin." In *Mystic Masque: Semblance and Reality in Georges Rouault, 1871–1958*, edited by Stephen Schloesser, 437-48. Boston: McMullen Museum of Art, 2008.

Kosinski, Dorothy M. "Gustave Moreau's 'La Vie de l'humanité': Orpheus in the Context of Religious Syncretism, Universal Histories, and Occultism." *Art Journal* 46, no. 1 (Spring 1987): 9-14.

Klee, Paul. *Creative Confession and Other Writing*. London: Tate, 2013. Kindle.

Kort, Wesley. *C. S. Lewis: Then and Now*. Oxford: Oxford University Press, 2001.

Lambert, Malcolm. *Franciscan Poverty. The Doctrine of the Absolute Poverty of Christ and the Apostles in the Franciscan Order, 1210–1323*. St. Bonaventura, NY: Franciscan Institute, 1998.

Larkin, Maurice. *Church and State After the Dreyfus Affair: The Separation Issue in France*. London: Macmillan, 1974.

L'Atelier Primavera et la décoration moderne, 1913–1923. Paris: Magasins du Printemps, 1923.

Lecoq, Jacques. *The Moving Body: Teaching Creative Theatre*. Translated by David Bradby. New York: Methuen Drama, 2009.

Lewis, C. S. *Christian Reflections*. Edited by Walter Hooper. Grand Rapids, MI: Eerdmans, 1967.

———. *God in the Dock*. Edited by Walter Hooper. Grand Rapids, MI: Eerdmans, 1970.

———. *Screwtape Proposes a Toast and Other Pieces*. London: Fontana, 1965.

Lock, Charles. "Michel de Certeau: Walking the Via Negativa." *Paragraph* 22, no. 2 (1999): 184-98.

Loder, James E. *The Logic of the Spirit: Human Development in Theological Perspective*. San Francisco: Jossey-Bass, 1998.

Logan, Steven. "Literary Theorist." In *The Cambridge Companion to C. S. Lewis*, edited by Rob MacSwain and Michael Ward, 29-42. Cambridge: Cambridge University Press, 2010.

Lossky, Vladimir, and Léonide Ouspensky. *The Meaning of Icons*. Translated by G. E. H. Palmer and E. Kadloubovsky. Yonkers, NY: St. Vladimir's Seminary Press, 1982.

Lynch, Cyprian, ed. *A Poor Man's Legacy: An Anthology of Franciscan Poverty*. St. Bonaventura, NY: Franciscan Institute, 1988.

Lyotard, Jean-François. *The Postmodern Condition: A Report on Knowledge*. Translated by Geoff Bennington. Minneapolis: University of Minnesota Press, 2010.

Mackey, Abby. "The Genesis Collective Gives Beaver County Artists a Voice." *Pittsburgh Post-Gazette*, August 11, 2022. www.post-gazette.com/life/goodness/2022/08/11/genesis-collective-beaver-art-mural/stories/202207240005.

Marcel, Gabriel. *Homo Viator*. New York: Harper & Row, 1962.

Marchiori, Giuseppe. *Rouault*. New York: Reynal, 1965.

Marcoulesco, Ileana. *Georges Rouault: The Inner Light*. Houston: Menil Collection, 1996.

Marion, Jean-Luc. *Crossing the Visible*. Stanford, CA: Stanford University Press, 2003.

Maritain, Jacques. *Antimoderne*. Paris: Ed. De la Revue des Jeunes, 1922.

———. *Art and Scholasticism*. Translated by James Scanlan. New York: Scribner & Sons, 1930.

———. *Georges Rouault*. New York: Harry N. Abrams, 1954.

———. "Georges Rouault." *Cahiers Jacques Maritain*, no. 12 (November 1985): 24.

————. *Untrammeled Approaches*. Notre Dame, IN: University of Notre Dame Press, 2017.

Maritain, Raïssa. *Les Grandes Amitiés*. 10th ed. Bruges: Desclée de Brouwer, 1965.

————. *We Have Been Friends Together; Adventures in Grace: Memoirs*. Translated by Michael S. Sherwin and Julie Kernan. South Bend, IN: St. Augustine's, 2016.

Marusic, Kristina. "These Are the New Titans of Plastic." *Sierra: The Magazine of the Sierra Club*, September 15, 2022. www.sierraclub.org/sierra/2022-3-fall/feature /these-are-new-titans-plastic-shell-pennsylvania-fracking.

McGrath, Alister. *C. S. Lewis: A Life*. Carol Stream, IL: Tyndale House, 2013.

————. *The Intellectual World of C. S. Lewis*. Oxford: Wiley-Blackwell, 2013.

McLaren, Brian. *Learning How to See*. Podcast. https://cac.org/podcast/learning -how-to-see/.

McManners, John. *Church and State in France 1870–1914*. New York: Harper & Row, 1972.

Merton, Thomas. "The Vatican Council and Sacred Art." *The Merton Seasonal* 35, no. 3 (Fall 2010): 3-5. www.merton.org/ITMS/Seasonal/35/35-3Merton.pdf.

Michalczyk, Susan A. "The Aesthetics of Shock: Baudelaire, Benjamin, Rouault." In *Mystic Masque: Semblance and Reality in George Rouault, 1971–1958*, edited by Stephen Schloesser, 193-204. Boston: McMullen Museum of Art, 2008.

Miles, Margaret. "Rouault and the Dynamics of Self-Deception." In *Mystic Masque: Semblance and Reality in George Rouault, 1971–1958*, edited by Stephen Schloesser, 109-16. Boston: McMullen Museum of Art, 2008.

Miller, Patti. "Reading Proust Aloud: 'How Can It Be That Deeply Flawed and Terrible Humans Have the Capacity to Create?'" *Guardian*, 12 November 2022. www .theguardian.com/books/2022/nov/12/reading-proust-aloud-how-can-it-be -that-deeply-flawed-and-terrible-humans-have-the-capacity-to-create.

Miller, Perry. *Errand into the Wilderness*. Cambridge, MA: Harvard University Press, 1956.

Morelli, George. "Healing the Infirmity of Sin: A Spiritual Nutshell." Antiochian Orthodox Christian Archdiocese of North America, 2009. http://ww1.antiochian .org/content/healing-infirmity-sin-spiritual-nutshell.

Mormando, Franco. "Of Clowns and Christian Conscience." *America* 199, no. 17 (2008): 18-20.

Nguyễn, vănThanh. *What Does the Bible Say About Strangers, Migrants, and Refugees?* New York: New City, 2021.

Nichols, Aiden. "The Dominicans and the Journal *L'Art Sacré*." *New Blackfriars* (January 2007): 25-45.

Noble, Louis. *The Life and Works of Thomas Cole*. Cambridge, MA: Harvard University Press, 1964.

North, Michael. *Reading 1922: A Return to the Scene of the Modern*. New York: Oxford University Press, 1999.

Nowinski, Sheila. "Creating Rouault's Legacy: 1945–1965." In *Mystic Masque: Semblance and Reality in Georges Rouault, 1871–1958*, edited by Stephen Schloesser, 399-409. Boston: McMullen Museum of Art, 2008.

Oreskes, Naomi. Introduction to *Encyclical on Climate Change and Inequality: On Care for Our Common Home*. London: Melville House, 2016.

Örsy, Ladislas. "Poverty: The Modern Problem." *The Way*, supplement 9, "Poverty" (Spring 1970): 7-15.

Padgett, Christopher. *Boom and Bust: A Journey from Beaver County to the Gulf Coast*. RiverWise, 2022. www.youtube.com/watch?v=PcD4zTV_RBw.

———. *Our Beauty, Our Place: Public Art in Beaver County, PA*. Genesis Collective, September 3, 2021. https://youtu.be/pVA3tC86ins.

Parker, James. "T. S. Eliot Saw All This Coming." *Atlantic*, January–February 2023. www.theatlantic.com/magazine/archive/2023/01/ts-eliot-the-waste-land-poem-anniversary/672231/.

Pascal, Blaise. *Pensées*. Translated by A. J. Krailsheimer. New York: Penguin Classics, 1995.

Patton, Sharon F. "A Divine Presence in the Art of Romare Bearden." *Prism* 15 (1992): 29-32.

———. "Memory and Metaphor: The Art of Romare Bearden, 1940–1987." In *Memory and Metaphor: The Art of Romare Bearden, 1940–1987*, 18-110. New York: Oxford University Press, 1991.

Paul VI (pope). *Sacrosanctum Concilium*. 1963.

Phan, Peter C., ed. *Christian Theology in the Age of Migration: Implications for World Christianity*. Lanham, MD: Lexington Books, 2020.

Pieper, Josef. *On Hope*. San Francisco: Ignatius, 1986.

———. *Über die Hoffnung*. Leipzig: J. Hegner, 1935.

Pinder, Kymberly N. "Deep Waters: Rebirth, Transcendence, and Abstraction in Romare Bearden's Passion of Christ." In *Romare Bearden, American Modernist*, edited by Ruth Fine and Jaqueline Francis, 145-61. Washington, DC: National Gallery of Art, 2011.

Place, Eric de, and Molly Kiick. "A Cautionary Tale of Petrochemicals from Pennsylvania." Ohio River Valley Institute, November 30, 2021. https://ohiorivervalley institute.org/author/molly-kiick/.

Polimeni, Emmanuela. *Léon Bloy, the Pauper Prophet 1846–1917*. New York: Philosophical Library, 1951.

Ponticus, Evagrius. *The Praktikos and Chapters on Prayer*. Translated by John E. Bamberger. Mulgrave, VIC: Cistercian Publications, 1970.

Pontifical Commission on Sacred Art. "Documents: 1952 Instructions on Sacred Art." *The Furrow* 6, no. 6 (June 1955): 368-72.

Possenti-Ghiglia, Nora. *Cahiers Jacques Maritain*. Kolbsheim, France: Cercle d'Etudes Jacques et Raïssa Maritain, 1985.

Printemps, Atelier Primavera. *L'Atelier Primavera et la décoration moderne, 1913–1923*. Paris: Magasins du Printemps, 1923.

Rasula, Jed. *What the Thunder Said: How* The Waste Land *Made Poetry Modern*. Princeton, NJ: Princeton University Press, 2022.

Read, Piers Paul. *The Dreyfus Affair: The Scandal That Tore France in Two*. New York: Bloomsbury, 2012.

Rookmaaker, Hans. *Modern Art and the Death of a Culture*. Downers Grove, IL: InterVarsity Press, 1970.

Rosa, Hartmut. *Resonance: A Sociology of Our Relationship with the World*. Translated by James C. Wagner. Medford, MA: Polity, 2019.

———. *The Uncontrollability of the World*. Translated by James C. Wagner. Medford, MA: Polity, 2020.

Rossi-Keen, Pamela. "Peering Through the Window: Divergent Treatments of Evil in the Works of Olivier Messiaen and Georges Rouault." In *Considering Evil and Human Wickedness*, edited by Daniel Keen and Pamela Rossi-Keen, 67-81. Oxford: Interdisciplinary, 2004. www.yumpu.com/en/document/read/6627874/daniel-e-keen-pamela-rossi-keen-inter-disciplinarynet.

Rouault, Georges. *Miserere*. Boston: Trianon, 1963.

———. *Soliloques*. Edited by Claude Roulet. Neuchâtel: Ides et Calendes, 1944.

———. *Souvenirs Intimes*. Paris: Frapier, 1926.

Rouault, Georges, and André Suarès. "Moreau." *L'Art et les Artistes* (April 1926).

"Rouault: Seeing Christ in the Darkness." Bowden Collections, accessed March 18, 2024. www.bowdencollections.com/rouault-darkness.html.

"Sacred Art and Sacred Furnishings." In *The Documents of Vatican II*, by Walter M. Abbott, SJ, 174-76. New York: Guild, 1966.

Sanzillo, Tom, and Kathy Hipple. "IEEFA Report: Financial Risks Loom for Shell's Pennsylvania Petrochemicals Complex." Institute for Energy Economics and Financial Analysis, June 4, 2020. https://ieefa.org/articles/ieefa-report-financial-risks-loom-shells-pennsylvania-petrochemicals-complex.

Schaefer, Jame. "The Virtuous Cooperator." *Worldviews: Environment, Culture, Religion* 7 (2003): 171-95.

Schloesser, Stephen. "1871–1901: Realism, Symbolism, Mystic Modernism." In *Mystic Masque: Semblance and Reality in George Rouault, 1971–1958*, edited by Stephen Schloesser, 23-43. Boston: McMullen Museum of Art, 2008.

——— . "1902–1920: The Hard Metier of Unmasking." In *Mystic Masque: Semblance and Reality in George Rouault, 1971–1958*, edited by Stephen Schloesser, 79-104. Boston: McMullen Museum of Art, 2008.

——— . "1921–1929: Jazz Age Graphic Shock." In *Mystic Masque: Semblance and Reality in George Rouault, 1971–1958*, edited by Stephen Schloesser, 133-56. Boston: McMullen Museum of Art, 2008.

——— . "1939–1958: Perpetual Pelegrinas." In *Mystic Masque: Semblance and Reality in George Rouault, 1971–1958*, edited by Stephen Schloesser, 341-56. Boston: McMullen Museum of Art, 2008.

——— . "Georges Rouault: Masked Redemption." In *Jazz Age Catholicism: Mystic Modernism in Postwar Paris, 1919–1933*, 213-44. Toronto: University of Toronto Press, 2005.

——— . "History as Revelation: Léon Bloy, Flannery O'Connor, and Symbolist Exegesis of the Commonplace." In *Revelation and Convergence: Flannery O'Connor and the Catholic Intellectual Tradition*, edited by Mark Bosco and Brent Little, 10-50. Washington, DC: Catholic University of America Press, 2017.

——— . *Jazz Age Catholicism: Mystic Modernism in Postwar Paris, 1919–1933*. Toronto: University of Toronto Press, 2005.

——— , ed. *Mystic Masque: Semblance and Reality in Georges Rouault, 1871–1958*. Boston: McMullen Museum of Art, 2008. https://archive.org/details/mystic masquesembooschl.

——— . "Notes on the Miserere Plates Exhibited in *Mystic Masque*." In *Mystic Masque: Semblance and Reality in George Rouault, 1971–1958*, edited by Stephen Schloesser, 157-80. Boston: McMullen Museum of Art, 2008.

Schneider, Laurie. "Donatello's Bronze David." *The Art Bulletin* 55, no. 2 (1973): 213. https://doi.org/10.2307/3049095

Schultenover, David, ed. *The Reception of Pragmatism in France and the Rise of Catholic Modernism, 1890–1914*. Washington, DC: Catholic University of America Press, 2009.

Schwartz, Richard C., and Martha Sweezy. *Internal Family Systems Therapy*. New York: Guilford, 2019.

Schwartzman, Myron. *Romare Bearden: His Life and Art*. New York: Harry N. Abrams, 1990.

Sherman, Daniel J. *The Construction of Memory in Interwar France.* Chicago: University of Chicago Press, 1999.

Sherrard, Phillip. *The Sacred in Life and Art.* Limni, Greece: Denise Harvey, 2004.

Siegel, Daniel J. *Mindsight: The New Science of Personal Transformation.* New York: Random House, 2010.

Siegel, Daniel, and Richard Schwartz. *The Myth of Unitary Self: A Dialogue on the Multiplicity of Mind.* DVD. Eau Claire, WI: PESI, 2015.

Silver, Kenneth E. *Esprit de Corps: The Art of the Parisian Avant-garde and the First World War, 1914–1925.* Princeton, NJ: Princeton University Press, 1989.

Silverman, Debra. *Van Gogh and Gauguin: The Search for Sacred Art.* New York: Farrar, Straus & Giroux, 2000.

Soby, James Thrall. *Georges Rouault: Paintings and Prints.* New York: Museum of Modern Art, 1945.

Sorett, Josef. *Spirit in the Dark: A Religious History of Racial Aesthetics.* New York: Oxford University Press, 2016.

Stăniloae, Dumitru. *Orthodox Spirituality: A Practical Guide for the Faithful and a Definitive Manual for the Scholar.* Waymart, PA: St. Tikhon's Seminary Press, 2003.

Taylor, Brandon. "The 1920s: Looking Forward, Looking Back." In *Make It Modern: A History of Art in the 20th Century*, 78-143. New Haven, CT: Yale University Press, 2022.

Thomas Aquinas. *Summa Theologica.* Vol. 4. Translated by Fathers of the English Dominican Province. Westminster, MD: Christian Classics, 1981.

Turner, Sidney. "The Vow of Poverty." PhD diss., Catholic University of America, 1929.

Vickers, Robert J. "Analysis: Gov. Tom Corbett's Plan to Give Tax Break for Shell Refinery Raises Questions About Jobs." PennLive, June 21, 2012. www.pennlive.com/midstate/2012/06/analysis_gov_tom_corbetts_plan.html.

Waldemar, George, and Geneviève Nouaille-Rouault. *L'Univers de Rouault.* Paris: Screpel, 1971.

Watters, Liam. "Creative Lift Off: How the Genesis Collective Is Shaping an Arts Community in Beaver County." Pittsburgh Foundation, August 1, 2022. https://pittsburghfoundation.org/creative-lift-off.

Wolterstorff, Nicholas. *Art Rethought: The Social Practices of Art.* Oxford: Oxford University Press, 2015.

List of Contributors

Sandra Bowden is a visual artist, patron, and art collector with Bowden Collections. Bowden has been interpreting Scripture and her own spiritual walk through mixed media for more than forty years. Bowden's work has been featured in books, magazines, and gallery shows across the United States, Canada, Italy, and Jerusalem. Her work fuses the vivid yet traditional imagery of the Old Testament—stone tablets and artifacts, Hebrew inscriptions, architectural depictions—with images of Christ's Passion, important music scores, and God's natural creations.

Leslie Anne Bustard was vice president of Square Halo Books and host of *The Square Halo* podcast. She was the coeditor of *Wild Things and Castles in the Sky: A Guide to Choosing the Best Books for Children* (2022) and the author of *The Goodness of the Lord in the Land of the Living: Selected Poems* (2023) and *Tiny Thoughts That I've Been Thinking: Selected Writings of Leslie Anne Bustard* (posthumous, 2024). Leslie was also the contributor to the Cultivating Project, the Black Barn Online, Story Warren, Anselm Society, and Calia Press, as well as having her poetry appear in other journals.

William A. Dyrness is senior professor of theology and culture and dean emeritus at Fuller Theological Seminary. A scholar of theology and the visual arts, Dyrness wrote one the first Protestant theological engagements with the work of Georges Rouault, called *Rouault: A Vision of Suffering and Salvation* (1971). His more recent work includes *Poetic Theology: God and the Poetics of Everyday Life* (2011), *Modern Art and the Life of a Culture* (with Jonathan Anderson, 2016), *The Origin of Protestant Aesthetics in Early Modern Europe: Calvin's Reformation Poetics* (2019), and *The Facts on the Ground: A Wisdom Theology of Culture* (2022).

Christina Felten is an artist and social worker. Creativity is deeply woven into her story through curiosity, wonder, self-worth, and therapy. She works primarily with heavy-body acrylics, building up layers of texture with modeling paste and other mediums before adding color. Her work is bold and expressive, yet her aim is to create pieces that invite meditation and calm. She paints intuitively, allowing drips, visible brushstrokes, and other imperfections to remain as a way of honoring radical self-acceptance. She loves playing with contrast, depth, and composition, and creating both dramatic and quiet areas within paintings. For Christina, art is a form of therapy, meditative and centering in a world that often feels too loud, too much, and too chaotic, holding space for the mystery where spoken language often fails.

Bryn Gillette is a painter and art teacher defined by his identity as an ambassador of Jesus Christ, a husband, and a father. He has been teaching full time for fourteen years while maintaining an active studio art practice. Gillette is currently the high school art and art history teacher at Charlotte Christian School, where his four children also attend. He is the cofounder of TeamOne:27, a nonprofit dedicated to serving the needs of Haitian orphans, and has spent much of his artistic time in the last decade as an advocate of Haiti's restoration. Whether raising up a generation of kingdom-hearted artists in the classroom, visualizing the global church as the Lausanne Movement's artist-in-residence, painting live as a visual scribe at a spiritual event, or serving a client artistically in his studio, Bryn's heart is to "make God's kingdom visible."

Thomas Hibbs is J. Newton Rayzor Sr. Professor of Philosophy and dean emeritus at Baylor University, having previously served as tutor at Thomas Aquinas College, professor and department chair of philosophy at Boston College, and president of the University of Dallas. His most recent publications include *Theology of Creation: Ecology, Art, and Laudato Si'* (2023), *Shows About Nothing: Nihilism in Popular Culture* (2020), and *Wagering on an Ironic God: Pascal on Philosophy and Faith* (2017). His book *Soliloquies* (2009) explores the connection between the work of Georges Rouault and Makoto Fujimura.

Josh Jensen was trained in representational oil paintings, but his work has evolved to more abstract themes in mixed media that focus on color and movement. His body of work is influenced by his established career as a marriage and family therapist. He finds that art and psychotherapy are perfect informants for each other. His distinct style continues to progress as he expands his vocabulary and practice of mark making and color composition. His work has always sought to strike a balance of exploration, seeking a high degree of access to "accidents" and commitment, using established techniques and standards. Josh believes the best art has a strong concept along with a strong aesthetic. He hopes that his work expresses a sense of gratitude and beauty, urging the viewer to see more than what initially meets the eye.

Rev. Helms Jarrell is an interdisciplinary artist who weaves stories together using mixed media, ceramics, needlework, and jewelry-making techniques. Her work intentionally integrates art, faith, and culture into organizing strategies to build people power and social change. Using the language of culture, art, story, and ritual, she aims to cultivate folks' sense of belonging, connection, and interdependence through visual art, engaging community, and facilitating workshops around community and justice issues. Helms directs a neighborhood-based community organization called QC Family Tree, and she is the organizing pastor of a church plant called Beloved Community Charlotte.

Soo Y. Kang is professor of art history in the Department of Art & Design and Honors College at Chicago State University. Her research areas are religious art and women's art of the twentieth and twenty-first century. She has presented and written on artists such as Paula Rego, Georges Rouault, Dorothea Tanning, and Maria Tomasula. Kang's books include *Rouault in Perspective: Contextual and Theoretical Study of His Art* (2000), *The Art of Maria Tomasula: Embodiment and Splendor* (2023), and the coauthored exhibition catalog *Georges Rouault's* Miserere et Guerre: *This Anguished World of Shadows* (2006).

Joel Klepac is a painter, licensed therapist, adjunct faculty in the School of Counseling and Pastoral Care at Asbury Theological Seminary, and psychology coordinator for the Orthodox Christian Association of Medicine, Psychology, and Religion. He studied fine art painting at Asbury University, where he was first inspired by the work of Georges Rouault. Later he worked in Romania for nine years, where he became Eastern Orthodox while working with children at risk and youth living on the street. During that time, he held painting exhibits in the local art guild gallery and designed and created oil paintings for the community center chapel. After completing a master of arts in marriage and family counseling at Asbury Theological Seminary, he worked in community mental health and then in a college mental health center until the present. Besides being a licensed marriage and family therapist, he was the art director of and a contributor to *Common Prayer Liturgy for Ordinary Radicals*, and his latest painting exhibit was titled "Apparition, Brilliance and Connection." He is also the author of *Miserere Mei: A Journey of Self-Discovery Through the Art of Georges Rouault* (2023).

Ryan Lauterio is a working studio artist specializing in painting, drawing, studio methods, curation, and art and theology. Ryan holds a bachelor of arts and a master of arts in studio art from CSU Sacramento, a master of fine arts in painting and printmaking from Virginia Commonwealth University, and three years of pastoral seminary-style theological training through Remnant Church in Richmond. Ryan is the director and curator of Shockoe Artspace and assistant professor as well as drawing studio area head at Virginia Commonwealth University. Ryan's studio work has been exhibited worldwide and included in several private and corporate collections, such as Capital One's extensive contemporary art collection. He has more recently codirected a multi-award-winning feature documentary called *The Builder* with photographer Nick Sietz. He is also the cofounder of the Maker Institute of Studio Art and Theology and has developed a comprehensive K-12 Christian art and education curriculum for homeschooling and Christian private schools called Made Makers—Christian Art Education.

Dave Reinhardt enjoys coaching people to improve their presentation skills as executive faculty with Ty Boyd, Inc. He studied English with a focus on creative writing at Ohio Wesleyan University and went on to study the intersection of theology and theater at the University of St Andrews in Scotland, where he received a master's and doctoral degree. In his spare time, he enjoys performing with Improv Charlotte and playing pennywhistle with the worship team at Storyhill Church. Dave lives with his family in Davidson, North Carolina.

James Romaine is professor of art at Lander University and the cofounder and vice president of the Association of Scholars of Christianity in the History of Art. He has edited several volumes, including *Art as Spiritual Perception: Essays in Honor of E. John Walford* (2012), *ReVisioning: Methodological Studies of Christianity in the History of Art* (with Linda Stratford, 2014), and *Beholding*

Christ and Christianity in African American Art (with Phoebe Wolfskill, 2017). His current book projects include *A History of Christianity in African American Art* and *The Three Dimensions of a Complete Artist: The Aesthetic of the Rev. Dr. Martin Luther King Jr in the Art of Tim Rollins and K. O. S.* His videos can be seen on YouTube at Seeing Art History.

Pamela Rossi-Keen is executive director of the Genesis Collective, whose mission is to support artists and their work, connect the public to art and creativity, and celebrate and enhance community development through art and storytelling. In addition, Rossi-Keen is adjunct instructor of humanities and the arts at Robert Morris University, an arts curriculum author for Lincoln Park Performing Arts Center, and has served as curriculum coordinator for Aliquippa Impact, a youth development organization in her hometown. Rossi-Keen serves in countywide education reform efforts and on various boards connecting art, education, and the public. She earned her doctorate from the Ohio University School of Interdisciplinary Arts, where she first began diving into Rouault's special nexus of art, culture, community, and theology.

Philippe Rouault is the great-grandson of Georges Rouault, and he works in investment banking and as a partner in a multifamily office. Alongside his professional activities, Philippe has been closely involved with the Rouault Foundation and his family to promote the works of Georges Rouault in the United States and around the world. He helped organize the Rouault and Fujimura exhibition at the Dillon Gallery in New York and represented the family most recently at the *Miserere* exhibit at Duke University.

Stephen Schloesser, SJ, is professor of history at Loyola University Chicago and the founding director of Loyola's Jesuit Heritage Research Center, having held previous positions at Boston College and the Weston Jesuit School of Theology. Schloesser is the author of *Visions of Amen: The Theological Aesthetics of Olivier Messiaen* (2014) and *Jazz Age Catholicism: Mystic Modernism in Postwar Paris, 1919–1933* (2005). In 2008, commemorating the fiftieth anniversary of Georges Rouault's death, Schloesser curated the Boston College exhibit and edited the accompanying catalog, titled *Mystic Masque: Semblance and Reality in Georges Rouault, 1871–1958.*

Melanie Spinks received a master of fine arts from Georgia State Atlanta in sculpture with a focus on ancient art-making and aesthetics. She went on to pursue her master of arts from Gordon-Conwell Theological Seminary to explore the spiritual and aesthetic connections between art, design, awe, and desire. Melanie has worked in the museum and luxury-design markets as an artist, builder, and curator for blue-chip designers and clientele, and she currently works as a researcher and strategist of digital design with Slalom in Charlotte, North Carolina. In her art-making, Melanie works in a variety of mediums, and she also has spoken widely on the intersection of art, spirituality, and creativity.

Rev. Wesley Vander Lugt is a pastor-theologian, writer, educator, nonprofit leader, and arts advocate. Vander Lugt is adjunct professor of theology and acting director of the Leighton Ford Initiative for Theology, the Arts, and Gospel Witness at Gordon-Conwell Theological Seminary in Charlotte. He is also the cofounder of Kinship Plot, a community of learning and practice that cultivates resonant relationships of every kind. Wes holds a PhD in theology, imagination, and the arts from the University of St Andrews, and his publications include *Living Theodrama: Reimagining Theological Ethics* (2014) and *Beauty Is Oxygen: Finding a Faith That Breathes* (2024).

Derrell Young is a pastor, church planter, chaplain, graphic designer, and poet with a passion to teach people to trust God, accomplish goals, and love hard. Derrell currently works at Atrium Health CMC as a chaplain, providing advanced spiritual counseling to address issues of grief and loss, spiritual concerns, and religious needs of patients, family, and hospital teammates. The mission of his graphic company, the William Group, is to offer branding services and expand a company's brand awareness. Derrell has eighteen years of dedication toward developing young adult ministries for ages eighteen to thirty-five, working in North Carolina (Raleigh, Greensboro, and Charlotte) and Memphis. Derrell holds a bachelor of arts in graphic communication systems from North Carolina Agricultural & Technical State University and a master of divinity from Gordon-Conwell Theological Seminary.

Image Credits

Figure F.1. Image courtesy of Bowden Collections. © 2024 Artists Rights Society (ARS), New York / ADAGP, Paris.

Figure P.1. Image courtesy of Bowden Collections. © 2024 Artists Rights Society (ARS), New York / ADAGP, Paris.

Figure 1.1. Used by permission of Philippe Rouault.

Figure 1.2. Used by permission of Philippe Rouault.

Figure 1.3. Used by permission of Philippe Rouault.

Figure 1.4. Used by permission of Philippe Rouault.

Figure 1.5. Used by permission of Philippe Rouault.

Figure 1.6. Used by permission of Philippe Rouault.

Figure 1.7. Used by permission of Philippe Rouault.

Figure 2.1. Image courtesy of Bowden Collections. © 2024 Artists Rights Society (ARS), New York / ADAGP, Paris.

Figure 2.2. Image courtesy of Bowden Collections. © 2024 Artists Rights Society (ARS), New York / ADAGP, Paris.

Figure 2.3. Image courtesy of Bowden Collections. © 2024 Artists Rights Society (ARS), New York / ADAGP, Paris.

Figure 3.1. Image courtesy of Kunsthaus Zürich. © 2024 Artists Rights Society (ARS), New York / ADAGP, Paris.

Figure 3.2. Image courtesy of Bowden Collections. © 2024 Artists Rights Society (ARS), New York / ADAGP, Paris.

Figure 3.3. Image courtesy of Bowden Collections. © 2024 Artists Rights Society (ARS), New York / ADAGP, Paris.

Figure 4.1. Image courtesy of Bowden Collections. © 2024 Artists Rights Society (ARS), New York / ADAGP, Paris.

Figure 5.1. Erin Ninehouser, used by permission.

Figure 5.2. Erin Ninehouser, used by permission.

Figure 5.3. Erin Ninehouser, used by permission.

Figure 8.1. Image courtesy of Bowden Collections. © 2024 Artists Rights Society (ARS), New York / ADAGP, Paris.

Figure 8.2. Image courtesy of Bowden Collections. © 2024 Artists Rights Society (ARS), New York / ADAGP, Paris.

Figure 8.3. Image courtesy of Bowden Collections. © 2024 Artists Rights Society (ARS), New York / ADAGP, Paris.

Color Plates Credits

Plate 1. Christina Felten

Plate 2. Bryn Gillette

Plate 3. Joel Klepac

Plate 4. Josh Jensen

Plate 5. Marlon Gist

Plate 6. Helms Jarrell

Plate 7. Image courtesy of Art Resource. © Romare Bearden Foundation/VAGA at Artists Rights Society (ARS), New York.

Plate 8. Image courtesy of Currier Museum of Art. © 2024 Artists Rights Society (ARS), New York / ADAGP, Paris.

Plate 9. Ryan Lauterio

Plate 10. Melanie Spinks

Visit https://ivpress.com/rouault for links to the web images not printed in this book.

General Index

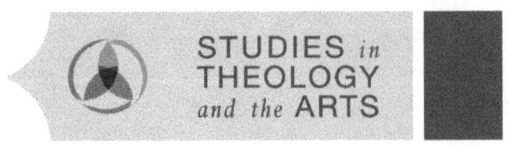

STUDIES *in*
THEOLOGY
and the ARTS

IVP Academic's Studies in Theology and the Arts (STA) seeks to enable Christians to reflect more deeply upon the relationship between their faith and humanity's artistic and cultural expressions. By drawing on the insights of both academic theologians and artistic practitioners, this series encourages thoughtful engagement with and critical discernment of the full variety of artistic media—including visual art, music, literature, film, theater, and more—which both embody and inform Christian thinking.

ADVISORY BOARD:

- **Jeremy Begbie,** professor of theology and director of Duke Initiatives in Theology and the Arts, Duke Divinity School, Duke University
- **Craig Detweiler,** professor of communication, Pepperdine University
- **Makoto Fujimura,** director of the Brehm Center for Worship, Theology and the Arts, Fuller Theological Seminary
- **Matthew Milliner,** assistant professor of art history, Wheaton College
- **Ben Quash,** professor of Christianity and the arts, King's College London
- **Linda Stratford,** professor of art history and history, Asbury University
- **W. David O. Taylor,** assistant professor of theology and culture, director of Brehm Texas, Fuller Theological Seminary
- **Gregory Wolfe,** publisher and editor, *Image*
- **Judith Wolfe,** lecturer in theology and the arts, Institute for Theology, Imagination and the Arts, The University of St. Andrews

ALSO AVAILABLE IN THE
STUDIES IN THEOLOGY AND THE ARTS SERIES